A GHOST IN THE CLOSET

Is There an Alcoholic Hiding?

A GHOST IN THE CLOSET

Is There an Alcoholic Hiding?

An Honest Look at Alcoholism

DALE MITCHEL

INFORMATION & EDUCATIONAL SERVICES

Hazelden
Center City, Minnesota 55012-0176
1-800-328-0094
1-651-213-4590 (Fax)
www.hazelden.org

Library of Congress Cataloging-in-Publication Data

Mitchel, Dale.
    A ghost in the closet : is there an alcoholic hiding? : an honest look
at alcoholism / Dale Mitchel.
         p.   cm.
    Includes bibliographical references.
    ISBN 1-56838-328-2
    1. Alcoholics—Rehabilitation—United States. 2. Alcoholism—
Psychological aspects. 3. Alcoholism—Religious aspects—Christianity.
I.   Title.
HV5279.M58   1999
362.292'0973—dc21   98-50581
                                                                 CIP

03 02 01 00 99 6 5 4 3 2 1

Cover design by Theresa Gedig
Interior design by Donna Burch
Typesetting by Stanton Publication Services, Inc.

Editor's note

Excerpts of material published by Alcoholics Anonymous World Services, Inc. (AAWS) have been reprinted with permission of AAWS. Permission to reprint such material does not mean that Alcoholics Anonymous is in any way affiliated with this publication or that it has read and/or endorses the contents thereof. AA is a program of recovery from alcoholism *only*—inclusion of AA materials in this publication, or use in any other non-AA context, does not imply otherwise.

All the stories in this book are based on actual experiences. The names and details have been changed to protect the privacy of the people involved.

*This book is dedicated to the ten to twenty million
still-suffering alcoholics, their families, their friends,
and all those engaged in the profession of finding a way
in which to eliminate or treat this awful disease.*

Contents

Foreword

The recovery path is like climbing a mountain by circular ascent—the same views reappear, but the perspective is changed each time. At each stage of recovery, alcoholics are challenged to alter their perspective to gain new information about the disease and about themselves, lest they slip into the chasm of relapse. Dale Mitchel has contributed uniquely to the literature on alcoholism and recovery. In the manner of Sigmund Freud, who was his own subject as he made his discoveries about psychoanalysis and the unconscious mind, Dale Mitchel has exhausted the literature on alcoholism, passing it through the filter of his own experience as an active, and now recovering, alcoholic. The result is this remarkable book.

The effect of *A Ghost in the Closet* is that of a dimmer switch, gradually illuminating more and more of a room darkened by ignorance, cultural bias, misunderstanding, and hostility. In a voice that is alternately objective and personal, he presents a comprehensive and compelling view of alcoholism and the recovery process. He shows us blindness and grandiosity as common aspects of this disease, shining a light on self-understanding and self-forgiveness along the recovery path. His chapter on the alcoholic mind is especially helpful to everyone who tries to understand this "cunning, baffling, and powerful" disease. For alcoholics and their families, as well as for all others, Dale Mitchel has taken the gift of his recovery and returned it a hundredfold.

On a personal note, in the thirty-plus years that I have struggled to understand this disease and be of some help to my patients, my greatest teachers have been my patients themselves. I am grateful for what I have learned from Dale in his recovery and in this book. I believe that readers will experience a similar gratitude.

JOHN T. NIEHAUS, L.I.S.W.
Cincinnati, Ohio

Preface

All of us have heard the varying myths and descriptions of alcoholism. Many of us have developed an ugly image of the alcoholic sitting under a bridge, unshaven, with a bottle of cheap wine in a brown paper bag. Others hold dear the thought of a co-worker, friend, or loved one joining us regularly for a happy hour that often turns into a "happy evening." Few of us feel that we have actually experienced the alcoholic life personally or knowingly. As this book has landed into your hands for one reason or another, let it serve no other purpose than to present through my eyes, those of a grateful recovering alcoholic, an overview of the facts, the fiction, and the information I have found helpful during recovery.

Hundreds of self-help books, therapists, manuals, tapes, journals, and teachings exist regarding alcoholism. Many of them I have experienced firsthand. But nothing has meant more to my continued recovery than talking with other alcoholics and "taking what I need and leaving the rest behind." There is no one answer as to what causes alcoholism or what can cure it. It is a plain fact that alcoholism affects more people than any other disease in the history of humanity. This fact alone has prompted me to study the far-reaching consequences of alcoholism and present the further-reaching differences in how we, as alcoholics, go through this life. If one were to consider the millions of recovering alcoholics and active alcoholics as well as their spouses, friends, family, and business associates, one could hardly walk through a single day without encountering someone affected by this disease. It is involved with crime and with success, with love and with hate, and it discriminates against no one.

Not until I accepted my alcoholism did I realize there is a commonality among those of us stricken with this disease. The theory of "Shameoboros" will be explained in chapter 7. This chapter describes some of the factors that I feel provide an open door for alcoholism to flourish, and how this alcoholic grew to understand it and continues to recover through this understanding. As an introduction to alcoholism, to both the alcoholic and the codependent, this book provides the information I took with me and the information I feel I needed to hear and understand to deal with this disease and begin a life of happiness.

I hope that the information provided in this book will help not only the active and recovering alcoholic in some small way but also just a few of the many people near and dear to the alcoholic. The only manner in which this help will be presented is a personal look at what this alcoholic thinks, feels, and believes. This in itself is a complex mixture of personality and behavioral traits. Perhaps by presenting this in a familiar manner, it may help readers understand that alcoholism is indeed a complex disease, yet there is a promise of growth, recovery, and happiness.

As I entered one of the best treatment centers for alcoholism in the world, full of denial and anger, I also entered with no prior knowledge of what alcoholism is or what it means, or any understanding that it can affect someone other than the actual alcoholic. As a prominent businessman, I felt that I certainly didn't belong in some treatment center and that I had nothing in common with the lowlifes with whom I was assigned to spend the next month. There I was, stuck in a dormitory-style room, with twenty-eight other addicts and alcoholics. Just a day earlier, I wouldn't have given any of these people two seconds of my valuable time.

What I came to learn quickly is that these are the kindest, most intelligent people I have ever spent time with. They are good people with a horrible disease. Among the people in my group we welcomed an airline pilot, a prominent cancer physician, a home builder, a priest, a counselor, an attorney, an engineer, a horse and cattle rancher, an auto dealership owner, several other business owners, a bartender, a nurse, a professional musician, a Hollywood movie director, a stockbroker, and many others. Alcoholism can affect anybody.

It didn't come to me until some time after graduating and leaving that all of us had several things in common. All of us had fallen to such a level of despair that we were unable to feel comfortable with ourselves in the world around us. Despite differences in social status, race, religion, and income, all of us felt uncomfortable in our own skins. We had isolated ourselves in such a way that the basic need for honest interaction with others was hidden. We had used our drug of choice to dampen the extremes of our emotions in a manner that best reflected our continuously changing moral standards. Simply put, we were all alcoholics. This belief is further strengthened every time I talk to another alcoholic and every time I listen to someone whose life is affected by an alcoholic. I feel that without an understanding of alcoholism and acceptance of it in our lives, we, as alcoholics, simply cannot heal. I also strongly believe that nonalcoholics could benefit from the views presented in this book. It may help them understand a loved one they feel may be affected by alcoholism. It is only this mutual understanding that will enable alcoholics to recover, loved ones to heal, and families to mend.

I am not a physician or in any way connected to the field of alcoholism, aside from my own personal insight and addiction. It is this personal insight, not scientific research, that yields the following pages. What I can promise is that through a dedicated recovery based upon much of what is written here, I have found, for the first time in my life, an inner peace and spiritual confidence that simply does not exist in any active alcoholic. I have been blessed with a wonderful marriage that was once far past the stage of ruin, three beautiful children who now actually enjoy my company, and a lifestyle that allows me to enjoy life on life's terms. Nothing in the following pages is new or revolutionary. It has all been said or written before. Where possible, I have listed the appropriate source for any referenced materials or writings, but I do not present this book as a summation of any quoted or researched materials. The theories, research, and conclusions presented are my understanding and interpretation of those writings and do not necessarily always present the intended findings of the original author.

What I have tried to accomplish in my writing is a book that will, in a simple form, help a few of those affected by alcoholism. I have tried to provide a simple explanation of alcoholism, the symptoms, the alcoholic mind, and the stages of recovery and relapse. My hope is that it may also provide comfort and be an aid to the active alcoholic. I have tried diligently to avoid excessive clinical presentations. Listed at the end of the book, however, are many references for further reading and research for those wishing to pursue this line of understanding.

This book is not intended as a manual or diagnostic tool for alcoholism. Each time I begin to believe that I have figured out the alcoholic personality, I meet someone who does not fit these stereotypical guidelines. I do, however, expect that most alcoholic and codependent readers of this material will find many similarities to themselves. The alcoholic has been analyzed and tested for years to find the singular common link. It does not exist.

Manuscript critiques of this book included comments that the book leans toward a textbook-style presentation. This was not my intent, but rather the book is driven by the scientific information presented to prove the disease concept. In no way do I present this information as all-inclusive or as a checklist of alcoholic traits. Many alcoholics may have only one or two of the many traits described; others may have all of those noted and more. Should an alcoholic become discouraged by the many negative personality traits described, I remind that person that the traits are presented only to help with the understanding that no alcoholic is terminally unique.

My most important goal when writing this book was selfish. I wanted only to study the available research and theories to aid my own recovery. As my incoherent notes grew into pages, sections, and chapters, they came to provide both a barometer of my past life versus my current life and a demonstration of my current gratitude for a spiritual and sober life. Soon, my notes began to look like the beginnings of a book. I became absorbed in a way I had never known. Could I actually possess the ability to put into words the many teachings and lessons I have learned in such a short time? Could I possibly provide a small level of comfort for another? It is this rough and crude compilation of my notes from the research I felt compelled to study that provides the following pages. I just had to find out if I truly have a disease or if I was simply a bad person. I had to read everything I could find on alcoholism. I spent time talking and listening to as many alcoholics as I could find, and find them I did. Most of the time in my car was spent listening to various recovery tapes (a practice I highly recommend to persons new in recovery). I was known by my first name at libraries and at bookstores. The Internet has over 108,000 current listings regarding alcoholism. Over time, I did my best to review some of them that contained new theories or information. They say that you can be too smart for recovery but never too stupid. I am convinced that many who knew me at this stage of my recovery wondered if I would ever make it. Nonetheless, this book became part of my recovery program, and I had to work it my way.

Many excellent books exist that I have found helpful in achieving a sober life. The majority of these books are far better researched and much better written than this one. I thank the authors of each of these books, as I have undoubtedly written many words from the subconscious recollections of their works. The combination of readings and teachings I felt compelled to study has helped me to begin to understand alcoholism and further helped me in a successful recovery program. Where possible, I have listed the books I have read and found helpful, as well as specific references at the back of this book.

What I have found, however, are few writings from the actual alcoholic. Writings that I did immediately connect with were seldom sitting on the local bookstore or library shelf. Writings from alcoholic to alcoholic were well disguised or left unattended. And although I felt closer to this type of source, the distinctions and commonalities of alcoholics were often not addressed, leaving me still to wonder if in fact I was a true alcoholic.

I wanted this book to be an honest personal interpretation of what I have found necessary to find a direction and to understand this disease. There had to be a sourcebook available to alcoholics, potential alcoholics, and the codependents of alcoholics that might briefly explain some of the commonalities of the disease. I was personally saddened by the family members' plight of having virtually no knowledge of alcoholism and addiction, and no time or desire to search out any materials to begin an understanding. Further, I found a need early in recovery to hear it all from someone else and to relate to others who had gone before me to accept alcoholism as a disease. It was simply the time—finally—to tell the truth.

Acknowledgments

I would like forever to express my love and admiration to my wife, Rebecca, for being the only person in the world to see the good hidden deep within my shell of deceit for so many years; to my beautiful children for providing the reason for my existence; to Lisa Reynolds for her compassion, ability to recognize an alcoholic in need, and friendship; to Joanne Lindy for introducing me to a possible life of happiness through sobriety and for helping to build a marriage once held together only by threads into a marriage now held together forever by love; to Jack Niehaus, responsible for an aftercare treatment and therapy process that enabled me to begin to grow into a level I never thought possible; to Fitz, John, Ken, Gertrude, Doug, and Eric—my first home group; to Dennis O., who took a scared and lonely man through the first tempting night out of treatment; to Joy Bannister, who first taught me to take a good look at myself and at how alcoholism affects our actions; to all of my peers at Hazelden–Shoemaker Unit, and to Phil Kavanaugh, our leader.

Special thanks to Mike and Maria, strangers who proved themselves true lifelong friends at a time when almost everyone else seemed to disappear from my life; to Jay A., Bill Z., Rick and Arlene, and, of course, Mark Gentuso and Jeff Rezzuto for proving that putting up with a person's ego long enough may eventually lead to something that is worth it at the end; to Rob M., my first sponsor, a gentleman and adviser, in addition to being a shining example. Bill Pittman, you have found yet another person whom you may call a friend, and I am honored by that fact.

To my manuscript editor, Kate Kjorlien, whose professionalism and patience guided me through the most difficult task of a properly coordinated presentation. To my brother Craig, my hero; and to Bob Z., the first person in my life who accepted me for who I was, for the good and the bad, as we grew together in recovery, and now a lifelong friend and brother; to all those who in some way or another helped with the early drafts of this book, ensuring my sober ego didn't get the best of me; and most important, to my Higher Power as I know Him, God, for His loving and patient understanding, His continued support, and His never-ending miracles.

Chapter 1

Introduction to Alcoholism

Alcoholism has been around since biblical times. The Bible contains over 150 writings of how alcohol affected people. James W. West, M.D., of the Betty Ford Center, reminds us that in the book of Genesis, once Noah had finally landed the ark on dry land, one of the first things he did was plant a vineyard. He then proceeded to pass out, stone cold drunk. This is probably the first written referral to some type of drunkenness (West 1997). Throughout both the Old and New Testaments, and throughout the history of humans, the effects of alcohol are often discussed in interesting contexts.

When It All Began

Others argue that even prior to the arrival of Jesus into our history, written accounts from ancient Roman philosophers detail the subject of drunkenness. Beer and wine are thought to have been made in ancient Turkey as early as 6400 B.C. (Berger 1992). Ancient Chinese writings indicate that drunks were executed as early as 1800 B.C. Robertson (1988) traces the first abuse of alcohol to Mesopotamia. Ancient clay tablets have been found dating to 4000 B.C. She also reminds us of references to blackouts in Greek mythology written by Euripides in his play *The Bacchae*. It would not be reaching far to imagine way back in history, when the storage of raw fruits was replaced by the natural spoilage and fermentation process, that some form of alcohol was being consumed. Throughout history there are accounts of how alcohol negatively affected the population of the day. In fact, at the point of Prohibition, it has been said that the United States was drunk. The per-capita consumption at the immediate pre–Prohibition time period was nearly five times what it is today. A scholar might argue that the temperance movement and later Prohibition had an effect on the United States that has lasted nearly seventy-five years.

There are written accounts of alcoholic behavior as early as the first voyage of the *Mayflower*, as its passengers spent six months at sea searching for a new continent. In fact, it is widely recognized that one of the reasons for the premature landing of the *Mayflower* was that the ship had begun to run out of supplies, including alcohol. Water would often run low or become contaminated, and the passengers would then use the crew rations of alcohol. There were negotiations upon landing at Plymouth Rock as to how much rum would be left for the crew for the return trip and how much left for the settlers.

Later, Captain John Smith is said to have been drunk when he first captured and imprisoned Squanto. Dr. Benjamin Rush (1784), a Revolutionary War hero and a signer of the Declaration of Independence, first described the symptoms of alcoholism as a deadly, progressive disease (Robertson 1988; West 1997; Brown 1995). In his writings, Rush accurately described cravings and held that the alcoholic was responsible during only the very early phases of use, until the alcohol actually took control of the drinking. This was quite an extraordinary conclusion considering the time period, the lack of research, and the poor information available. I personally believe that if the information superhighway available now had been available at the time of his writings, Rush would have changed the course of history, disproving the mistaken belief that the alcoholic fails through poor willpower.

Around this same time in U.S. history there are accounts of bleeding people to their deaths in hopes of expelling the demons and hysteria associated with an alcoholism diagnosis. In 1804, Dr. Thomas Trotter, a Scottish physician, astounded his peers and was perhaps the first to upset the prevailing viewpoint that only moral degenerates became drunk. His challenge of the ethical and religious overtones of the century, advocating the disease concept of alcoholism, started a division in the opinions of the church and scholars that continues today (Warner 1993).

Much later, Mark Twain described in detail and with some accuracy, in his novel *The Adventures of Huckleberry Finn,* the rigorous and horrific results of alcoholism and alcoholic withdrawals. Huck witnesses his own father in dire pain (D.T.'s) due to alcoholism (Milam and Ketcham 1981).

During the temperance movement early in the twentieth century, the Anti-Saloon League actually advertised *The Effect of Alcohol on Sex Life* (Menninger 1973). Below is an early printed example of the outlandish thoughts of that time and shows just how misunderstood alcoholism has been throughout the years. The published poster (typos and all) looked something like this:

Alcohol Inflames the Passions,
thus making the Temptations to Sex-Sin unusually strong.
Alcohol Decreases the Power of Control,
thus making the resisting of temptation especially difficult.
Alcohol Decreases the Resistance of the Body to Disease,
thus making the result of the disease more serious.
The influence of alcohol upon sex-life
could not hardly be worse.
AVOID ALL ALCOHOLIC DRINK ABSOLUTELY!

A couple of years after Prohibition was repealed, Dr. Norman Jolliffe, a trustee at Bellevue Hospital in New York, became certain that alcohol use could not be treated effectively unless alcoholism was viewed as a primary disease. He convinced his colleagues to bring together a distinguished research team to study the biological effects of alcoholism and obtained funding for the study from the Carnegie Foundation. Jolliffe assigned E. M. Jellinek, a noted physiologist, to lead and carry out the study.

In the early modern recollection of alcoholism, many treatments were thought to reduce the craving for alcohol and in some cases eliminate the disease altogether. These treatments, which sometimes bordered on torture, are evidence of the misunderstanding of the disease early in the research and development of alcoholic treatments. Madill et al. (1966) administered a drug (succinylocholine) intravenously to a group of alcoholics immediately after they drank their favorite alcoholic beverage. The drug induced respiratory paralysis and the feeling of death. This treatment was continued on the same patients for some time to create an aversion to alcohol. It was hoped that this feeling of death would be remembered prior to any future use and would stop the alcoholic from using alcohol altogether. It seemed to work for a few months. Upon the premature conclusion of their research, the group published their impressive findings as evidence of the ability to eliminate in alcoholics the desire to drink. Many in the field of therapeutic treatment of alcoholism initially jumped onto this bandwagon. It wasn't until follow-up research that they realized although the subjects experienced nausea, fear, tremors, disgust, and rejection toward alcohol, the treatment truly did not stop them from drinking. In fact, it was noted that this same pain was often the excuse to drink for some of the subjects. Many simply switched to another alcoholic beverage, but no substantial abstinence and sobriety rates were found. Some experienced psychological repercussions and some analysts thought dual disorders had occurred.

In other treatment procedures, electric shocks were given when alcoholics tasted or even smelled alcohol. Some researchers during this same period believed that induced overdrinking would cause a permanent aversion to alcohol. We all know how effective this is as we remember the "hangover promise." Many narcotics and other drugs were given to cause an array of discomforts when the alcoholic drank, but the drinking continued nonetheless. As late as 1970, certain researchers joined the growing experimentation of treating alcoholics through administering LSD and other hallucinogenic drugs in hopes of curing alcoholism (Vaillant 1983). None of these treatments worked, although many were so excitedly accepted at first that this type of experimental research was allowed to continue for some time. A heroin addict friend I have, now fully committed to recovery, said to me: "Heck, with LSD, who needs alcohol?"

Obviously the study of alcoholism has been around for a long time. More obvious is a history of the continued ineffective, unrealistic, and misunderstood diagnosis of alcoholism as a primary disease. As research on many known diseases also took painstaking experimentation of trial and error, an alcoholic should harbor no ill feelings for the injustice done in early recovery treatments. We should thank every one of the attempts for trying in some small way to find a cure. Perhaps one day, through the continued caring of individuals engaged in research on alcoholism, the cure may be found. These men and women at times have put their reputations on the line to help others. We must remember that not so long ago, and even in some circles today, research on alcoholism has been regarded as a fool's bet.

Without my marriage counselor having read some of this research, I would have never found the road to recovery. Without the mountains of research materials, personal stories, opinions, and hypotheses, there would not be the outpatient treatment support services nor the inpatient, full-term recovery centers that exist today. Nonetheless, many people enter their personal programs with much success and without these advantages.

Alcoholism as a Disease

In 1950, E. M. Jellinek was publishing the results of his research. This eventually led to the modern-day medical acceptance of alcoholism as a physical disease. In 1941, Jellinek published what was then considered a groundbreaking work of the subtypes of alcoholism. He associated these subtypes with different degrees of social, physical, and psychological impairments. In 1964,

Jellinek's work developed into the concept for "A Chart of Alcohol Addiction and Recovery," later regarded widely as "The Jellinek Curve" (see page 12). This graph (or time line) depicts the levels and behavioral traits usually associated with varying stages of alcoholism, including recovery. Although this chart cannot be all-encompassing, it clearly reveals that this is a progressive disease that can be arrested only with abstinence. In reviewing this chart, alcoholics often relate that they experienced symptoms and behaviors of several stages at the same time, while not feeling that they had progressed to the full extent of the next stage. Jellinek's book *The Disease Concept of Alcoholism* (1960) is still held in high regard as the first major contribution to the field of alcoholic research. Most recovering alcoholics will tell you that this work, taken in its entirety, is perhaps the most concise view of potential symptoms at various stages of the disease and of the progressive nature of the disease. Jellinek held that the disease was progressive and that the progression was unstoppable as long as the alcoholic continued to drink.

Although some have taken issue with the Jellinek analysis and hypothesis, in my opinion, there has never been any reasonable, accepted, concrete, scientific proof to support the opposite side of the theory. One of the reasons for this lack of proof is that alcoholics tend to lead anonymous lives and avoid involvement in research. Where proof has been presented against the progressiveness of the disease, the research used has often eliminated the members within the research pool who have died or left during research due to the use of alcohol. Also, that research often did not maintain a sufficient use of individuals involved with a relapse after a term of documented recovery. Jellinek believes that loss of control and craving for alcohol are inseparable but that the alcohol use is a response to a physical need—a need, he believes, that is due to a complete adaptation of cell metabolism to alcohol. He attributes the psychological need for alcohol to the alcoholic's false belief that additional alcohol use will reduce the problems and tension in life.

Cloninger, Bohman, and Sigvardsson (1981) defined alcoholism as "a heterogeneous set of behaviors that includes any pattern of alcohol intake that causes medical and/or social complications." Let us emphasize, alcoholism is perhaps the only disease in the world more easily recognized and diagnosed by behavioral patterns than by direct physical changes.

Wallerstein (1956) wrote, "Alcoholism is a symptomatic expression of deep-seated emotional difficulties" in response to Sherfey's (1955) hypothesis that alcoholism was secondary to behavioral and psychiatric states of mind in his sampling of 161 alcoholics. Syme (1957) then concluded his analysis of the MMPI (Minnesota Multiphasic Personality Inventory) results of over one thousand alcoholics. He believed that the more social or psychological problems the alcoholic had, the more the need for alcohol. All of these different studies still had one common denominator—alcoholism is a terrible disease.

Today the American Medical Association, the American Psychiatric Association, the American Physiological Society, the Department of Health, Education, and Welfare, the American Society of the Aging, the American Public Health Association, and numerous other governmental and health-related organizations and associations worldwide call alcoholism a physical disease. The Presbyterian Church became the first religious organization to recognize alcoholism as a disease in 1946 at its 158th general assembly.

Understanding a little about the insurance industry can also support the disease concept, as the majority of insurance providers now include in their disease coverage alcoholism and drug-related treatments. Only the World Health Organization (WHO) places alcohol in a category all alone, somewhere between a habit-forming and an addiction-producing function. The WHO's definition of an addiction-producing drug requires that the majority of the drug's users become addicted to it. In the case of clinical alcoholism, use of alcohol causes addiction in only a minority of users. It is estimated that this "minority" in the United

States alone lands somewhere between ten and twenty million suffering alcoholics.

Dr. Steven Hyman, of the Mind, Brain, and Behavior Initiative at Harvard University, is widely regarded as one of the current experts on alcoholism as a disease. He believes that in the most vulnerable of people, alcohol affects the long-term functioning of the brain and these changes are the basis of the behavioral changes in addicted people (1976). Hyman lists numerous factors that he believes cause vulnerability to alcoholism. Among these are heredity, developmental and environmental factors, a lack of behavioral alternatives, learning and child rearing, psychiatric illnesses, physical pain, emotional stress, peer pressure, and simple availability. Schuckit (1980) clearly found in his research with the children of alcoholics that many already maintain a lower capacity to convert acetaldehyde in the brain before they have ever had one drink of alcohol, supporting that heredity (to be discussed later) plays a part in who becomes an alcoholic.

In recent years, research has advanced to address the brain chemistry, heredity, and physical addiction of the disease. Medical scanning equipment, similar to the MRI and MRS scan equipment widely used for brain analysis, is currently being developed that researchers hope will show the movement of the neurotransmitter fluid called serotonin within the brain. It is now understood within the medical profession that alcohol addiction is more likely in some people than in others and that this addiction occurs within the brain.

Many studies now point to serotonin and the reduced level of neurological impulses capable of transmitting through this fluid in alcoholic brains. This effect reduces reasoning abilities in the alcoholic mind and is said also to cause an exaggerated level of emotional thought processes. As I will discuss later, many researchers have found evidence that people addicted to alcohol may have decreased levels of serotonin, particularly during the early withdrawal period (Milam and Ketcham 1981).

It is now a plain and proven scientific fact that alcoholism is indeed a disease. The disagreements lie more in the differences in terminology and the physical and psychological differences that are involved with alcoholism. It is said that this disease affects more people than all of the cancers combined. Alcohol is one of the most psychoactive drugs in the United States. It is further said that one person dies every four to five minutes because of alcoholism or an alcohol-related action. Alcoholics do not want to be alcohol dependent. The high suicide rate among recovering alcoholics indicates that many recovering alcoholics would rather die than drink again.

We have enormous sympathy for the cancer patient lying in a hospital bed, yet we still place many alcoholics in sanitariums and psychiatric wards. Of the nearly one million new spousal and child abuse and neglect cases reported each year in this country alone, over 60 percent are attributed to alcohol use. Over 60 percent of wife-battering cases indicate that the husbands had been drinking when the violence occurred (Russell 1982). From 35 to 64 percent of all traffic deaths involve alcohol (Milam and Ketcham 1981). The rate of alcoholism among rapists is as much as three times that of the general population (Rivers 1994), and between 39 and 50 percent of all rapes and 60 percent of all sexual offenses involve alcohol (Roizen 1997). An alcoholic is much more likely to die from a fall than a nonalcoholic (Department of Health and Human Services [DHHS] 1984). Over 86 percent of homicides are attributed to alcohol use (Roizen 1997), and suicide risk is increased over the national average by as much as 20 percent in alcoholics (DHHS 1984). Up to 80 percent of all suicides involve alcohol, and 30 percent of recorded suicides are the direct result of alcohol use. Schmidt and Popham (1979) present information that one-third of all alcoholic deaths are from suicides or accidental deaths such as drowning, fires, falls, or car crashes. Alcoholics have an estimated natural life span that is ten to fifteen years less than their nonalcoholic friends. Pernanen (1991) found that 42 percent of violent crimes reported to police involved alcohol use, while 51 percent of the victims believed that their assailants had been under the influence of alcohol.

Alcoholism, in one way or another, costs the United States over fifty billion dollars per year (Vaillant 1983). Alcohol abuse and alcoholism now account for more economic and social damage than any other public health problem in the United States.

Knowing these facts, why then do we as a humane people continue to ignore and misunderstand this terrible, far-reaching, progressive disease? The *Cincinnati Post*, March 16, 1998, reported that nearly 25 percent of all patients admitted to a general hospital today are in some way affected by alcohol use.

In general, today's society still regards alcoholism and alcoholics to be moral degenerates, failures devoid of any willpower or self-esteem. In 1979, Yankelovoich, Skelly and White, Inc., in a survey funded by General Mills, found that over 60 percent of all people surveyed still believe that alcoholism is a sign of weakness. Recent surveys hold that alcoholism is still generally regarded as a lack of willpower. Gordis (1976) reported in the *Annals of Internal Medicine*, "The treatment of alcoholism has not improved in any important way in 25 years."

Jellinek uses a simple graph to support his theory of a progressive disease. It is presented here (page 12) to allow those touched by alcoholism to review the road ahead and reflect on the road behind. Jellinek believed that even after a prolonged abstinence, an alcoholic who reverts back to drinking, or relapses, would almost always reach the same point of use and behavior that occurred before abstinence, and the disease would begin to progress beyond that point rapidly.

I used the Jellinek chart for some time during early recovery to promote the idea that I was not an alcoholic. In my opinion, I had not experienced the identified traits to the full extent or in the same order. Upon reflection, I see now that I did experience many more of the traits than I had admitted, and in fact, I find the chart quite accurate in timing of the disease. I have further found that the progressive nature of the disease itself almost requires that the alcoholic return quite quickly to the same point of alcoholic consumption and behavioral traits exhibited before abstinence.

It is this experience that allows me to recommend that perhaps an outsider's viewpoint of the alcoholic as related to this chart would be helpful as a diagnostic reference. An outsider who may be close to the alcoholic is perhaps better able to see within the alcoholic the behavioral traits Jellinek describes, while the alcoholic probably has a strong case of denial. The outsider must, however, be an individual who is not too close to the pain and anguish of being involved with an active alcoholic. The Jellinek chart should not be used as a tool to prove the damage the alcoholic has caused but as a reference toward understanding the progressiveness of the disease.

The Myth of Willpower

Since I first thought of myself as an active alcoholic, I have been amazed at how alcoholics are treated by others and how others view alcoholism. I need only to be reminded that I once believed those same thoughts to gain any compassion for people who to this day, despite all the medical and scientific data available, believe it is a matter of willpower. I ask those who subscribe to this theory to look upon the thousands incarcerated in our jails and prisons due solely to their alcoholism and drug addictions. Look upon the millions of ruined families, careers, marriages, businesses, politicians, and the like—due solely to alcoholism. Sit in on an Alcoholics Anonymous group session or meeting and hear the story of a recovering alcoholic who in a fit of desperation and drunken loneliness put a pillow over his ten-month-old baby's face while she slept, only to be stopped just in time by his wife. I had the opportunity to hear that story. We all cried as he cried, and we all understood the emptiness, loneliness, desperation, and total lack of willpower he was facing.

This is not to say that all alcoholics fall this far down the scale, but it does remind us that we all have the potential to fall that far and further. We all have our own bottom. This man is now a ten-year recovering alcoholic, a deacon in his church, a successful businessman who maintains a happy, spiritual, and wonderful life with his wife and ten-year-old daughter. Gaining willpower was

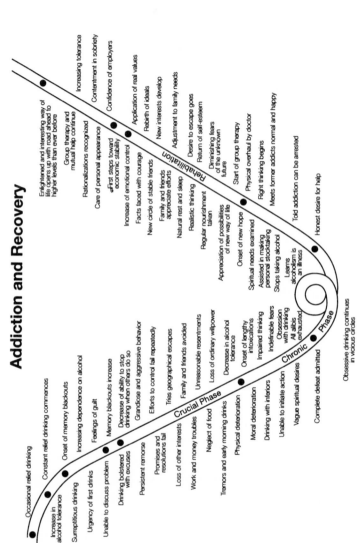

The Jellinek Curve

Addiction and Recovery

Taken from a presentation by the late Dr. E. M. Jellinek at the Yale Center of Alcohol Studies in 1950 (Springborn 1992).

not his salvation. He would be the first to admit his willpower is no stronger today than ten years ago. A different Higher Power has given him the strength and faith to stay in recovery.

Understanding the physiological and psychological dependency in the disease helps one understand that alcoholism has nothing to do with willpower. In fact, alcoholism has little to do with any outside source and nothing to do with an ability to decide. Theories exist on both sides regarding the physical or mental dependency on the drug alcohol. As a depressant and as a stimulant, alcohol fools the most scholarly of researchers. The largest problem for researchers studying alcoholism is that the disease is both psychologically and physically affecting. The clinical researchers find fault in the undocumented truths; the therapists find fault in the lack of proper subjects; they both find fault with the government agencies, and on and on. The one common link in this research is that nearly everyone agrees scientifically that alcohol is addictive to the actual alcoholic.

Maslin (1994) fears that alcohol is simply a self-addictive prescription against depression and a way that unhappy people try to combat their sadness. Ludwig (1988) has identified "nine basic overlapping patterns of thought and attitudes that seem to predispose to drinking" that will be discussed in chapter 2.

What I would like to get across is that alcoholism is no joyride of self-indulgence. Nor is it a social means of fellowship gone astray. Only through recovery have I come to understand that many factors totally out of my control played a role in how I became an alcoholic. Further, many experiences throughout my life affirmed and reaffirmed my sense of not belonging. No matter how popular I was, how many awards or promotions at work I received, how many friends I had, I just could not feel happy inside or with myself. I am not proud of who I became, but I now accept responsibility for it. Few outside a close circle of people knew what I was feeling. Like those surprised by a suicide of a close friend or family member, I, too, still surprise many people with honest statements about my past feelings and actions. Chapter 2, "The Alcoholic Mind," will explain how this is all

possible. I assure you, however, that willpower had absolutely
nothing to do with my alcohol and other drug use. I could move
mountains if I wanted to, and often did. When it came to alcohol,
an unconscious pattern of thought took away any knowledge that
there was anything wrong, so why did I need willpower? It is not
called willpower when someone sits alone at home for days,
drinking alone, passing out, then waking up with a terrible hangover and going through life like nothing happened. "Physiology,
not psychology, determines whether one drinker will become addicted to alcohol and another will not" (Milam and Ketcham
1981).

Addiction

Addiction to alcohol has been widely studied for many years.
One camp holds that the addictive nature is due to the physical
differences of the human body and brain in an alcoholic versus
a nonalcoholic. Until recently, another camp held that the addiction was a psychological and moral problem. The fact is that
alcoholics are physically addicted to the continued use of alcohol. Continued and progressive use causes emotional, physical,
and psychological pain. The alcoholic drinks more to help alleviate the pain and change the mood. Addiction is the inability to
have any choice about the compulsion to continue the progression of use. Alcoholics begin to drink excessively for psychological reasons, but become addicted for physical reasons (Gorski
and Miller 1986).

Many books devoted to addiction can be summarized like this:
addiction is the complete and total loss of willpower. Addiction is
the loss of choice. Addiction to alcohol as well as other mood-
altering drugs strips the user of compassion for self. The user becomes further isolated and removed from all that was once
important without ever realizing that change has occurred. What
is most startling about addiction is that the user can hide the addiction from most loved ones for years, through an occasional
resurfacing of the old self. Much as a baby learns that crying may
result in something to eat, an addict learns to manipulate others

in many ways. Even when the possibility emerges that someone has realized this deep, dark secret, the addict is so threatened that he or she can rationalize behavior and use, even to the point of belief in being entitled to continued use, as it harms no one but the addicted.

There seems to be two distinct differences in the processes that motivate addiction. The first is a process whereby the alcoholic is rewarded through an action that brings pleasure. When such a process becomes repetitive, it is called *positive reinforcement.* "Normally, this process functions to sustain motivation for behaviors essential to the individual or species, such as eating, drinking, or reproductive behavior—evidence suggests that alcohol and other drugs are chemical surrogates for such natural reinforcers" (Roberts and Koob 1997; Di Chiara 1997; National Institute on Alcohol Abuse and Alcoholism [NIAAA] 1996, no. 33). In other words, the use of alcohol can actually be more powerful and rewarding than natural reinforcers, initiating an increased addiction.

The second process occurs after the brain has undergone certain adaptive changes to continue working properly despite the presence of alcohol. When alcohol is removed during abstinence, many abnormalities can occur that can cause enormous pain and discomfort. There is then a motivation to use alcohol so as not to experience this pain. This process is called *negative reinforcement.*

Approaching addicts with any discussion of addiction that may threaten continued use can actually be a stimulus to further use and further isolation. Until addicts have begun to sink to some level of despair, with the realization that not only has past use contributed to problems but also continued use will promote future problems, they can simply not be helped. But in most cases, once users begin to accept that use has caused problems, they may be willing to grasp the concept of addiction. In fact, many addicts and alcoholics, while in recovery, have said they eventually welcome the concept of their addiction, if only to hold on to an initial excuse for some of their prior behavior.

As will be discussed later in this book, the alcoholic (and addicted) mind requires inner forgiveness and a release of some of the guilt and inner shame for recovery to be possible. For an alcoholic to begin a recovery program without this action is useless in most cases. A nonalcoholic or nonaddictive personality has great difficulty accepting the addiction and willpower premise because it is a characteristic they do not share. It's impossible for someone who allows a drink to be unattended long enough for the ice cubes to melt to understand an alcoholic's lack of control regarding alcohol. All of us judge the world through our own colored glasses. It is difficult for the nonalcoholic, effectively guarded at all times by willpower, to comprehend an alcoholic's powerlessness over alcohol yet full capability of exercising willpower on so many other difficult decisions.

Powerlessness

An addict devoid of willpower is absolutely powerless over his or her drug of choice. This is perhaps the single most important basis to every recovery program for both the addict and the codependent. Without an acceptance of powerlessness, addicts hold on to the premise that they are in control and that they therefore can quit on their own, but they just don't need to quit. Codependents, believing that they have some responsibility to help their loved ones, also believe that they should be able to control their loved ones' behavior. In fact, most codependents are mirror images of their addicted loved ones when it comes to the need to control. Without letting go and detaching with love, neither can recover. A nonalcoholic can no more control the alcoholic than the alcoholic can control his or her drinking. Once willing to accept powerlessness over alcohol, the alcoholic has taken the first step toward recovery.

Acceptance of powerlessness has been shown to occur through counseling, self-help programs, the Alcoholics Anonymous program, and even personal reflections but is always necessary to recovery. Realizing powerlessness is the first step to asking for help.

All treatment centers for alcoholism based upon the Twelve Steps of Alcoholics Anonymous begin with this First Step: "We admitted we were powerless over alcohol—that our lives had become unmanageable" (*Alcoholics Anonymous* 1976).

To help edge alcoholics into this acceptance of powerlessness, it is best to help them realize that past problems and ill-fated behaviors occurred usually when using or drinking. That those problems and behaviors most likely would not have occurred had they not been drinking is not difficult to prove. This is walking a fine line of accusation and is usually presented best by another alcoholic. It seems that many treatment centers have found that group counseling with alcoholic peers can steer the active alcoholic in the right direction. For some reason, we all tend to listen best to those who have experienced the same level of pain and can share the disastrous effects drinking has had on their lives. Having realized that he or she is not terminally unique, the alcoholic is then capable of accepting that many recovering alcoholics were much farther down the road to death and have fully recovered. This realization in some cases is the only muscle behind an active alcoholic having a desire to turn around a life of despair.

Denial

Many alcoholics have promised their spouses, after inflicting emotional or physical pain during a drinking bout, that this will be the last time. More important, the alcoholics promise themselves that this will be the last hangover, the last missed morning of work, the last ill-spoken words to a loved one, or the last time a child's birthday is forgotten. These promises are usually made with the best of intentions; they are a defense mechanism against the reality of the effects of alcohol. An alcoholic begins to believe the lies and has no concept that he or she is indeed sick. No words of advice, no threats, no loss is too great for the majority of active alcoholics to endure. An alcoholic lives in a constant state of denial. Denial actually provides the alcoholic with an acceptable alternative system with which to view the world (Brown 1995). It occurs only after the alcoholic ceases to choose the use of alcohol freely. Once the need for alcohol becomes the centerpiece of the alcoholic lifestyle, an internal conflict is born between the innate need for self-control and the subconscious need for continued use. The only subconsciously practical means with which to rationalize this extreme difference in regulatory beliefs is denial.

The main intended result of drinking and drugging is to change a mood. It can include trying to calm down after a hectic day at the office, to celebrate an accomplishment or event, to enhance a social occasion, to liven any gathering, to soften a frustration or resentment, to ward off threats and fear of life itself. It stands to reason then that no outside force can solve this dilemma. An alcoholic is fighting emotions much scarier from within than any that are external. Dr. Harry Tiebout (1953), a pioneer in alcoholism research, wrote that denial allowed the alcoholic to manage frustrations by ignoring the reality of a growing lack of control. Stephanie Brown (1995) explored denial as "a means to reconcile the internal conflict between this desperate need to continue drinking and using drugs, and the accumulating evidence of the destruction likely if drinking and drug use continue." She went on to add that alcoholics may subconsciously support denial while continuing to grow closer to their own worst stereotype of an alcoholic with each passing day.

Many alcoholics must sink to a level that is so dangerously frightening, there is simply nowhere else to turn but finally to accept help. The level itself varies greatly for every alcoholic. Some do indeed end up under a bridge or in a jail, but just as many are perfectly functioning professionals at work, while secretly destroying their private lives. To finally welcome help can be accomplished only from within and only through first opening the door to a reduction in denial about the disease itself. Although some alcoholics do indeed begin programs and lives of complete recovery on their own, this is the exception and not the norm. It is effective for only a small percentage of alcoholics and only in the primary and early stages of alcoholism.

One gauge of denial I have developed is referred to as the

"room key theory." Imagine a person who has never been to a gambling casino and has never dropped a single nickel into a slot machine. Should someone suggest that the person has a gambling problem, that person simply cannot open the door even to go to that room. There is no denial for something that doesn't exist. Imagine an extremely skinny person being told she or he has an overeating problem. Again, the person simply cannot go to that room, does not even comprehend where in the world the commentator is coming from. Now, tell an alcoholic that you think he or she has a drinking problem and hear a list of thousands of different answers, excuses, and denials.

Many alcoholics have promised to cut back or have actually stopped drinking for a few months or even years to prove they were not alcoholics. They quickly take the key, open the door, and easily enter that room. Imagine that skinny person I mentioned promising not to eat as much for a few months or to lose weight to show there is no overeating problem.

In my case, a six-month abstinence from alcohol actually gave me a license to drink as much as I desired, because I had "proven" I was obviously not an alcoholic. To celebrate the end of the sixth month, I installed a hard liquor fountain at my company Christmas party (instead of champagne) and tried to do a shot with every person who entered the front door. By 7:30 that night, after approximately thirty shots of cognac, I raised my glass to toast the room and passed out, falling over backward onto a dinner table in front of all my clients, my employees, and my friends. This was the first episode of having a complete blackout for an extended period of time. I spoke with many people over the next few weeks who were at the party. Many of them told of having extended conversations with me after I got up off the floor. To this day, I do not remember anything about that night after the now infamous event. My own brother tells a story of carrying me up the stairs to my bedroom. Guess what? The next morning I still didn't think I had any real drinking problem. Denial stands for "don't even know I am lying."

Tolerance

A true indicator of alcoholism is tolerance. First of all, for anyone to drink enough alcohol to develop a tolerance level for it should in itself be a red flag. What all alcoholics experience is a steady increase in tolerance levels with increased usage of their drug of choice. Sitting down and writing a personal history of use generally indicates a pattern of beginning with a drink or two a week, then a drink or two a night and a few extra on weekends, then on to several drinks a night, maybe one during the day, and so on. Eventually, alcoholics settle into a pattern whereby their entire life revolves around the next drink.

Many alcoholics function as completely normal, successful people in their careers and some even in their families. At some point, however, it is a given that the tolerance level will increase, and the alcoholic consumes more and more. Some do indeed get to extremely dangerous levels that affect their health, sneaking bottles and drinks at every occasion, while some are lucky enough to get into treatment before they reach this level. Left untreated, an alcoholic will continue to increase the level of consumption again and again (Jellinek 1960). For some it starts with the first drink, and for some it may take twenty years, but if history presents a case, sooner or later the majority of alcoholics continue to increase their drinking level and the behavior that goes with excessive drinking. Menninger (1973) states: "The physiological and psychological effects of alcohol are mediated by the personality and cultural backgrounds of those that use it," indicating the differences in tolerance growth levels within alcoholics.

It wasn't until I reviewed my first usage history on paper with a staff counselor that I realized that perhaps my tolerance and usage had increased and I should consider cutting back, at least during the workweek. But I was still certain I was not an alcoholic. To me, enjoying a few beers while working outside on the yard on Saturdays, then progressing to the couch for a couple more over a ball game on TV and a short nap was absolutely normal. Of course a mixed drink or two were in order while I showered up to go out for a nice dinner, then a couple of cocktails before dinner at the restaurant, and a couple more while the meal was enjoyed. And after all, no dinner was complete without a few cognacs to enjoy afterward with a nice dessert. Most often, dinner was complete by 8:30 or 9:00, so the evening was still young. My gang then enjoyed the rest of the evening at a nice bar, where the machos would begin the ritual of shooting cognacs with beer chasers. Imagine, before leaving the restaurant, before beginning really to drink, I had consumed over fifteen alcoholic beverages—and I didn't have a problem.

With increased tolerance, I wasn't getting drunk, and most who did not know me could not ascertain that I had had more than a drink or two. Imagine the intake on evenings when I did get drunk. What began to happen, and what seems to be common among many alcoholics, is that my tolerance level actually began to drop. Where I could once finish a bottle of Grand Marnier alone without any problems, I was getting tipsy after four or five "simple drinks." I can remember thinking that perhaps there might be some kind of problem. I was focused on the wrong problem as I began to wonder if my age was getting the best of me and I should begin to exercise more or eat before I drink. This is the point where I was capable of convincing myself that the world centered on my judgments. My behavior was my God-given right, and drinking was one of those rights.

From forgetting that I was a father of three talented and beautiful little girls, to forgetting what my wedding vows meant, I was capable of making any excuse for my behavior. More important, I truly believed my excuses. The numbness of my tolerance was so mood-altering that nothing else seemed to hold any importance unless it became a crisis. As my tolerance levels increased, so did my consumption. As my consumption increased, I fell deeper and deeper into my own isolated world of fear. This fear provided the impetus to "stinking thinking," whereby all of my thoughts were alcoholic-based, self-centered explanations to my self for my behaviors. The alcoholic begins thereby to drink more and more, with the frequency increasing with almost every use. The toxic effects (discussed later in this book) begin to cause scientifically documented, bizarre psychological and emotional imbalance.

Alcoholics develop tolerance when their brains compensate for the disruption caused by the alcohol in both their bodies and their behaviors. Some studies have shown that impairment within the same drinking session actually lessens with continued alcohol intake for some alcoholics. Whatever the brain chemistry, or whatever the reasons behind it, tolerance levels do increase in alcoholics, while those levels do not increase in "social drinkers."

Other studies have shown that tolerance is greater when drinking occurs in a familiar, drinking-type environment. For example, McCusker and Brown (1990) found that "environmental-dependent tolerance" occurred when men were asked to perform a specific task in two separate environments while drinking. One environment was officelike, the other barlike. The men performed the same task much better when tested in a barlike environment. When tested in an officelike environment, they felt uncomfortable with the formality and knowledge that it was inappropriate to drink in that environment.

"Learned tolerance," on the other hand, occurs when new tasks are learned while drinking. Later, when drinking again, these tasks are performed easily while many other new tasks are performed with some difficulty and lesser success (LeBlanc et al. 1973; Vogel-Sprott 1979; Vogel-Sprott et al. 1991).

Scientific Alcoholism

If alcohol were invented and introduced today, it probably would not be approved by the Federal Drug Administration (FDA) for over-the-counter sales. Some believe that the final by-product of alcohol, once the body has removed all the sugars and the alcohol has undergone a complete breakdown, is a chemical similar to that left over in the body once heroin is broken down.

Alcohol use and overuse affect many parts of the body and brain, starting in the stomach, where it is almost immediately absorbed into the bloodstream. The effects of alcohol vary in every individual, with the amount of alcohol consumed and the length of time involved in continued use. In smaller quantities alcohol reacts as a stimulant. As larger quantities are consumed, alcohol begins to act as a sedative. After prolonged use, the effects change, requiring more alcohol consumption to achieve a stimulant effect and also allowing the chemical processes that occur in depression to occur more rapidly.

The strength or alcoholic content of a beverage has an additional effect on the absorption rate, with the stronger drinks being absorbed quicker. Lack of food in the stomach can speed absorption, as there is nothing to dilute the alcohol. Different kinds of mixers or additives within the beverage can also affect absorption rates of the alcohol. Generally, natural mixers such as water and fruit juices can slow the process, and artificial mixers, such as sodas and treated sugar by-products, speed the process. As most people initially dislike the taste of alcohol, it has been found that the onset of drinking behaviors often includes the mixing of alcohol with something sweet.

Once the alcohol enters the bloodstream, it is routed throughout the body in a race to the small intestine, the liver, the lungs, the heart, the brain, and virtually every other organ within the body, including the muscle tissue. Research suggests that the processes leading to the development of alcoholism, however, reside largely in the brain. Approximately 25 percent of the alcohol is immediately absorbed into the blood system. For this reason, we will focus on the effects on the brain and the process occurring throughout consumption. The brain itself is protected by dura mater that allows only the most basic of molecular structures to enter the brain canal and later the spinal cord. This is required to feed the brain oxygen and water, keeping it fresh and vibrant while maintaining a balance of fluids required for neurotransmitters involved in our thinking processes. The terms *epidural* and *subdural* refer to the layers above and below the dura mater protecting the brain. Alcohol affects the layer below the dura mater—the brain itself. Alcohol has a simple molecular structure that includes water and can therefore pass quite easily into the brain while many other drugs cannot. When large amounts of alcohol enter the brain structure, many things occur, including a negative effect on reasoning and the central nervous system.

Most of us have heard of the thousands of destroyed or dead brain cells after a night out. This isn't too far off the truth, as studies have shown that with continued alcohol use, the brain tissue decreases in volume. Berger (1992) believes that alcohol causes the red blood cells to clump together. His analysis of other scientific research on alcoholism leads him to assert that this larger mass has difficulty traveling throughout the bloodstream to carry the normal (and needed) supply of oxygen to the brain. Brain cells come under duress in as little as five minutes without oxygen and begin to die after periods longer than fifteen minutes. "In time, alcohol abuse alters brain cell function, shrinks the cerebral cortex, and throws the hormonal system so out of balance that, some doctors think, it induces the body to shut off production of natural euphoriants. Without these euphoriants, the theory goes, drinkers fall into mental distress" (Robertson 1988).

Our body works hard to eliminate foreign substances, including alcohol. Many areas help in this elimination but none as much as the liver. Once alcohol enters the liver, it is actually attacked by enzymes called *dehydrogenase ADH,* killing two hydrogen atoms within the molecular structure of alcohol and forming a new substance called *acetaldehyde,* a highly toxic (deadly in large quantities) agent that causes many of the symptoms of a hangover. The liver then enlists another enzyme in the body to break down acetaldehyde into acetate, which is, in time, converted to carbon dioxide and water, then finally eliminated from the body as waste. Data from two relatively new studies underwritten by the National Institute on Alcohol Abuse and Alcoholism (NIAAA) suggest that dehydrogenase may be associated with resistance and vulnerability to alcohol (NIAAA 1998).

To better enable a basic understanding of the brain and how alcohol may affect the normal brain processes, we must review a short description. All brain functions, including addiction, involve active communication between different nerve cells, called *neurons*, located in the brain. Each of these connects with thousands of other neurons that are kept separate by microscopic spacings called *synapses*. The directional impulses, or messages, are carried across these synapses by chemical fluids called *neurotransmitters*. Each neuron maintains a receptor protein capable of responding to only one specific type of message but that can indirectly affect the conversion of messages from other neurons into changes within the receiving neuron, called *signal transductions* (Shepherd 1994). When these receptors are activated, it causes an increase or decrease in the neuron's responsiveness to additional messages (NIAAA 1996, no. 33). These neurons are known to support many long-term changes in the brain environment, such as the presence of alcohol (Grant et al. 1979; Grant 1987).

Once acetaldehyde builds up within the brain, it also inhibits the use of some of our amines, or the neurotransmitters that help control reasoning, by keeping their enzymes busy. Alcohol's effects on genes may alter the structure and function of specific receptors that involve intoxication and physical dependency. Further, alcohol's effects on genes is thought to alter the proteins involved in the signal transduction. These amines then store up for possible future use and interact with the acetaldehydes to form *isoquinolines*, a substance similar to opiates. Some say that these isoquinolines are possibly the birth of a desire or need for continued alcohol use, while others question whether they actually act negatively upon the opiate receptors in our brains. The brain is invaded by leftover acetaldehydes that cause mental confusion, then by unnatural levels of amines that are mixed with opiatelike isoquinolines that can also cause delusional thinking.

The key neurotransmitters (or neuromodulators) involved with normal reinforcement include a group of chemicals (dopamine and endogenous opioids) similar to morphine. These chemicals seem to amplify pleasurable effects and the extremes of rewarding activities in addition to helping to maintain the drinking behavior (Froehlich 1997). Di Chiara (1997) describes how the neurotransmitter dopamine acts as the reward center in the brain. This is thought to contribute to motivation and reinforcement of alcohol consumption. The receptor for another neurotransmitter known as *gamma-aminobutyric acid (GABA)* is thought to be the major inhibitor neurotransmitter of the brain. It is believed that alcohol induces changes in this neurotransmitter and contributes to alcohol dependence and tolerance as well as to the predisposition to alcoholism.

Researchers are making great efforts to find out the specific use of acetaldehydes and neurotransmitters in the brain and whether there is a link to addiction within the alcoholic. In the early 1970s, Wallgren and Berry concluded in their work that stimulation occurs with low doses of alcohol and depression occurs with high doses. Other researchers have shown that neuron activity itself is stimulated by low alcohol use and depressed by higher levels of use.

One of the natural amines within the brain that is thought to be common to alcohol preference and overuse is *serotonin*. Serotonin helps to regulate many of our mental and bodily functions and also helps to modulate reinforcement (Grant et al. 1979; Grant 1987). In 1968, Meyers and Veale performed experiments on rats that proved three important points. First, rats that were given a chemical to increase the normal levels of serotonin in the brain drastically reduced or completely quit drinking water treated with alcohol when they had been choosing it over regular water for some time. Second, when THP (the product of acetaldehydes and dopamine) was injected into the rats' brains, it caused rats that normally rejected alcohol altogether to drink it excessively. Third, rats that naturally had lower levels of serotonin in their brains had a higher tendency to drink alcohol. This was confirmed by Murphy with a study on alcohol-preferring and alcohol-nonpreferring rats. In a follow-up study in which the serotonin levels were artificially increased and decreased, it became evident that when more serotonin was present, the rats reduced their alcohol intake; when the serotonin was decreased, the alcohol consumption increased (Murphy 1980).

According to Dr. David Lovinger, serotonin levels also appear lower in human brains of alcoholics than in the brains of non-alcoholics (Lovinger 1997). It is also thought that the serotonin interaction with dopamine may promote the intoxifying and rewarding effects of alcohol use in alcoholics. *Glutamate* is believed to be the major excitatory tool of the brain. Some studies have shown that the receptors that control glutamate's actions are also affected by alcohol, possibly creating part of the dysfunction associated with alcoholism.

This research is the basis for the belief that, regardless of user willpower or preference, a mysterious set of chemical reactions within the brain causes a desire or need in alcoholics to drink. Many studies that have focused on the effects of alcohol on the brain have provided fundamental proof that alcoholics exhibit different levels of chemical abnormalities within the brain. It is not known whether alcoholics are born with these brain chemistry abnormalities or whether they are effected over time. It is not known what psychological event, if any, may trigger changes. Furthermore, it is not yet known what exactly results from the alcohol or the alcohol breakdown within our systems. But what is slowly becoming an accepted theory is that these abnormalities do exist within the alcoholic brain, through no fault of the alcoholic. Alcoholics have a different brain makeup from that of non-alcoholics, and it seems that many areas of the brain are negatively affected by alcohol abuse.

Heredity

Goodwin (1976) first claimed a theory of heredity as the primary cause of alcoholism. Studying a research pool of adoptees, he found that birth children of alcoholics, even if separated from their alcoholic parents at birth and adopted by nonalcoholics, had a 400 percent higher rate of becoming alcoholics than birth children of nonalcoholics. This research questions the Freudian claims of environmental and parental factors as the primary seeds of alcoholism. Goodwin's results dismiss the notion that problem drinking (nonalcoholic) and alcoholism are in any way related. In fact, he takes a rather bold stance when he states that problem drinking appears to be caused by emotional problems, while alcoholic drinking is caused by heredity. Pickens et al. (1991; see Vaillant 1985) later studied 169 same-sex pairs of twins where at least one had sought treatment for alcoholism. They found a much greater concordance of alcohol abuse and dependence in identical twins than in fraternal twins. Other studies show that the percentage of brothers and sisters born years apart who both become alcoholics drops lower yet if they are not born to alcoholic parents.

Cloninger hypothesized that so-called Type II alcoholics (see page 39), characterized mainly by having an early onset of problems due to consumption, have a more heritable form of alcoholism and are quite antisocial. Schuckit (1992) emphasized the argument that the antisocial behavior is more likely to be heredity-based than is the actual alcoholism.

Blum et al. (1991) studied the marker referred to as the *dopamine (D$_2$) receptor* within the brain. They found this receptor to be more present in alcoholics than in nonalcoholics. In animal studies, this D2 receptor has been linked to brain functions relating to reward, reinforcement, and motivation. Although the Blum studies have not been duplicated, a number of researchers believe that dopamine may affect the intensity or severity of alcoholism but may not be the cause of the disease.

A few years earlier, Kissin and Begleiter (1972) addressed the fetal alcohol syndrome (FAS) of babies born of alcoholic mothers. Because babies eat and drink what their mothers do, if the mother drinks, even to a small degree, so does the baby. Damage to brain tissue in an unborn baby has been shown to be directly linked to the mother's alcohol consumption. Where two glasses of wine might make a mother a little tipsy, imagine what it must do to a baby with virtually no defenses against alcohol. While brain tissue loss in adults due to alcohol abuse can often be regrown or replaced, the effects of fetal brain exposure to alcohol are found to be permanent. In addition, animal research has shown that the earlier in the pregnancy the fetus is exposed to alcohol, the more permanent and severe the damage may be to the unborn baby. The damage that can occur in just the first couple of weeks into pregnancy can range from many developmental disorders to limb deformities.

Over twelve thousand babies are born each year in the United States with physical and mental disorders as the result of their exposure to alcohol during gestation. If in fact heredity and brain chemistry combined can be triggers of alcoholism, it stands to reason that many of us are born alcoholics. Who knows the amount of alcohol necessary to trigger the addiction? Is it a glass, a case, or a drop?

Once genetic factors that cause alcoholism are isolated, it is a sure bet they will be present in both parent and child. Milam and Ketcham (1981) believe that a baby may be born an alcoholic. Years later, when taking that first drink, the addiction is instantly triggered. This may support the fact that some alcoholics experience late-stage addictive problems and withdrawal symptoms upon taking their first or second drink. Robertson (1988) wrote: "To date, there is only one proven predictor of alcoholism, the strongest of all—a family history of alcoholism." Vaillant (1983) included a similar thought in his analysis when he answered the question of how alcoholics were different. He said that future alcoholics were more likely to come from ethnic groups that tolerated adult drunkenness, were more likely to be related to other alcoholics, and were probably antisocial.

Much earlier Menninger (1938), one of the pioneers in alcoholism research prior to and during the Alcoholics Anonymous movement, stated that alcoholism was only considered a hereditary trait by the "older psychiatrists." Furthermore, he stated, "Alcoholism cannot possibly be a hereditary trait, but for a father to be an alcoholic is an easy way for a son to learn *how* to effect the retaliation he later feels impelled to inflict" (Vaillant 1985). Goodwin and others have helped dispel this theory through their research, but it is mentioned here to stress the constantly changing dialogue and opinions regarding alcoholism and its causes.

In his book *The Natural History of Alcoholism*, Vaillant (1983) sums up the research of Jellinek (1960), Snyder (1962), and Heath (1975) with this statement: "The attitudes toward drinking and the socially sanctioned drinking practices surrounded by which a child learns to drink play an important role in the development of subsequent alcoholism." The McCords (1960) and Gluecks (1950) have held that dysfunctional families with many problems, as reflected by a childhood environmental weakness scale, invariably produce children who are later afflicted with alcoholism. Many others have also laid forth theories that alcoholism is often influenced by environmental factors. As this book unfolds, we will also see that it is difficult to find one concrete cause of alcoholism, as this disease attacks us at virtually every opportunity and within every fiber of our bodies, our minds, and, indeed, our souls. The fact remains that this is a disease caused by a variety of unknown sources.

The idea that alcohol runs in families and may have genetic influences has been discussed for decades. Beginning in the 1970s (Goodwin 1971–1976; Cotton 1979), many studies began to prove that it does run in families, but whether it is because of the child's home environment or because of inherited genes is still in dispute.

Stress

The term *stress* is often misunderstood both in terminology and in the effect on the human brain. Stress is most used to describe the conscious feeling of tension, anxiety, and pressure. Although mainly thought of as harmful if prolonged or intense, stress is often worn as a badge of honor by people making their livings through stressful situations. The way the brain works with stress is a highly complicated network of activity involving the central nervous system, the cardiovascular system, and the adrenal system. As a purely subjective action (except when used in clinical terms regarding physiological processes), the stress response varies in all individuals.

Many researchers have found that high levels of stress may influence drinking and alcohol abuse (Sadava and Pak 1993; Jennison 1992). As discussed in the section on heredity, Cloninger found that stressful early childhood experiences have an association with alcoholism. A number of animal studies further concluded that there is a direct relationship between alcohol consumption and unavoidable stress (Volpicelli 1987; Nash and Maickel 1988). In both humans and animals it has been shown that drinking appears definitely to follow stress (Kalant 1990; Pohorecky 1991; Nash and Maickel 1988). In studies with mice placed in an open maze, inducing stress, it was found that alcohol reduced anxiety in these mice. Furthermore, when mice were given alcohol before being placed in sections of the maze they had come to avoid, they would spend more time in the maze. In a study of monkeys, Higley (1997) explored the relationship that alcohol has with being peer-raised or mother-raised and how isolation may influence drinking. First, he found that drinking in monkeys taken from their mothers and then peer-raised was much higher than monkeys raised by their mothers. Second, when the mother-raised monkeys were later isolated from their peers, they drank to the same extent as peer-raised monkeys. Last, in all model groups, the animals that displayed more anxiety were the animals that also drank more alcohol (Higley 1991).

An excellent example of an alcoholic causing more problems through the perceived solution to his problems is what I call the "cause-and-effect stress syndrome paradox." Alcohol abuse is known to increase the adrenaline levels within us, and adrenaline is known to create stress. In other words, alcohol produces the same physiological stress that the alcoholic is trying to avoid or eliminate.

One of the theories behind the continuation of internal stress and the alcoholic paradox is that as children, our negative experiences can be put into a permanent playback mode on our "subconscious tape recorders." We continue to re-explore the past over and over again throughout our lives, without being aware of doing so. As each occasion occurs, we continue to fail to resolve the issues and have our stress reaffirmed not only through this failure but also through the guilt associated with the continued alcohol use.

Although it may well be a narrow (and Freudian) focus to include childhood experiences as a predisposition to alcoholism, it is rare to find an alcoholic who has no shame-based feelings of inadequacy generated during early childhood.

Blackouts

One of the most misunderstood by-products of alcoholism is the blackout. Quite different from passing out due to excessive drinking, an alcoholic experiencing a blackout is totally functioning and often seems totally normal to an observer. The difference is, once the blackout episode has ended, the alcoholic has virtually no memory of what she or he did or what happened during that time period. Blackouts have been known to last as little as an hour or as long as a few days. They have occurred early in the disease, late in the disease, or not at all, but are most prevalent and regular in the later stages of alcoholism. I am an example of one who dismissed the concept of blackouts, even in early recovery. But once I began truly to review my past, taking a fearless personal inventory, I realized that blackouts did indeed exist while my disease and drinking were active.

A professional engineer I know well experienced a blackout the very first time he drank. One of the last times he drank, he became "conscious" with two cases of empty beer on the passenger seat of his car, while driving his car in a different state, over six hundred miles away from his home and from where he started his trip. An airline pilot I've spoken with was thought to have had blackouts while flying, though he admits only to having blackouts in his hotel room before flying. To this day, he cannot accept the possibility that he might have flown a plane during a blackout, yet he cannot explain why many moments in his memory are gone forever.

This phenomenon often explains the memory, or lack of memory, the morning after a fight with a spouse during a heavy drinking episode. It is similar to walking into a room and forgetting what you are to do there.

In major heart surgery, it is not uncommon for the recovering patient to have lost short-term memory details, such as a phone number or a combination to a lock. It is said that this is due to being under anesthesia for a prolonged period of time. The effects of prolonged, excessive drinking can have the same effect on short-term memory, with the alcoholic having an even greater chance of never recalling the loss than a recovered heart patient.

It is important to note that while providing comfort to an alcoholic during recovery, it is not recommended that blackouts be accepted as an excuse for past behavioral problems. An alcoholic must be held accountable for any behavior. But remember that forgiveness is giving up hope for a better past, and moving on.

Most researchers and alcoholics alike agree on this point: blackouts tend to occur for the first time during the middle stages of the progression of alcoholism and become more frequent in the later stages. This is not the case for all alcoholics but seems to be the normal chain of events.

The Alcoholic Test

Quite simply, no one true test of alcoholism exists. Currently, over a hundred testing and evaluation procedures are used to gauge alcoholism. All of these tests identify a series of behavioral patterns common to most alcoholics that can exemplify alcoholism in its purest and most clinical form. The problem is, in using only this test or that test to make a quick decision regarding alcoholic dependency, one can often exclude those poor alcoholic souls who do not fit the exact parameters noted. Or one may include non-alcoholics who out of coincidence may fit several alcoholic behaviors. Only the alcoholic is capable of knowing the truth about his or her alcoholism, and only after a suitable period of recovery and abstinence.

The SMAST, or Short Michigan Alcoholism Screening Test, maintains a greater than 90 percent accuracy for the identification of alcoholism. The alcoholism-indicating responses are shown in parentheses. If your answers match only three or more of the following questions, most professionals would yield a diagnosis of alcoholism. Only two matching answers indicates a possibility of alcoholism (Selzer et al. 1975).

Short Michigan Alcoholism Screening Test

1. Do you feel you are a normal drinker? (By normal we mean you drink *less than* or *as much as* other people.) (No)
2. Does your wife, husband, a parent, or other near relative ever worry or complain about your drinking? (Yes)
3. Do you ever feel guilty about your drinking? (Yes)
4. Do friends or relatives think you are a normal drinker? (No)
5. Are you able to stop drinking when you want to? (No)
6. Have you ever attended a meeting of Alcoholics Anonymous? (Yes)
7. Has drinking ever created problems between you and your wife, husband, a parent, or other near relative? (Yes)
8. Have you gotten into trouble at work because of drinking? (Yes)
9. Have you ever neglected your obligations, your family, or your work for two or more days in a row because you were drinking? (Yes)
10. Have you ever gone to anyone for help about your drinking? (Yes)
11. Have you ever been in a hospital because of drinking? (Yes)
12. Have you ever been arrested for drunken driving, driving while intoxicated, or driving under the influence of alcoholic beverages? (Yes)
13. Have you ever been arrested, even for a few hours, because of other drunken behavior? (Yes)

I have hundreds of other barometers to use in evaluating alcoholism. What I have found is that all alcoholics have allowed drinking to affect their personal lives and, in most cases, without their knowledge. Asking the following ten simple questions of a suspected alcoholic can help gauge whether that person is in need of help.

Many alcoholics truly believe that they can alter the results of psychological testing, and frankly, despite scientific proof to the contrary, I believe them. If they know the reason for the question, they can respond accordingly. Asking the following questions over a period of time may prove beneficial. Again, the alcoholism-indicating responses are in parentheses. All of the diagnostic tools boil down to one question: Has alcohol in any way caused a problem in your life?

A Diagnostic Analysis

1. Do you ever drink to unwind or to celebrate? (Yes)
2. Have you ever had a fight with a loved one after drinking? (Yes)
3. Can you drink more than most people you know? (Yes)
4. Has your tolerance for alcohol increased over the years, or do you drink more than you used to? (Yes)
5. Do you ever skip an event because alcohol is not being served? (Yes)
6. Has a loved one ever offered to drive after a night of drinking? (Yes)
7. Have you ever thrown a party where no alcohol was served? (No)
8. Have you had more than three hangovers in the last three years? (Yes)
9. Has anyone, including a loved one, ever told you that you drink too much? (Yes)
10. Have you ever missed any work due to drinking, even if only an hour? (Yes)

Following is a survey which Whitfield (1987) modified and adopted from the Children of Alcoholics Screening Test (Jones and Pilat 1993), The Family Alcohol Quiz from Al-Anon, and The Howard Family Questionnaire. A "yes" answer to only two questions suggests that someone in your family has a good chance of having a drinking problem. A "yes" answer to four or more questions indicates a definite drinking problem within your family.

Family Drinking Survey

1. Does someone in your family undergo personality changes when he or she drinks to excess?
2. Do you feel that drinking is more important to this person than you are?
3. Do you feel sorry for yourself and frequently indulge in self-pity because of what you feel alcohol is doing to your family?
4. Has some member's excessive drinking ruined special occasions?
5. Do you find yourself covering up for the consequences of someone else's drinking?
6. Have you ever felt guilty, apologetic, or responsible for the drinking of a member of your family?
7. Does one of your family member's use of alcohol cause fights and arguments?
8. Have you ever tried to fight the drinker by joining in the drinking?
9. Do the drinking habits of some family members make you feel depressed or angry?
10. Is your family having financial difficulties because of drinking?
11. Do you feel like you had an unhappy home life because of the drinking of some members of your family?
12. Have you ever tried to control the drinker's behavior by hiding the car keys, pouring the liquor down the drain, etc.?
13. Do you find yourself distracted from your responsibilities because of this person's drinking?
14. Do you often worry about a family member's drinking?
15. Are holidays more a nightmare than a celebration because of a family member's drinking behavior?
16. Are most of your drinking family member's friends heavy drinkers?
17. Do you find it necessary to lie to employers, relatives, or friends in order to hide your family member's drinking?
18. Do you find yourself responding differently to members of your family when they are using alcohol?

19. Have you ever been embarrassed or felt the need to apologize for the drinker's actions?
20. Does some family member's use of alcohol make you fear for your own safety or the safety of other members of your family?
21. Have you ever thought that one of your family members had a drinking problem?
22. Have you ever lost sleep because of a family member's drinking?
23. Have you ever encouraged one of your family members to stop or cut down on his or her drinking?
24. Have you ever threatened to leave home or to leave a family member because of his or her drinking?
25. Did a family member ever make a promise that he or she did not keep because of drinking?
26. Did you ever wish that you could talk to someone who could understand and help the alcohol-related problems of a family member?
27. Have you ever felt sick, cried, or had a knot in your stomach after worrying about a family member's drinking?
28. Has a family member ever failed to remember what occurred during a drinking period?
29. Does your family member avoid social situations where alcoholic beverages will not be served?
30. Does your family member have periods of remorse after drinking occasions and apologize for his or her behavior?
31. Are there any symptoms or nervous problems that you have experienced since you have known your heavy drinker?

Rivers (1994) best reviews the theories of both Cahalan (1970) and Plaut (1967) that describe problem drinking as an interference with one's function rather than any specific drinking behavior. Time is spent in Rivers's wonderful book listing additional definitive traits of alcoholics from Cahalan, Knupfer, and Pattison and Koffman. Even Chafetz's illusions of a definition of safe or moderate drinking for the alcoholic are reviewed, although most maintain that the terms *safe* and *drinker* are not possible in the same sentence when discussing alcoholism. Most alcoholics in recovery are convinced, through trial and error (or, better stated, relapse), that total abstinence is absolutely necessary for long-term recovery. This honest approach by Rivers in presenting the clinical findings of experts such as Pattison and Koffman—that take issue with mainline organizations such as the National Council on Alcoholism, who they feel often ignore the more popular theories on early-stage alcoholic symptoms—is a valuable addition to any recovery program, and I have found it useful in mine.

Milam and Ketchum (1981) rely on one simple diagnostic tool as the strongest of all indicators: the disease's profound progression. "Alcoholism does not do a little damage and then suddenly stop its attack. If the alcoholic continues to drink, he will not be able to reverse his psychological problems; they will only get worse," they write. Again, a review of the Jellinek theories and the Jellinek curve provide an earlier and much more detailed expression and analysis of this same concept.

Types of Alcoholics

Although the medical and psychoanalytical professions tend to agree that there are two distinct classifications of alcoholics, as an alcoholic myself, I welcome the descriptions found in Alcoholics Anonymous that include all those other active alcoholics who do not exactly fit within those two classifications. All in all, I have never found an effective means of describing all alcoholics in one or two categories. In that vein, the following should provide enough insight to allow a personal analysis of both the questioning alcoholic and the codependent.

A study of Swedish adoptees (Cloninger et al. 1981) and their biological and adoptive parents presented the Type I alcoholic as influenced more by environment than heredity. The onset of symptoms usually does not occur until after the age of about twenty-five. The personality traits of this group include psychological dependence and an inner knowledge of some kind regarding this dependency. The Type I alcoholic tends to admit and, in some cases, accept that the root of the problem is alcohol, but can use this same acceptance to avoid blame long enough to continue drinking for some time. The sense of denial can include a warped sense of blame.

The Type II alcoholic is more influenced by heredity and is younger. These alcoholics are said to be more antisocial and have a more difficult time in abstinence. The Type II alcoholic has often grown up in an alcoholic household with little understanding of a functioning family life, thereby making the behavioral patterns all the more acceptable. This alcoholic has grown up with and developed a deep sense of isolation and solitude (Cloninger 1987). A model later explored at the University of Connecticut described a similar typology called Type A and Type B, whereby the Type B disorder tends to be more severe than Type A (Meyer et al. 1983).

The Big Book, the manual for Alcoholics Anonymous, describes four categories of alcoholics (*Alcoholics Anonymous* 1976, 108–10). These categories are paraphrased below.

1. A heavy drinker that is constant or occasional. The drinking may be slowing up the alcoholic mentally or physically, but she or he does not see it. Often a source of embarrassment, the alcoholic is certain he or she can handle the liquor and that it does no harm. This alcoholic would be insulted if called an alcoholic.
2. This alcoholic is showing a lack of control and is unable to abstain even when possessing the desire. He or she now admits being occasionally entirely out of control when drinking but is positive things will get better. Business performance and relationships with friends may be suffering. The alcoholic is worried at times and is now aware of being unable to drink like other people. This alcoholic is often remorseful after heavy drinking but still begins to drink again thinking he or she can drink moderately.
3. This alcoholic has gone much further than the other two. Friends have slipped away and his or her home is in ruins. She or he admits being unable to drink like other people but still can't understand why. This alcoholic may have come to the point of desperately wanting to quit but being unable to do so.
4. This alcoholic can become violent and may have been placed into one institution or another. Often this alcoholic appears insane

when drinking, and even doctors shake their heads and
recommend committing this person.

Milam and Ketcham, in their book *Under the Influence,* break
down the categories into three distinct stages: The *early and adaptive stage,* where the alcoholic's tolerance level begins to rise. This
adaptation, they describe, is a tool for survival. The *middle stage* is
announced through an increase in penalties outweighing the
benefits of drinking. Although the exact point of movement from
the adaptive to the middle stage is not clearly defined, it is recognized as the point where the size of cells actually increases to
accommodate the alcohol. The *late* or *deteriorate stage* is representative of a total loss of control, overexcited brain chemistry and
brain damage, and physical damage to the body.

In any description of an alcoholic, several other subcategories
can be found that can also accurately describe the progressive nature of the disease. The *social alcoholic* is still at or near peak performance at work and at home but has just begun the first step in
a slow downward spiral of full-blown alcoholism. Using social and
business activities as excuses to drink and accepting and planning social and business activities around events where alcohol is
present are red flags. I have lost many possible friends over the
years because of not accepting social invitations from them in
fear that they may not drink up to my standards. The social alcoholic begins regular private drinking at home, ending each workday with the customary drink or two, or more. So as not to look
different, he or she may begin to sneak a drink or two when out
with others and will most often be the sport who orders another
round for everyone at the table, although everyone else still has
the better part of their drinks left. Few people, if any, have noticed any drinking problem, as at this stage, it is quite easy to hide
all but the most intense of problems from others.

The *problem-drinker alcoholic* has a pattern of drinking that
causes lack of responsibility as problems begin to occur at home
and at work. Denial is in full force at this stage, and the alcoholic
is now actively massaging the technique for dealing with future

threats to his or her use of alcohol or other drugs. Despite occasional problems driving or with the law, fights with loved ones and co-workers, and the onset of enormous resentment and guilt, problem drinkers are beginning a pattern of alcohol abuse. They maintain no concept of drinking for taste and often think about their next drink. Little time comes between drinks, as drinking has become an almost daily routine. They are beginning to hide drinking more, surrounding themselves with people who accept and often share their level of consumption, and they may be known by their first names at local taverns. This stage is usually the onset of isolation, and these alcoholics find themselves pulling away from family and loved ones to find security through alcohol itself and the "warm fuzzies" shared with other drinkers.

The *dependent alcoholic* has a deep dependency on the continued use of alcohol and has lost all desire to handle life on life's terms. This alcoholic uses alcohol as the drug of choice to change from one mood to another, often forgetting the prior mood with every few drinks. At this stage, the alcoholic becomes incapable to quit drinking, and activities once enjoyed are eliminated from the calendar altogether. Occasional binge drinking begins in this stage, and tolerance levels grow with almost every binge. Most of the people around notice when this alcoholic has been drinking. Family members and friends run from confrontation after drinking, as tempers tend to flare, and everything becomes everyone else's fault. This is the stage where different forms of mental and physical abuse of others can begin to occur. Although occasional abstinence can still occur to prove a point, this alcoholic holds a "dry drunk" mind-set throughout the periods of not drinking, knowing all the while it is just a short-term sacrifice and soon the glass will be full again. Obvious relationship problems occur at this level, and this alcoholic is typically involved in self-serving pleasures. Even when surrounded by people, this alcoholic has withdrawn into an inner isolation of despair and low self-esteem. Knowing no other alternative, this alcoholic often turns to some type of prayer on his or her terms. Offering deals and negotiations with God, as though they might actually have something that God needs, becomes commonplace. At this level, the alcoholic knows there is a problem, but denial is so practiced by now, he or she believes the problem is most certainly not with the alcohol. This alcoholic is too sick to maintain any rationality of thoughts that would allow him or her to understand the problem.

The *addicted alcoholic* has fallen to stereotypical levels most often thought of by outsiders. Drinking alone is much more prevalent, and drinking anywhere, including under the proverbial bridge, has become natural. Binge drinking is now a much more normal part of the pattern, while at the same time tolerance levels jump and dip drastically. A friend whom I have come to know in recovery was well into the addictive stage and explained his daily departure from the office lunch to buy and drink a full fifth of vodka under a nearby bridge before returning to work. He explained how he enjoyed being the king under the bridge, with local homeless people looking up to him as the leader and provider of daily vodka. He had his spot where he sat, like a favorite barstool he used to have at an upscale bar. He said that during this period he was totally comfortable with all of this and looked forward to visiting his friends each lunch hour. The addictive alcoholic is in the chronic stage of the disease. Left unattended and without help, death is near for this alcoholic. Intervention is a must if this alcoholic has not yet realized a need for help. The obsession has become so strong that there is little else this alcoholic can think about. Blackouts are common, and delusional thinking becomes the normal state of affairs. Denial allows this alcoholic to rationalize virtually any behavior.

At this stage, obvious physical and psychological problems occur. The addiction has robbed this alcoholic of any ability to choose. This person has noticeably changed in appearance and attitude and can grasp no other concept but that one more drink will not hurt. A binge for this alcoholic can last days, and morning consumption can almost become necessary. This alcoholic has as much a problem when she or he does drink as when not.

Withdrawal symptoms can occur within less than a twenty-four-hour period without a drink. Recovering alcoholics who had entered this death-trap stage of alcoholism recall that they often made conscious decisions that another drink was more important than life itself. For those alcoholics who to this day live in this state of fear, I add you to my prayers every night. The majority of alcoholics who have progressed this far down the scale have at some point attempted to quit drinking, and many have been in and out of jails and treatment centers several times. Having failed at sobriety on so many occasions, they have the most difficult time accepting the possibility of a sober life and often continue to relapse without an effective program.

It is important to point out the difference in definitions and typologies of alcoholics. I leave the typologies to professionals engaged in the study of alcoholism as a disease, and I write here about the many definitions used by so many authors and researchers. In the 1950s, the World Health Organization defined alcoholism as a simple dependency on alcohol that causes physical and mental disturbances, while also having a negative effect on personal relationships. To date, this definition best puts all the existing definitions into one sentence, while ignoring the concept of a disease.

In late 1970, Wanberg and Knapp looked at the subgroups they thought occurred within the other known alcoholic types. These subgroups included using alcohol for stress relief, socialization, self-assurance, and regular patterned drinking. Since then, many others have taken great effort in describing and redescribing the varying groups and subgroups of alcoholics. They have been examined in physical, mental, biological, and physiological manners to group them within certain therapeutic divisions for treatment recommendations. Add in the likely prospect of additional nonalcoholic psychological disorders, and the task becomes quite uncomfortable.

Psychologists, therapists, and researchers alike have had difficulty grasping or accepting all the different views and classifications. Brickman et al. (1982) tried to put many of them together in one form when he listed four distinct categories of alcoholism based solely upon the "responsibility model." In that, it seems we all wish to find who is responsible as a means of cleaning our own slate. I found this representation unusually accurate.

Brickman's Models of Alcoholism

- *The Moral Model*—The alcoholic is responsible for the problem, the use, and the cure.
- *The Medical Model*—Alcoholism is a disease, and therefore, the alcoholic has no responsibility for either the problem or the cure.
- *The Compensatory Model*—The alcoholic must be handicapped emotionally in some way, so is not responsible for the problem of alcoholism but is responsible for the cure.
- *The Enlightenment Model*—The alcoholic is totally responsible for the problem but, because of the need for intervention by a Higher Power or outside source, not for the cure.

All of the varying attempts at a truly definitive description or type of alcoholic seem to have many similarities. As complex as the disease is, once all of the theories are boiled down, they share the same simple premises: Alcoholics cannot stop drinking alone. Use of alcohol affects the lives of alcoholics in a negative fashion. The alcoholic's use of alcohol results from a need to change his or her current perception of life experiences. And finally, alcohol use by alcoholics is fear based.

The Dry Drunk

The expression *dry drunk,* used in alcoholic circles around the world, refers to an active alcoholic mind-set while in abstinence. Until the alcoholic enters recovery, abstinence means little. The alcoholic still maintains alcoholic thoughts, patterns, and behaviors. Although the violent and combative "always right" thought process may seem to subside, the alcoholic mind continues, knowing full well that use of alcohol can and will continue at some future point. A dry drunk alcoholic is dangerous in that abstinence provides a level of righteousness or self-approval for drinking at a later date. Alcoholics who do not accept their alcoholism believe that alcoholics can't quit drinking, and can therefore use short periods of abstinence to reinforce their denial. I have experienced many dry drunk alcoholics in Alcoholics Anonymous meetings, convincing themselves, and everyone else in the room, of their recovery, only to see them fall off the wagon weeks or months later. This alcoholic does not always have the outward drunken attitudes and actions one may assume. This person has an innate ability to function socially without using alcohol but has not in any way lost the inner turmoil and beliefs of the alcoholic mind.

Again, most alcoholics use a period of dry drunkenness to solidify their alcoholism, not to work on recovery from it. A period of abstinence, no matter the length of time, is totally ineffective unless the alcoholic is both involved in a true program of recovery that includes working with other alcoholics and is living an inner spirituality-based lifestyle.

Social Pressure

To an active alcoholic, the social pressure to drink that is prevalent in our society opens the door to despair. The day before I left for treatment, one of my best friends, my attorney, my banker, and a social contact all called and left messages to "meet for a drink." It became so ironic to me at that moment, that here I was, prepared to leave for a four-week treatment facility, and all of my phone messages were centered on drinking. Most alcoholics in professional business fields will tell you that drinking is actually required for their jobs. Salespeople have long been stereotyped as always wining and dining their clients. Even in recovery, by people I thought grasped the concept of alcoholism as a disease, I have been asked why I can't have just one drink.

Another type of social pressure, particularly noticed by a person in recovery, is the withdrawal of friendship by those who prefer to continue to drink. It is often discussed how a person in recovery should expect to lose some or most existing friends, particularly if they drink or use other drugs. A person I had thought of as a good friend, a friend whom I had named as the trustee of my daughters' trusts, has totally withdrawn from my life in less than one year. This same person once called nearly every week, if only to share a funny joke or story. There is one theory that people like this are afraid of recovery, as they see themselves or their own hidden disease in the mirror. Another theory is simply that some people, not happy with their own spiritual program, find contentment in seeing the failure of another. This theory is convincing because many alcoholics have probably exhibited such a sense of self-centeredness that nearly anyone could find joy in seeing that stripped away. Regardless, the withdrawal of friendship is mentioned here only as an example of the invisible type of outside pressure that can hinder recovery programs.

It is at times difficult to walk a dry road in a society that looks at the nondrinker as boring or as a "holy roller" who cannot handle his or her liquor. Comments about not being able to handle liquor can cut to the quick, particularly to an alcoholic who could easily drink a fifth before noon. In my profession, for example, I received no less than ten bottles of liquor for Christmas from outside associates on an average year. The year I entered recovery, I received three sets of pilsner glasses from three different family members as my Christmas gifts. And I didn't have a problem? Alcoholism is perhaps the only disease that is so misunderstood that society will actually pressure you into relapse unless you are blessed with a strong recovery foundation.

A quick story regarding the prevailing attitude that drink accompanies the man and spirituality does not: Two local politicians are running for Congress. One is receiving bad press. I have spent some time researching which of the two I will support. As a businessman, I have received requests for money from both camps. The man receiving bad press is being called a "Bible thumper" by members of the other camp. They have filed numerous ethics violations against him to disparage his religious beliefs and stature as an honest man. Having visited the fund-raiser of his opponent, I realized that the liquor was free and free flowing. It came to me how some people were voting against this other man because he is a "Bible thumper." Imagine, most people say they have a sound religious or spiritual foundation, and then they vote against someone solely for standing up for spiritual beliefs. I do not know which of these candidates is better for the job, nor do I intend on studying the matter any further. But I can tell you which of the two I will vote for.

Children are taught at a very early age in our school systems to "just say no" to drugs. But there exists no national school program for our youth to learn about alcohol and alcoholism. The social pressure develops early in our children, simply by watching us, their parents. Most children begin to pull away from their parents when they are around six or seven years old. This is also the time in which we, as parents, begin to pull our nurturing away and put the pressures of the life ahead on their shoulders. Parents should and must nurture their children, enabling them to see—through example, not through words—the benefits of a healthy, spiritually honest lifestyle.

The United States annual alcohol consumption has increased from approximately two gallons of ethanol per person in 1950 to over three gallons in 1980. This is social pressure in the purest form. Imagine the consequences to our schools if children went home with knowledge about alcoholic traits and symptoms and started talking to the alcoholic parent or parents about what they had learned. The denial from the parent could extend all the way back to the classrooms. It is sad to review the 1991 report to Congress from the secretary of the Department of Health and Human Services (DHHS). This report states that a survey of high school seniors indicated that over 32 percent admitted to being, or said most of their friends had gotten, drunk at least once a week. Could this be an indication of the future generation of alcoholics?

Another type of indirect social pressure is gossip. Life is full of people who make themselves feel better by talking about others. Father Martin, in my opinion one of the best speakers in Alcoholics Anonymous, once spoke at an AA convention on this very topic. He said that gossip was the unconscious tribute to those more fortunate by those less fortunate. I have found gossip to be one of the first frightening parts of recovery. As I've spent the better part of my life living without regard for the consequences, it is no wonder people found it amusing to talk about me. In looking back, it is almost comical to remember that 99 percent of the stories were totally untrue. I must have done quite a job in hiding the truth, because the truth is much worse than what was said. Nonetheless, in early recovery we hold on to many of our old memories, habits, and behaviors. Among them are the resentments that develop when other people talk about you or upset you. This is even more prevalent in active alcoholics. Faced with the truth on many occasions, alcoholics will do anything to protect their inner selves from being hurt by the truth; this includes learning to believe their own lies. As an active alcoholic, I endured years of both physical and emotional pain. I thought that initial recovery would provide singing angels, when in fact a single word could crush me. This pressure provided several instances of cravings and several occasions of resentment toward others that led to cravings.

Diagnostic Alcoholism

What are the behavioral patterns, thoughts, and actions that might help us to better identify ourselves as alcoholics? Many of the questions used in alcoholic testing are truly diagnostic, but what about those inner thoughts that are easily hidden from testing, and most certainly from loved ones? Having spent the better part of my life judging the world by my standards, I found that one of the difficulties in recovery is in not prejudging as alcoholics people with alcoholic traits. Many people have the same character defects as part of their natural makeup that alcoholics possess, but they are not alcoholics. One must be extremely careful not to use diagnostic alcoholic traits and characteristics as proof of alcoholism. They may indeed be a tool to aid in a professional's analysis of alcoholism, but they are sometimes traits also shared by nonalcoholics.

Understanding the alcoholic mind, if that is possible, is the key to understanding alcoholic traits and alcoholism. If a person is having trouble in any particular area of life due to the use of alcohol, the odds are great that the person is an alcoholic. These odds grow with each case of repeated problems due to drinking and become stronger when the person does not see the problems around himself or herself.

Another diagnostic tool is when a suspected alcoholic begins to lower personal standards to those of his or her behavior. In a long discussion one night, an active alcoholic near rock bottom and I discussed our own moral standards that we had both begun to breach. His comments were interesting when explaining how he had constantly lowered his standards as his behavior began to worsen. Although consciously still aware of holding strong religious and moral standards, his actions were now becoming acceptable for himself while still unacceptable for others. These actions became the edge of the envelope for self-acceptance, with the envelope constantly redefining itself through the behaviors.

Hitting rock bottom, as described in the Big Book of Alcoholics Anonymous as a prerequisite for an alcoholic becoming willing to accept help, is disregarded in recent research. It is now felt that rock bottom for some alcoholics can be to the extent of permanent physical and psychological damage and should not be allowed to progress to that level. What we shall rely on in the context of this book is that rock bottom shall equal any type of crisis in the alcoholic's life that forces the alcoholic into recovery. This varies greatly for each individual. With each alcoholic, a "worst thing" seems to occur at nearly every new event. Rarely do we see things getting better. Like a floating raft with a hundred holes, once one problem has been mended, another leak springs up just as fast.

Earth People

Once involved in recovery, many alcoholics humorously refer to sober nonalcoholics as "earth people." This paragraph is dedicated to those alcoholics who now accept that for years they have lived up in the clouds with contempt for those more fortunate and well-grounded people. The emotional extremes that alcoholics experience daily are impossible for non- alcoholics to understand. The gift of alcohol to an alcoholic is a way always to maximize the intensity of the emotion. Highs are much higher and lows are much lower, hence the phrases *living in the clouds* and *earth people*. Although used in reverence, the term *earth people* is used primarily as an indication and admission that past alcoholic thoughts and beliefs were alien thoughts and quite different from those of nonalcoholic people living on earth. Similar to a woman being unable to describe childbirth to a man, an alcoholic cannot explain the inner turmoil of alcoholism to an earth person.

Codependents

Virtually anyone close to or involved in an alcoholic relationship can be labeled a *codependent*. A term usually used for the husbands, wives, parents, siblings, and children of alcoholics, a codependent is simply the other half of an alcoholic mind-set. Wegscheider-Cruse (1985) describes codependency clinically as "preoccupation and extreme dependence (emotionally, socially, and sometimes physically) on a person or object." Whitfield (1987) expands the definition in his description: "problematic behavior that is associated with living with, working with or otherwise being close to an alcoholic."

Widely believed to subconsciously inherit the same type of control and compulsive needs as an alcoholic, a codependent is in need of as much or more recovery as the alcoholic. This fact most often escapes the understanding of the codependent until involved in some type of personal recovery. Why should codependents accept any responsibility for the alcoholic's behavior and disease? They should not. But they must accept full responsibility for their relationship with the alcoholic that has not only affected their lifestyle and behavior but also perhaps caused a change in themselves. Furthermore, codependents must take a good, hard look at themselves in regard to how they have enabled the alcoholic due to their own shortcomings.

Codependents must detach with love from the alcoholic to have any chance of recovery for themselves or the alcoholic. This does not necessarily mean walking away from the relationship (although at times this may be the only answer). It does mean to detach themselves from the relationship so they can let go of the belief that they can in some way control the alcoholic.

Codependents cannot give the alcoholic recovery and sobriety. What they can often give is support from a distance, patience, tolerance, understanding, and an effort toward their own personal recovery from the pain alcoholism has caused them over the years. It is not until well into recovery that an alcoholic can begin to feel compassion for the pain that he or she has caused others. Conversely, it is not until well into their own recovery that codependents can accept that they, too, were involved in the emotional turmoil and perhaps, for some, were part of the problem. A spouse of an alcoholic often takes complete control of the household, the children, the social calendar, the finances, and many other aspects of family life. The alcoholic is more than eager to relinquish this responsibility to gain the freedom of an alcoholic mind-set. Missed children's birthdays, late-paid bills, and missed dinner engagements are then the responsibility of the codependent in the eyes of the alcoholic—an enabling of sorts.

Once recovery has begun, it is just as difficult for the alcoholic to become involved again in these areas as it is for the codependent to relinquish responsibility for these areas. A spouse who has experienced heartache due to extramarital relationships by the alcoholic is not ready to forgive and forget. At the same time, a recovering alcoholic is taught to let go of the past and forgive herself or himself for past behaviors. These two thought processes will not mix and often are cause for failure in recovery and potential for relapse.

Both the codependent and the alcoholic must enter into some type of recovery for the relationship to begin to heal and grow. Many a codependent has begun to heal, leaving the alcoholic behind. Many an alcoholic has begun to recover, leaving the codependent behind. To heal together, both must work their own program, independent of the other. In any marriage, there are problems to work out. Codependents must become sensitive that just because their spouse has acted in an awful manner for years doesn't mean that they do not have their own set of actions that should be evaluated.

When in recovery, an alcoholic must develop self-forgiveness and leave the past behind, without shutting the door on it. Having not had suitable explanations or apologies from the alcoholic for past behaviors, codependents have a hard time forgetting the past. They want answers, explanations, and apologies. They probably deserve this, particularly when it is likely that the alcoholic has hidden, denied, and run from confrontations regarding his or her behaviors while still drinking. There comes a stage in alcoholic recovery that demands that alcoholics pay amends to those they have hurt in the past. These amends, however, must be on the alcoholics' terms, must not cause any additional pain to those they have hurt, and must be made only when they are fully prepared through recovery to make them.

This may mean that codependents receive less information than they feel that they deserve at the time. For example, a wife who has been dealt the blow of infidelity from her alcoholic husband may never learn the details that would cause additional pain and bad feelings. The best amends that the husband could possibly give is never to do it again. While it is easier to repay stolen money when making amends during recovery than to repair hurt feelings and broken hearts, it is still a most difficult task to ask anyone to atone completely for past behaviors. A codependent must be patient with this concept and willing to accept that the alcoholic is obviously recovering as shown through new actions and amends. To demand additional amends or atonement from an alcoholic is only to invite the possibility of relapse. The purpose is not to dig up the past needlessly, but to use it as an inventory to adjust any present-day behavior before mistakes happen.

By and large, codependents have plenty of their own healing to do and should also enter some sort of recovery program. Realizing the alcoholism is not their fault is often asking a lot of the codependent. It is imperative to point out that codependents must do this for themselves, not for the alcoholic. There is little codependents can do for the recovering alcoholic except to offer some support. Codependents must work their own program, and alcoholics must work theirs. These are independent from each other but essential for mutual healing to occur. And at the risk of causing quite a stir, who is to say that part of the problem is not the fault of the codependents?

Codependents must try to understand that the alcoholic is physically, emotionally, and psychologically sick. They must detach with love and refuse to become embroiled in the behaviors, excuses, and denials. Codependents cannot accept any responsibility for the alcoholic's unhappiness and must work their own programs to find a conscious security in this fact.

Al-Anon, an Alcoholics Anonymous–based program of codependents (cofounded by Lois Wilson, wife of Bill Wilson) offers the same Twelve Step program that is used by recovering alcoholics in achieving an inner peace. It also provides insight into the fact that codependents do not have unique problems in dealing with an alcoholic. What often occurs in this program is a self-realization that the codependents also have issues to work on. Furthermore, these issues are often similar to the type of personality and behavioral problems of the alcoholic. Many codependents discuss learning after some time in the program that they had become enablers. Grasping for some level of control over their mate and their lives, enabling spouses often find control to be a self-rewarding substitute for an intimate, personal relationship with their alcoholic spouses and visa versa. This is an extremely complex issue to deal with and work through for any person and often requires the therapeutic enforcement of an Al-Anon peer group, counseling, or both.

Having lost intimacy in the relationship, the alcoholic and the codependent have separately defined needs that require separate healing. Though they may work on the same issues, they work them from different sides of the fence. Both are feeling like complete failures in their ability to enhance the other's life. Both wonder why they cannot make the other happy. The codependent wonders why he or she can't help the alcoholic quit drinking, and the alcoholic wonders why she or he is being asked to quit. The fact is, no one can give someone else happiness. Happiness comes from within and results from a self-assured confidence in the way we are living our lives. Both the alcoholic and the codependent have been stripped of this feeling. The parent feels responsible for the child's drinking just as the husband feels responsible for the wife's drinking, and the wife for the husband's. A program for codependency recovery is just as important to the codependent as to the alcoholic and should be administered with or without the alcoholic's recovery in a separate program.

Chapter 2

The Alcoholic Mind

The best description of an alcoholic mind that I have found is this: "An egotist with an inferiority complex." One of the hardest things for people to accept hearing from an alcoholic is that they are lonely and feel inferior to other people. With a mastered ability to deceive, an alcoholic holds his or her pain deep below the levels of public perception. Similar to all other earth people putting up a wall of deception to hide their emotions when needed, an alcoholic lives in such a state of fear of being found out that outward appearances and actions often lean toward egotism. This fear is not based solely upon being found out to have a drinking problem but being found out to be unhappy or anything less than normal.

That many alcoholics are often eventually "found out"—but few are known to be unhappy, lonely, and insecure except to those around during initial recovery—is proof enough of this thought.

Eventually an alcoholic becomes incapable of hiding the alcoholism but still can hide the many actions and behaviors that were fear and insecurity based. Codependents and alcoholics alike have the option of blaming all of the past behaviors on the alcohol as a drug. These behaviors will not begin to change until the alcoholic and the codependent can accept that abstinence alone, without a strong recovery program, is only a dry drunk. Behind every alcoholic there is a wide range of inner thoughts and character defects that must be addressed in recovery by both the alcoholic and the codependent. Gordis (1976) wrote: "Changes in personality or mood are now recognized to be largely the consequence of alcoholism, not the cause." In the early 1980s, researchers thought they had a handle on the cause of this behavioral change—a loss of thinking power after alcohol use. Some found in their research that both alcoholics and nonalcoholics alike lost thinking power the day after drinking, proportionate to the amount of alcohol consumed, not necessarily the frequency of use.

The Alcoholic Ego

It is difficult for a nonalcoholic even to imagine living in a state in which one actually likes oneself as a person, because liking oneself comes so naturally to most sober people. Alcoholics do not like or trust themselves, much less understand themselves. These feelings hidden beneath the egotistical and self-centered thought processes brought on by acute alcoholism are difficult to find and even more difficult to come to terms with. Words like *ego, conceit, self-centeredness,* and *selfishness* are fighting words. Small wonder any person would do all that is needed to mask these thoughts. Alcoholics can even trick themselves into believing their own actions are normal and not self-centered. This trick is further strengthened because alcoholics are often compassionate and giving people when not caught up in the drinking personality.

In a pleasant talk with a chaplain at Hazelden, a renowned treatment center located outside St. Paul, Minnesota, I was surprised by his view on this subject. Having sat through thousands of meetings (and Fifth Steps) with alcoholics discussing their moral inventories, the chaplain had heard it all. Part of working on recovery in Alcoholics Anonymous (AA) includes this honest moral inventory and private discussion of the inventory with another. It is referred to as the Fourth and Fifth Steps of AA. To be helpful to recovery, this inventory must include all of the recognized character defects and past improper behaviors. It must also, however, include the good traits and past actions of the alcoholic. This particular chaplain shared with me that the majority of the alcoholics he had met with are much more compassionate and giving to others than most other nonalcoholics he knows. From simple favors for friends, to donations to charities and volunteer work, he was amazed at the level of self-sacrifice the average alcoholic was capable of. It is this occasional good deed that can keep a failing alcoholic marriage together for years after it is ruined by alcoholism. It is this resurfacing sensitivity that can fool all those near and dear into believing it may only be the alcohol, not the disease, that is causing the problems. An alcoholic ego is capable of the very best as well as the very worst emotional actions and behaviors.

What is most important to recognize is that the alcoholic ego is a mask meant to disguise and protect the fragile shell behind it. The ego is used for protection against an array of common psychological misgivings. It is the alcoholic's only way to gain acceptance and to provide himself or herself with continued examples of power, influence, popularity, and grandiosity.

The Chlorine Test

Imagine swimming underwater in a chlorine-treated pool for hours on end. The water begins to burn your eyes, your outlook is blurred, and you want to clear your vision. You hear things differently, and at times you cannot understand what is being said above the water. You reach the point where you do not want to be underwater any longer and you wish that the pool were not treated with chlorine. You lose perception of what is happening above you in the fresh air.

As you continue to swim, you begin to feel more alone in the water. Very few others are swimming underwater, and most seem to be enjoying themselves above the water. You become more in tune with your own movements and thoughts, and have a hard time recognizing or understanding the movements of others above the water. Despite repeated requests from friends and loved ones to get out of the pool as you surface every once in a while for a breath of fresh air, something forces you to dive again into the chlorine-filled water.

Like a recurring nightmare, there is still a sense of sanity hidden within you that tells you it can't really be happening to you, but you continue to dive. With each new dive you tell yourself that this will be the last, but again you dive into the water. At times you find yourself reasoning this bizarre nightmare into thoughts that tell you how special you are to be able to continue to do this. You begin to believe that it is actually normal, and others are missing the fun. This vision is like the life an alcoholic lives every day.

A Bottle of Soda

An alcoholic mind goes through an amazing thought process for the simplest of normal thinking. When asked if he or she would like a bottle of soda, an alcoholic can consider a thousand scenarios before answering. Why did he ask me if I wanted a soda? Is she out of soda? Does he think I need a diet soda? Maybe she only has cans. Maybe he thinks I shouldn't be offered a drink or a beer. Does she think I drink too much? Is he one of those "holy rollers" who doesn't drink? Should I have brought a soda? Should I have offered her a soda first? What kind of soda does he have? What if I don't like what she has? Would I have to finish drinking it?

Imagine living this way each minute of each day for years on end. Then add the effects of excessive drinking. An alcoholic truly does have the ability to turn the best intentions into the worst plans. If a total stranger simply walks past an alcoholic in a hallway, an alcoholic might wonder if that person likes him or her or what that stranger thought of him or her. This is the behavioral pattern bordering on depression that can be the cause for the alcoholic to continue to drink. In fact, many alcoholics are eventually diagnosed as also having depression or another dual disorder. Obviously most earth people would hardly notice the stranger walking by, let alone devote energy into trying to understand the stranger's thoughts.

The Scales of Justice

One way in which an alcoholic tends to rationalize behavior is through performing occasional good deeds, then placing the deed on the good side of the scales of justice. It is subconsciously hoped that these good deeds will eventually balance the bad behaviors on the other side of the scales. Although this is a simplistic manner in which to evaluate the inner workings of an alcoholic mind, it is important to note that alcoholics can and do perform a variety of good deeds and behaviors. What is unusual is to talk with alcoholics in recovery and hear how for the first time they unconsciously do things for the benefit of other people. In the past, although others may have received some benefit, the alcoholics would grasp the event as a rationalization and benefit to themselves. Granted, it is better to give than to receive, but with most alcoholics it is necessary to give to receive.

Referred to as "due deeds" in alcoholic circles, some alcoholics speak of actually becoming upset over the response they receive from the person for whom they have done a good deed. The alcoholics did the deed with a preconceived notion of what type of gratitude was expected and deserved in return for that deed. When a reward or thank-you is less than expected, the alcoholics may become upset and feel slighted. Resentments may build against the person receiving the deed. The alcoholics feel rejected, and what started out as a good intention contributes to continued drinking.

Keeping score of any giving to another human being is part of alcoholism. It becomes part of the essence of denial in that it enables one's subconscious constantly to rationalize behaviors and continued usage. To this day, I can remember all the "good things I did for others" while drinking. One exciting part of recovery is that now I not only do not keep score, but I enjoy every moment filled with the possibility of somehow helping another person.

Another aspect of the scales of justice is the private and inner change that occurs in those who hold the scale. While drinking, alcoholics do things for themselves. In one way or another, all things affect them; every decision, deed, response from another, and change in perception has some effect on the alcoholic. The alcoholic holds the scale. Presents are often bought for others with the intention of showing off, receiving a present in return, paying off a "due bill," or some other benefit. On the other hand, while in recovery, the scale is thrown away or given to a Higher Power, and recovering alcoholics find themselves doing things for no one in particular and for no particular personal benefit. From picking up a piece of sidewalk trash to giving friendly advice to a newcomer, recovering alcoholics slowly learn to give of themselves because it is the right thing to do and the right way to live.

Recovering alcoholics will speak of doing the same community service work they had done for years while drinking, yet for the first time are receiving inner gratification solely from doing the work. One good example is my own work as Santa Claus every Christmas for a local orphanage, hospitals, retirement centers, and friends. For years I did this work and enjoyed doing it but was sure to mention it to others throughout the year as my badge of service. It was important that I could use this simple act as a means of proving to myself and others that I was a good person to do such a nice thing.

In sobriety, the very first Santa event I attended was for a long-term-care nursing center. The tears welled in my eyes as I went from person to person knowing that I might be their one and only visitor over the Christmas holiday. Several asked for hugs, and many wanted just a few seconds with Santa Claus to ask for a simple Christmas gift. Many more, mentally disabled with age, strokes, and disease, simply stared at me as though I were the real Santa, but all of them smiled. Several of them reached out a tender hand to give me a gentle touch. Each person in that room shared a joy, however small, in seeing Santa Claus. For the first time, that joy came back to me tenfold because I was doing it for them not for me. This is the first time I have spoken of it since. When the event ended, I sat in my car for a few moments, then began to pray with gratitude and thanks for being chosen and allowed to be a part of such a wonderful moment.

Send in the Clown

An inherent part of virtually every alcoholic is the need to be liked by others. As an insecurity- and fear-based disease, alcoholism tears away the very fabric of self-worth. Despite an outwardly secure, if not arrogant, personality, alcoholics struggle with the need to be accepted by themselves and others. While discussing the concept of alcoholism and low self-worth with my wife during recovery, the words she spoke will stay with me for life. I explained that despite what I had tried so hard to lead her and others to believe while drinking, I maintained a low self-worth and most certainly did not like myself or my actions. She stated that she couldn't even imagine going through life without loving oneself. We as alcoholics rarely, if ever, have feelings of self-esteem and self-love. Without grasping this concept, nonalcoholics cannot understand the alcoholic mind.

For this reason, early-stage alcoholics will go out of their way to be accepted and liked by others. It promotes self-worth in an extremely distorted manner. Often becoming the clown at parties, willing to bear the brunt of jokes to help others have a good time, alcoholics will indeed send in the clown when required. There is no behavior too extreme if it results in laughter, love, false admiration, sensuality, or simply a feeling of acceptance. This acceptance doesn't need to come from anyone the alcoholic knows or admires. It just needs to be there. Like a child crying for attention, alcoholics reach out in the only manner available at the time. In the boardroom, the home, the bar, or the shopping center, alcoholics must reach out for acceptance at every chance, because daily they are reminded that they are punished not *because* of their actions but *by* their actions. A shame-based alcoholic may find it necessary to bring attention to a character defect in a flamboyant and arrogant way, to tell the world it is not a defect at all but an attribute to be proud of. The easiest way to accomplish this is to send in the clown.

Fear

When listening in at most Alcoholics Anonymous meetings, I am constantly reminded how the majority of our emotions are fear based. Many of the most deeply rooted emotions disturbing the average alcoholic are fueled by fear. *Fear* stands for frustration–ego–anxiety–resentments. To live in fear day after day, no matter the consequence, is fuel enough for just one more night of drinking. One more opportunity to change a mood and alleviate or forget the fear for a moment is most welcome.

To live in fear and live with the fear-based emotions that follow is probable cause to take whatever steps necessary to hide from these fears. To help an alcoholic through recovery is to try and understand that these fears, like a nightmare, are felt deep within the soul and are realistic to the alcoholic though they may seem silly to earth people. Much of the emotional turmoil felt by an alcoholic is, of course, fear based. In effectively reviewing the emotional issues engulfing the alcoholic mind, it is difficult, if not impossible, to find one that is not in some way fear based.

Assuming that fear is the grandfather of low self-esteem and insecurity, one can also assume that if alcoholics can learn to eliminate the fear-based emotions and begin to recognize true feelings instead, they will be able to adjust the irrational behavior that has warped their reasoning system through alcohol use.

All of fear is inferiority based. Although the following list is only the beginning of a much longer list of fear-based emotions, it gives a snapshot of the thought processes involved in alcoholic behavior. Living in this constant state of fear causes alcoholics to overthink nearly every situation. There is no way they will consciously allow the fear to be exposed. Accepting that fear-based emotions reside at the root of most personality shields, alcoholics can benefit by learning that there is nothing to be afraid of, providing they have faith in a Higher Power capable of handling any situation.

Fear is one of the reasons why diagnostic depression and dual disorders are so common in an alcoholic yet are often unrecognized. It is also an occasional cause for a diagnosis of depression alone for alcoholics intent on lying to their physician about their use of alcohol.

Fear-Based Thoughts and Emotions

Fear of being disliked	Financial instability
Fear of being deserted by loved ones	Fear of not belonging
Humiliation	Rejection
Fear of being unwanted	Consequences of breaking laws
Job insecurity	Inadequate sexuality
Poor performance	Parental rejection
Poor parenting	Religious and moral failures
Peer pressure	Physical appearance
Fear of imperfection	Fear of failure
Fear of criticism	Rage
Resentments	Denial
False expectations	Control
Fear of being found out	Manipulation

Fear-based emotions often cause resentment. Resentments enable the insecure and fear-based mind to rationalize the decision to dislike someone or something. Because resentments are one of the most frequent reasons why an alcoholic relapses, one should evaluate the causes of resentments and the various methods of coping with them. Focusing on fear and insecurity will help recovering alcoholics to focus inward, accepting the part of the resentment they own or caused, and may allow a therapeutic endeavor to occur wherein they are eventually secure enough that they do not need to put others down through resentments.

Guilt versus Shame

At the root of all alcoholism is a shame-based personality and low self-worth. It is imperative that we can differentiate between guilt and shame prior to moving forward in recovery. Understanding this difference enables us finally to accept responsibility for our past behaviors that cause us feelings of guilt (and take responsibility for them) and to rationalize the things done to us that cause feelings of shame.

Shame-based people do not believe that they have done something wrong. Rather they believe that they *are* something wrong. People with shame-based personalities are their own worst critics. Quite simply, shame is "being" and guilt is "doing." Bradshaw (1988) states: "Shame as a healthy human emotion can be transformed into shame as a state of being. As a state of being, shame takes over one's whole identity. To have shame as an identity is to (subconsciously) believe that one's being is flawed, that one is defective as a human being. Once shame is transformed into an identity, it becomes toxic and dehumanizing." Guilt results from voluntary actions, and shame results from involuntary actions.

Opinions vary as to where the first feelings of shame begin, but some believe that the infant in a highchair remembers the finger-pointing parent much later in life. An average parent says the word *no* to a child twenty-five times each day. By the age of ten, a child has heard the word *no* 91,250 times, based upon this average. Combine this with excessive parental criticism, a vulnerable alcoholic mind, or any other of a number of shame-producing influences, and you have built a wide-open door for the onset of mind-altering addictions later in life. All of us have heard or seen the stories of the schoolchild who comes home with a report card of all A's and one B. The parent only focuses on the one B, and the child receives no acknowledgment for being a good enough student to earn the A's. Without some type of affirmation, criticism is the hardest of all things to accept. Excessive criticism will lead to an inner belief of self-worthlessness in any person. It is my belief that throughout child rearing there exist thousands of opportunities for shame-based criticisms and rejections to occur without any premeditation.

In listening to hundreds of stories in AA meetings, I have yet to hear one that was not shame or fear based in one way or another. Although most were related to unintentional parental or childhood scarring of some sort, it is not the purpose of this section to focus on this as the only cause. Bradshaw (1988) discusses the concept of the "no tell rule" whereby children are taught early not to discuss certain family issues outside of their home. He believes this is a cause of the dysfunctional family and further indicates the importance of a normal parenting process for a healthy nonalcoholic life.

While in treatment, I was impressed by how, at some point during my discussions with each individual in my group, feelings of shame were shared. Sexual abuse, poor parenting, peer pressure, religious teachings, and educational embarrassment were all deeply felt and deeply remembered by the alcoholic. To a listener, some of the more painful memories might sound frivolous, yet to the alcoholic they were extremely painful and often brought on tears during discussion. Each person remembers experiences as they were perceived at the time. Until that perception can be changed, the pain lingers. One gentleman, over seventy years in age, began his life story with ease and continued until he came to the point of informing us he was once yelled at and rejected by his mother. At this point, he began to cry uncontrollably and had a hard time finishing his story. All this for an event that had happened over sixty years earlier! Others recounted similar stories of their youth, tears flowing over the littlest of things. Some had terrible stories to tell of beatings, of sexual abuse, of unbelievable punishments and embarrassments. All held on to these feelings throughout their lifetimes. All had begun to believe they were worth less than others because of these events.

Shame is an emotion based upon feelings; it is not to be confused with guilt, a feeling based upon actions. Ronald and Patricia Potter-Efron do an excellent job of differentiating between the two in their book *Letting Go of Shame*. What is most direct in the book is the information that states how true humility is required to let go of shame. The authors explain that "shame tells us that people are better or worse than us. Humility tells us they are equal to us." Shame is generated through the subconscious emotions from something that happened to us in the past, while guilt is a conscious feeling of something that we have done in the past.

What interested me were the defense mechanisms that the Potter-Efrons point out for the shame-based personality. In reviewing the list, I was impressed to find parallels between the defense mechanisms of the alcoholic and the shame-based personality. I believe it would be foolish to ignore this when reviewing and trying to understand the alcoholic mind.

Although alcoholics most certainly have reason to feel guilty for years of actions that fell below even their own moral and social standards, in recovery they also find themselves reviewing shame-based past environmental influences and experiences. At this point it is often difficult for the alcoholic to give up control, control being one of the most frequently used cover-ups for shame (Bradshaw 1988). A recovering alcoholic has no choice but eventually to give up the control and manipulation of others to enter into successful recovery.

It is uncanny to find so many recovering alcoholics sharing their experiences and inner beliefs regarding their lowered self-esteem due to no fault of their own. These beliefs are transformed into a variety of improper defense systems that, when helped along by a vulnerable alcoholic mind and plenty of drink, become the essence of their personalities. Shame is something that must at some point in recovery be forever shed. Guilt is something that the alcoholic must recognize as fact and eventually deal with through accepting responsibility for actions.

Bradshaw (1988) presents an excellent case of "shame spirals" whereby he believes that shame exists as an independent personality from our true being. The feelings of shame, he believes, are self-talk based on learned past beliefs about ourselves and the people around us. Certain words or events can trigger old shame-based feelings and thoughts. These triggers are referred to as "anchors." Bradshaw supports the therapeutic efforts of Bandler (1978) with a relatively new approach called neuro-linguistic programming (NLP) to combat these shame-based feelings.

Essentially, it is a program that helps individuals change their perception of personal history.

According to Bradshaw and some transactional analysts, over twenty thousand hours of these prerecorded anchors exist in a typical mind. These triggers can cause a shame spiral leading to shame- and guilt-based personality traits. In working with a therapist using NLP methodology, a client can be taught to create a new anchor that will be used as an association tool to replace the negative, shame-based recording. Although it takes some time and a qualified therapist, it is nonetheless an effective way to help the recovering alcoholic re-address past shame-based feelings in a positive manner.

For example, once into recovery, alcoholics can better recognize past shame-based emotions from parental shaming as simply poor parenting. It is usually recognized that the parents acted out of love but were simply not good at the parenting the child may have required.

For an alcoholic finally to realize that she or he is and always has been loved by the individual who has provided an inner sense of rejection and shame over the years is an accomplishment that provides inner self-assurance and aids any recovery program. In many cases, finding out that the parent was no better or worse than anyone else and that the rejection and shame were self-prescribed enable the recovering alcoholic to move on to other more conscious, fact-based feelings. Once an alcoholic recognizes the difference between shame and guilt, he or she may begin to accept responsibility for guilt and reject shame-based feelings of low self-esteem.

Guilt is an emotion that can become a positive attribute. Learning from past mistakes is what life is all about. The AA program teaches us to focus on the reasons behind the guilt, make the necessary amends when possible, then put the issue to bed. The Big Book says we never want to forget our past, nor do we want to close the door on it. It is this past that can provide us the potential to realize the great changes occurring during recovery.

The feelings of guilt from improper behavior in the past, however, must be dealt with and forever released.

When I was drinking, I was a jerk but simply did not know it. That fact accounted for most if not all of my irrational and self-centered behavior. In recovery, I now know every time I am a jerk—quite a difference. This allows me occasionally to stop it before it happens, occasionally to make immediate amends for the behavior, and occasionally to realize that I am human. Without the benefit of the experiences of my past behavior, I would be unable to see the differences in lifestyle and the new behavior that accompanies my recovery. This refers to the guilt associated with effects of my past behaviors. If the shoe fits, then wear it, as the old saying goes. Although at times I wish it were possible, I cannot make the past go away. I do not want to shut the door on my past because I can learn from it.

The emotional ties to shame, on the other hand, should be eliminated from our being altogether. Shame is not a healthy emotion and is one that we must come to realize is a fear-based misinterpretation of past events in our lives. We have no guilt in shame. We did nothing to cause the shameful experiences, nor should we now maintain the unconscious rage that builds up when these emotions are left unattended. One of the greatest tools for full recovery is a healthy feeling of self-worth and self-esteem. This is nearly impossible to achieve in a shame-based personality.

What can occur in the alcoholic is a propensity to develop a number of defenses to combat the inner turmoil of shame-based thoughts. When in recovery, the majority of these defenses and actions can be dangerous and may provide fuel for relapse. While drinking, the alcoholic uses these defenses and actions to dig deeper into a world of isolation, denial, and low self-worth.

It is for this reason that the alcoholic must work on a matter-of-fact understanding that no shame exists in guilt. In other words, remember the things that you have done wrong and learn from your mistakes. Forget the things that you have no control over but that have caused feelings of shame. Better yet, begin to realize that no one has the power to "cause you" to have any feelings whatsoever. You do this to yourself by allowing the feelings to live rent-free in your head. Shame is something that our own minds develop deep within who we become. Often, upon full analysis of the specific action or actions that may have planted the feeling of shame, we will find that the perception of that same action is much different.

Defenses against Shame*

- Denial—denying the parts of life that bring us shame, forcing our real problems out of our consciousness.
- Withdrawal—temporarily pulling away from others with loss of interest and energy.
- Rage—driving others away so they cannot see our defects. This is most likely to occur if we believe others are deliberately trying to humiliate us.
- Perfectionism—trying to hold off shame by striving to never make a mistake or to do everything perfectly.
- Arrogance—acting superior to everybody or insisting that others are full of defects. (Arrogance has two parts: grandiosity and contempt.)

- Exhibitionism—making a public display of behavior that we would prefer to hide. For example, if we cannot read well, we might call special attention to this handicap in a flamboyant way, perhaps to convince ourselves and others that it does not bother us.

It is obvious that the mind is invincible when it comes to the ability to substitute one protective personality for a lesser, more insecure or vulnerable personality. "Alcohol may be the enactor's attempt to douse this fury. Using liquor to unwind, to feel mellow, to relax and to forget may actually be an unwitting attempt to take the edge off wrath" (Maslin 1994).

* Potter-Efron and Potter-Efron 1989, 123–24

All at Once

One of the disturbing attributes of an active alcoholic is the attempt to juggle all the balls at once. Having begun to intertwine yesterday's problems and successes with today's happenings while still worrying about what tomorrow will bring, the alcoholic begins to melt all the days into the present. What is often seen at the office as an uncanny ability to remember or to think ahead is often a mixture of too many worries at once. The problem with this lifestyle is, of course, the inability to focus. When engulfed with all the problems and successes of the past while attempting to worry about what tomorrow may bring, today is a most difficult arena in which to live. What can happen in this mode is a mixture of what really did happen, what is really happening, and what is the appropriate plan for tomorrow. Many alcoholics actually retrace yesterday's actions by talking with friends about what was said and done. Although totally different from a blackout, this propensity to mix thought processes can cause a similar reaction to events that happened but are not easily recalled.

This phenomenon has been referred to as the *caveman syndrome.* Ponder the caveman sitting high up on a hill watching the sunrise as his day begins. There is no thought of yesterday's hunt, no thought of what the hunt might be like tomorrow. All thoughts are focused on the hunt of just one day. Should he deviate from these thoughts with past worries and future burdens, the caveman may go hungry for a long time. The caveman does not need it all at once. He lives life on life's terms. He focuses on one moment at a time. He does not mix the thoughts of yesterday and tomorrow with today's needs. While alcoholism causes a need for everything to come at once, for patience to become a foreign concept, and for not knowing when things are becoming a burden to handle all at once, it also robs the drinker of the ability to identify the needs of today and act solely upon those needs. In this regard, all too often the drunken past becomes the true history.

Never Enough

How foolish it must seem to an outsider to watch an alcoholic obtain goal after goal, success after success, and still want more. The concept of "enough" to an alcoholic is totally nonexistent. There is never enough sex, enough success, enough money, enough laughter, enough friends, enough drinking, enough anything. This premise allows the alcoholic to lower personal standards to a new level and provides yet another avenue for "more," particularly when raising standards hinders the ability to have more of something due to the difficulty in obtaining it through the real world and real rules.

It is not the kill that excites the alcoholic, it is the hunt. Self-worth is measured by "how much," not by "how happy." It becomes an uncanny ritual to see oneself exploring new behaviors, knowing all the while they are simply the result of wanting more than the next person. Like children always outdoing each other with a larger fish story to impress their friends, alcoholics have the most important people in the world to impress—themselves. The problem is, since alcoholics cannot be impressed much by outside influences, they judge the world by their standards and actions. Everything happening has some influence on the alcoholic. There is never an event that happens to someone else; it has happened to the alcoholic. There is never enough emotional input even though little feelings are put out. Enough is simply a concept that cannot be understood until well into recovery. Suddenly the simplest of things have meaning, and suddenly the alcoholic can take a moment to enjoy. Eventually it leads to a belief that enjoying life, one day at a time, provides much more happiness than trying to enjoy it all at once.

Inadequacy

Every person occasionally experiences self-doubt and feels inadequate. In every alcoholic is a complete feeling of total inadequacy. There is no reward to the alcoholic at the peak of his or her game.

No success is too big, and every failure is a measurement of self-worth. Rejections occur in a way that has little to do with the situation and everything to do with the value of the person. People become objects while the alcoholic is withdrawn into a state of depression fertilized by feelings of inadequacy. Although never admitted, the alcoholic lives in a world that demands perfectionism and grandiosity to survive. Defense mechanisms serve to hide these troublesome feelings but always include an inner desire to be normal. Feeling judged at every turn in life only provides alcoholics with an immense passion for improvement in their being. They are their own worst critics and can even turn outright compliments into an internal struggle with inadequacy. It is only upon a thorough review of their inventory and honest discussions with others that a sense of self-worth can emerge.

Alcoholics, like most people, have a deep need to be liked by others. The difference with alcoholics is that their actions at times are solely the result of a desire to be liked. They must learn to eliminate the need to compare themselves with others. Alcoholics have the ability to change their behavior as they perceive the situation may require. The bad news is that their perceptions, dulled by the alcohol and decreased levels of accurate reasoning, are often incorrect. Alcoholics set unrealistic goals. They can assume they are liked when they are not and vice versa. It is for this reason that their actions are often out of sync with what the situation calls for. Oswald (1976) writes: "As emotional development continues, the child takes on a sense of identity or self-concept. Much of this self-concept is derived from the child's measuring of his adequacy as defined by others."

As a diagnostic problem, this behavior and self-doubt can all too often lend themselves to clinical depression. It is imperative that the feelings of inadequacy are appropriately discussed with a physician or psychologist to ensure that additional treatment is not required. Alcoholics must allow themselves to become vulnerable to recover. This can be extremely painful at times after years of living in a state of conditional love.

Normal, everyday depression can occur with anyone dealing

with feelings of guilt and shame, but to feel depressed every day is, to an alcoholic, a possible sign of other physiological problems. To feel depressed unless one is drinking is a guarantee that alcoholism exists and an obvious reason to seek help.

The process of the Fourth and Fifth Steps of the AA program involves creating a moral inventory of one's past. This provides a chance for the recovering alcoholic to deal with some of the past guilt, shame, and trauma that have not yet been effectively dealt with over the years. The list is broken down into many separate sections involving emotional behaviors that result in this hidden guilt and shame. The importance of this list is not only to begin to recognize past unacceptable behavior but also to come to grips with some of the fear-based emotions like guilt and shame that may be hidden within the behavior.

Whitfield presents a list he calls "Some Terms for Mental, Emotional, and Spiritual Trauma That May Be Experienced by Children and Adults" in his book *Healing the Child Within*. When reviewing this list, as he relates it to a dysfunctional family, I was struck with how his term *trauma* relates to the feelings of inadequacy and how early childhood trauma of the type listed yields a belief system later in life that is shame-based and inadequacy centered.

Whitfield's (Inadequacy) Trauma Terms

Abuse: Physical
      Mental
      Emotional
      Spiritual

Abandonment	Neglecting
Shaming	Withdrawing/
Humiliating	withholding love
Degrading	Not taking seriously
Inflicting guilt	Discrediting
Criticizing	Invalidating
Disgracing	Misleading
Joking about	Disapproving

Laughing at	Making light of or minimizing
Teasing	feelings, wants, or
Manipulating	needs
Deceiving	Raising hopes falsely
Tricking	Responding inconsistently or
Betraying	arbitrarily
Hurting	Making vague demands
Being cruel	Stifling
Belittling	Saying, "You shouldn't feel
Intimidating	(anger)"
Patronizing	Saying, "If only (you were
Threatening	better or different)" or,
Inflicting fear	"You should (be better
Overpowering or bullying	or different)"
Controlling	Limiting

Grandiosity

One of the most active ingredients in the mind of the alcoholic is the subconscious necessity for grandiosity. As mentioned earlier, not only is this a defense mechanism in response to low self-esteem brought on by guilt, shame, and inadequacy, but it also becomes the subconscious essence of an alcoholic's being. It must be made clear that alcoholics do not consciously say that they will act out some role to be accepted by others. This occurs because of the continued alcohol use. Over time, it is not unusual for alcoholics to begin to believe that they are equal to or better than the next person. Always picking up the tab, being the big tipper, and buying things just to buy them all become part of the routine. Grandiosity comes in all forms. There exist a number of ways in which to act out this favorite role. Typically, aggressiveness takes the place of assertiveness by violating the boundaries of others.

As a supplement to true intimacy—a lost art for most alcoholics—grandiosity gives the alcoholic the ability to dismiss any true and necessary closeness with others. By staying at the forefront of the stage, a grandiose person may alter, through behavior modifications, the need of intimacy into one of false pretense and false feelings of affection. By simply acting as though we are something different, something that we think is better than what we perceive ourselves to be, we allow ourselves to hide from what and who we truly are.

Grandiosity begets aggressiveness. Aggressiveness begets getting what you want now and doing what it takes to get it now, regardless of the consequences. The actions of grandiosity eliminate the need for the risk that is required to develop an intimate relationship with another. When people eliminate this risk by taking control of situations, they also minimize the possibility of rejection and pain. The only person the alcoholic is fooling with this behavior is herself or himself; therefore, actions of grandiosity do not need to be witnessed. It is not uncommon to find that recovering alcoholics acted above it all when in total solitude. This reason is proof that this behavior is a result of the inner desire for alcoholics to trick themselves into believing that they are acceptable.

We have all heard of those "living in a shell," or those who have "built a wall around themselves." Consider the actions of grandiosity just that—a wall built high and strong enough to protect alcoholics from the painful truth of who they may be, a wall built for the sole purpose of preventing a clear view of the inner workings of a complex and insecure person.

Antisocial Behavior

Often, many personality disorders (and dual disorders) exist in alcoholics. What is debated is whether they existed prior to alcohol use or are a result of alcohol use. Due to this debate, the American Psychiatric Association (APA) has recommended that therapists observe the alcoholic for a minimum of four weeks after abstinence before making a diagnosis. It stands to reason that whatever research the APA based this statement on would also support that an alcoholic could expect to see personality changes within this same time period. This is clearly a benefit to any alcoholic entering recovery. There may now be a clinical point in time to look forward to in regard to any recognizable changes being made in the alcoholic belief systems, attitudes, and behaviors.

Among the many "disorders," antisocial personality disorder (ASPD) tends to be one of the most prevalent in alcoholics. Brown (1995) points out that antisocial behavior is approximately 10 percent higher in alcoholics than in nonalcoholics. More specifically, an alcoholic man is four times more likely to become or be antisocial than a nonalcoholic man, and a woman is twelve times more likely. Brown reviewed a couple of studies that show that approximately 35 percent of all alcoholics may have antisocial personality disorder. The findings, however, emphasize that childhood stress and behavioral disturbances may have existed prior to alcohol use, which then predispose the person to alcohol abuse and personality disorders. Without leaving out the possibility of alcohol-based disorders, Brown states: "Intoxicating substances can produce a combination of toxic, organic effects on brain function and reinforcement of regressive behavior. This combination may result in a personality disorder that is secondary not primary to alcoholism and drug dependence."

This is not to say that all alcoholics have several personality disorders. Many alcoholics have at least some of the traits included within the descriptions of other disorders. The isolation required in hiding from one's own truth certainly provides an avenue for uncommon antisocial behavior.

Perfectionism

Another purely defensive tool to protect an imperfect and insecure person is perfectionism. The false pride that is generated by seemingly perfect work and actions is enormous. Lee Iacocca once spoke about his takeover of Chrysler. On the first day of interviews with his top-level management team, one manager spent the hour talking about his organizational skills, work ethic, and not having taken a vacation in years. Iacocca supposedly fired him on the spot.

There is no perfection in this world, and we as human beings are most certainly incapable of being perfect. Anyone who believes they are perfect needs to be brought back down to earth to see that false pride clouds the view and their actions are self-serving. Perfectionists are not perfect. They are, however, incapable of admitting their mistakes. There are many roads to get to the same place, but perfectionists can't understand or follow directions on any road but their own. Perfectionistic, grandiose, and self-centered behavioral traits are common in alcoholics only to the extent that they protect alcoholics from pain. A feeling of being invincible and perfect leads to a deterioration of physical health and the ability to relate to others. Becoming one who judges the world through a private and distorted viewpoint only drives the alcoholic further underground and into a world that is muddied by a false concept of righteousness.

Self-Centeredness

A by-product of the alcoholic mind-set is a belief that the world revolves around our feelings. Self-centeredness introduces us to stubbornness and defiance. We become individuals completely lacking in empathy. Everything affects us in one way or another. A man caught in an illicit affair by his wife may worry first about what this may do to his reputation long before thinking about the pain he has caused his wife or children. To the earth person, this may sound like an awful and distorted mind-set. It is indeed. But it is also a mind-set that the alcoholic is incapable of dispelling. It simply comes without warning. Once into recovery, all alcoholics are amazed to look at their own moral inventories to see the ugliness that has surrounded them. When a boss or co-worker dies, an alcoholic may first worry about the personal effects before thinking for a moment about the pain and suffering of the deceased person's family. All things in the world are thought somehow to affect the alcoholic in some way.

This mind-set and the drug of alcohol force the alcoholic to view the world through only his or her eyes. One AA joke states that an alcoholic invented the modern-day toilet seat. The reason that there is a hole at the end of the seat was to keep it from hitting the alcoholic on the back of the neck when leaning over the toilet at the end of a day's hard drinking. This type of impaired and distorted judgment feeds a self-centered ego. After all, if we judge others as objects and judge the world by our own standards, how easy it is to live. We begin to live life on our terms. This should not, however, be confused with conceit.

A self-centered mind-set is meant to protect and hide us. It allows us to see ourselves as acceptable. It allows us to manipulate others without truly knowing that we are engaging in this behavior. Control, for a self-centered alcoholic, is a necessity. It is also recognized as a cover-up for other, more extreme subconscious emotions (Bradshaw 1988). Without controlling others, our world can fall apart and our ideals become threatened. It is for this purpose that alcoholics surround themselves with people who allow them to have the control and believe that the world is theirs to rule. This is *enabling*, a trait often mastered by the codependent.

It should be noted that being extremely gracious and giving can still fall within the self-centered lifestyle, particularly as a benefit and means to seeing the world as a good place and ourselves as good people. It is this mixed bag of behaviors and emotions that often confuses the codependents and those close to an alcoholic.

Feelings versus Emotions

It has been said that an alcoholic lives only in emotional extremes. Through an effective dramatization of both the highs and the lows, the alcoholic always presses the envelope of emotional development. Alcoholics drink to change a mood. Whether to soften a frustration, to make a bad feeling better, or even to make a bad feeling worse, our emotions are constantly being fed by alcohol. Many nonalcoholics should be able to grasp this concept, as they have also spent teary-eyed moments over drinks with friends. Alcoholics have mastered the ability to use drink for this same basic need to release or change a mood.

To effectively enter a program of recovery, alcoholics must find the difference between emotions and feelings. Emotions are simply internalized actions and extremes, often not rationalized through an honest look at the situation at hand. Feelings deal solely with how things affect us personally. Fear, resentment, guilt, rage, anger, denial, stress, and frustration are emotions alcoholics live with but do not know how to deal with. Understanding, tolerance, love, trust, spirituality, and compassion are feelings shared with others.

Until alcoholics have learned this difference and have gained the ability to feel instead of think, recovery is not possible. We must learn to rationalize our emotions through a nondistorted thought process and begin to feel the pleasures and weight of the world on our shoulders. To regard everything as a cause of our own happiness without seeing the effects on others is to look at the world through a pessimistic and distorted view. In recovery alcoholics will still have problems, but they will also, sometimes for the first time in their lives, be able to recognize and enjoy the many small wonders that occur every day. Emotions are the most difficult to control. They occur deep within our subconscious and boil up so often without warning. Feelings are conscious representations of the happenings around us, brought on by the rationalization of each event as it occurs.

Intimacy

Having spent years in isolation, hiding from all types of threatening emotions, alcoholics most often lose the ability to recognize or practice true intimacy. Bradshaw (1988) reasons that alcoholics should not be trusted or expected to be reliable in any relationship. This most certainly inhibits any intimacy. His thoughts are based upon the reliable premise that if alcoholics protect themselves from intimacy, they will not be disappointed.

Often confused with sexuality, true intimacy can occur with both males and females. Intimacy is essentially what happens as a *result* of honest and open sharing, not necessarily *during* that sharing. Sex is never intimacy per se; it is the result of intimacy. Allowing yourself to be vulnerable through sharing honest feelings, thoughts, and emotions can provide a sense of intimacy that can be cause for love and long-term relationships with a spouse or a friend. Alcoholics are far too protective to allow people to come that close to their essence and therefore reject most advances of intimacy. To fulfill a follow-up need after or during a period of successful recovery, alcoholics can benefit greatly from therapy involving the methods of communication producing an intimate and honest lifestyle. Despite having to learn how finally to deal with our own emotions and feelings honestly during recovery, there will come a time when we must learn to both listen and express ourselves in a new manner that can open a door to a whole world of intimate relationships. The vulnerability required to allow intimacy to develop is reason enough to take things slowly when first entering recovery. The possibility of further rejection is not something a newly recovering alcoholic should be expected to handle.

Compulsive Behavior

A result of the various components of the alcoholic mind is true and addictive compulsive behavior. Having lost over time the ability to evaluate the truth in their behaviors, thoughts, and actions, alcoholics move through life in either fifth gear or neutral. There exists no "in between" in their lifestyle. Alcoholics move, and move quickly, to satisfy the urge to be accepted by others and themselves.

Please note that the ability has been lost to act or think any differently. This is not the result of a decision. We alcoholics have over time found various behaviors and thought processes, fed by denial and inadequacy, that protect us from the pain that surrounds our lifestyle. Any possible means to escape the torment of guilt and shame is fed through actions that cause more guilt and shame, and the cycle continues.

Various symptoms are associated with the potential for compulsive behavior. Among these is preoccupied counting. Compulsive addictive behavior often exists in the person found counting the number of brick rows on a wall, the number of design patterns repeating in wallpaper, and so on. Nothing is too silly to count. Often the alcoholic is not aware that this propensity even exists, until pointed out by others.

Excessive housecleaning, a perfectly organized desk, a workshop or sewing room with everything perfectly placed points not only to a perfectionist but also to a possible compulsive personality. Add the long-term effect of alcoholism and the alcoholic mindset and one ends up with an out-of-control individual with nowhere to turn but to self-pleasure and gratification, often regardless of the consequences. Psychoanalysts and psychiatrists alike have written thousands of pages regarding the compulsive personality. It can be summed up as the person who thinks and acts out of control.

Often after regrettable actions, an alcoholic controlled by compulsive behavioral traits will feel guilty and recognize that the actions were improper. At the time, however, these actions were not reasoned, nor were they analyzed for possible future effects on the alcoholic or others.

Although these actions could be understood as being uncontrolled and often unintentional, to begin recovery, the alcoholic must still be held accountable for his or her actions. Until alcoholics recognize that they are powerless over these actions and alcohol, no recovery can occur.

Compulsive personalities make decisions without fully weighing the effects. Without this conscious effort to analyze their decisions, active alcoholics are often stripped of the ability to recognize right from wrong. They compulsively go to a place that they would normally not go and often only recognize this fact after they have been there.

Add to that our alcoholic propensity to protect ourselves from rejection and any sense of lowering our secret inner self-worth, and one gives birth to a personality intent on rationalizing the most destructive and compulsive of decisions. Compulsiveness breeds the impulsiveness that becomes the essence of decision making. As protection from the wrongs of these impulses, we lower our standards and drink more. This is most often when we require the most control of other people and begin to surround ourselves with those who may succumb to our will. At this point, we are capable of gaining reinforcement for behaviors through the evidence of others joining or sharing those improper behaviors.

Gorski and Miller (1986) place the major compulsive behaviors into eight specific groups:

1. Eating/Dieting
2. Gambling
3. Working/Achieving
4. Exercise
5. Sex
6. Thrill Seeking
7. Escape
8. Spending

There are those who subscribe to the theory that a compulsive behavior is simply an exerted need to control. After all, even in the examples from Gorski and Miller, all of the alcoholic behavioral types could have in common a subconscious effort to control something in life. Having lost control of most everything else, this is one way to provide instant self-esteem and gratification. These compulsive natures do not disappear with or during recovery, but the recovering alcoholic learns to deal with them in a normal and productive manner. The compulsiveness can be kept in check through an understanding of one's own good self, eliminating the need to provide false levels of self-acceptance.

Some believe that denial is also deeply rooted in compulsiveness and control. It is easily understood that alcoholics compulsively deny their problems and disease, but it takes careful listening to find that they also try to control their denial compulsively.

Violence

Sadly enough, it is well known that alcohol abuse can lead to violent behavior. Depending on the alcoholic's natural emotional state, the violence is expressed in different ways. An introvert becoming violent may only mean raising the voice or becoming critical and angry at his or her spouse or children. For more extroverted individuals, it may mean physical violence.

The extent of violent behavior includes homicide, rape, and other horrendous actions. Many codependents in recovery programs of their own would argue that emotional violence is just as painful as physical violence. A violent temper, for example, does not necessarily include the need to throw things, hit people, or become physical in any way. Alcoholics can be violent in a passive manner.

Most alcoholics, as most others in the real world, fall somewhere in the middle of the aggressively and passively violent behaviors. The danger is that most alcoholics exhibit varying levels of violent behavior at some point during their drinking careers. Many of the alcoholics I have met were never violent before acute alcohol dependence and have never been violent since entering recovery. In fact, most have found the difference between healthy assertiveness and unhealthy aggressiveness. Some have described the use of violence as their last act during their last intoxication or as the first indication that they may have had some type of drinking problem. This lends itself to the theory of deflation of ego or rock bottom, to be discussed later.

The most disturbing piece of the puzzle is the dual effect of violence. It surrounds alcoholism and further perpetuates it in some cases. Not only does alcoholic behavior, through consumption, trigger the aggressiveness in alcoholics, but the victim is often led to alcohol consumption and overuse as a tool to control internal turmoil. Reiss and Roth(1994) and many other researchers and scientists agree that there is a two-way relationship between alcoholism and violence (Froehlich 1997). This occurs through the disruption of normal brain reasoning due to the chemical processes involved in alcohol overuse.

As alcohol weakens the normal brain mechanisms that restrain aggressive, compulsive, and impulsive behaviors (Gustafson

1994), it can lead to an alcoholic's misreading or misjudging normal social cues. Misinterpreted cues are perceived as threats and can cause a violent impulse (Miczek et al. 1997; Cook and Moore 1993). This is an important part of the cycle to understand. Although many studies have attempted to blame alcohol use alone as a cause of violent behavior, no proof has been found. That many alcoholics become overly passive is one indication that using violence is not always the reaction of all alcoholics. What is agreed upon is that, when the alcoholic mind perceives (rightly or wrongly) a threatening situation, most research subjects take this threat or provocation, mixed with intoxication, as a reason to use violence.

Serotonin, as discussed earlier, is thought to be one of our behavioral inhibitors. Decreased serotonin, common in alcoholics, is also associated with increased impulsivity and aggressiveness (Virkkunen and Linnoila 1996). This line of research was substantiated by Higley et al. (1996) in a study of monkeys with low serotonin levels. They exhibited increased alcoholic consumption and excessive aggression. "Interestingly, among both macaque monkeys and humans, parental neglect leads to early onset aggression and excessive alcohol consumption in the offspring, again correlated with decreased serotonin activity" (Higley and Linnoila 1997; NIAAA 1998).

Isolation

Any one or two of the common traits of the alcoholic mind might be cause enough for anyone to take a road of isolation. Alcoholics, however, share many of the traits outlined in this chapter. It is no small wonder that the alcoholic then falls deeper and deeper into a pattern of isolation. It is a safe place to live, unaffected on the surface by the interruptions and judgments of others. Faced daily and hourly with impaired judgments that are known to occur as quickly as with the first drink or two for even nonalcoholics, alcoholics must become isolated to accept themselves and to avoid the continued possibility of rejection. This isolation can occur socially, professionally, or simply mentally. In a group care center, the recovering addict and alcoholic are required to interact with others. Isolation is frowned upon in this setting and is a definite obstacle to any long-term recovery. Alcoholics have the ability to sit with a group of friends at a professional baseball game and actually isolate themselves. This type of isolation is the hardest for an outsider to understand and recognize.

Conversations are superficial and mean little to the alcoholic in a state of isolation. The mind is elsewhere and most certainly not on the situation at hand. We maintain our own little world of safety, a "shell," and no penetration into this shell can occur except during the most intense or drastic of situations. This is particularly important for the codependent to understand while spending hours trying to convince the alcoholic that she or he is on the wrong path.

Isolation becomes, at times, the only means by which the alcoholic finds acceptance. The loneliness attributed to the isolation can be the reason for some to drink—yet another example of the alcoholic cause-and-effect relationship that helps to perpetuate the disease.

Sensitivity

Although alcoholics are generally self-centered individuals focusing on the world as it affects them, they also possess a heightened sensitivity to their emotions and, at times, their feelings. I have always been amazed that, despite my professional accomplishments, I never once felt adequate or successful in my business endeavors while I was an active alcoholic. While the compliments didn't change that, criticisms I received are forever branded in my memory. Within the home, the workplace, and the social environment, most alcoholics become overly sensitive to any question of their adequacy. This sensitivity causes many of the behavioral traits outlined in this chapter. To overimagine the negatives and to reject the possibility of the positives enable the alcoholic to wander down a path of hurt feelings and overintensified beliefs. Each alcoholic will tell you of the overpowering urge to find a state of mind without this pain.

Rites of Passage

Many alcoholics look back upon their lives prior to drinking with a confusion regarding the many rites of passage they were denied. Followers of Freudian theory hold that the alcoholic, having been weaned too soon, substitutes the bottle as an oral stage supplement for the mother's breast and feeling of total security. People who subscribe to this theory believe that this frustration as children turns to anger and then to inward guilt for feeling angry at their mothers. The drinking, therefore, solves the problem of the oral fixation with the bottle. It punishes the alcoholic for bad thoughts against his or her own mother through the continued use of alcohol and releases inhibitions toward authority figures (Rivers 1994). Drinking can be more easily understood as a lack of the rite of passage from childhood into adulthood.

Despite the American myth that all fathers talk to their sons and that all mothers talk to their daughters about the birds and the bees, few of us have truly had this luxury. Many little boys were never taught by their fathers how to play baseball, shave, put on a tie, build something, or even drive. Many little girls were never educated by their mothers about boys, makeup, cooking, or even how to dress their dolls. And most certainly, the conversations around the household rarely focused on sexuality. This lack of a formal passage into adulthood shared with a parent is the foundation for dysfunctional family values and can perpetuate itself generation after generation.

In my household there was never a discussion about alcohol and its effects. That would have been much too threatening to my father with a double scotch in his hand. I do believe, however, that had some of these rites of passage occurred earlier in my lifetime, it would not have been quite as easy to make up the standards of the world as I felt they should be. The world as we know it today was a completely different place when I was a child. Our parents didn't have the luxury of numerous studies on parenting and alcoholism as a disease. Despite many important ground-breaking studies on the disease concept, it seems that only the scholars were aware of them at the time. Alcoholism was something that was kept in the closet, as a ghost, not to be seen. Discussions of overdrinking centered only on the nature of one particular action related to one particular evening of drinking. Many comedians of the day made a good living imitating drunken behavior, and many of the television and film stars were rarely seen without a drink in their hands. It was the American thing to do. In short, drinking itself became a rite of passage into adulthood, most particularly for men. We were taught early that we should celebrate with a drink, console ourselves with a drink, and use a drink for every sort of social and professional entertainment.

Most anyone can look back on their youth and see some of this lost parental coaching and rites of passage involving alcohol. We discuss it here only in the context of an alcoholic mind-set, impaired through reduced levels of serotonin in the brain, through years of isolated self-centeredness, through the sedative qualities of alcohol itself, and then molded by a lack of closeness with our parents. As we review various forms of parenting involving the rites of passage into adulthood, we see that the distortions of our youth are only emphasized in our alcoholic adulthood.

As already touched on, classic Freudian psychoanalysts suggest that alcoholism is a subconscious substitution for masturbation or oral gratification. Many alcoholics are indeed nail-biters, smokers, or gum chewers, but it is difficult to find the link scientifically to a suppressed sexual urge. A more acceptable explanation of this primary addiction was put forth in the late 1950s by many noted writings that suggested that an earlier rite of passage may have been interrupted through a dysfunctional family event.

It is also this lost rite of passage that often emerges as an environmental influence on heredity-based alcoholics. Although there is no concrete evidence that alcoholism is genetic, it has been widely accepted and proven that the risk of alcoholism is greatly increased (some say by as much as 20 percent) if one comes from a family with an alcoholic parent. The number of studies regarding this issue is increasing, providing enough data to allow a formation of a rational acceptance of the heredity- and genetic-based alcoholic theories.

It would be difficult to argue that this continued alcoholic circle, devoid of any true rites of passage, would not have some effect on future alcoholics. We all require love and reinforcement. Dismissing the theory that lost rites of passage play an important role in our self-esteem would be to ignore the effects of environmental and learned influences.

The nurturing of our children must include the understanding that we, as the parents, must give them the required tools for a smooth passage into adulthood. These tools certainly change for every child, but the commonality with all of them is that we provide lifelong memories of self-assurance and support. While actively drinking, engulfed in our own isolation, self-centeredness, and problems, we can easily overlook the needs of a love-starved child. Children are inadvertently taught by alcoholic parents to develop scripts by which to live. Alcoholic parents in recovery can give children the chance to choose a life that best suits them, based upon honesty, without pretense, and with the security of a nonalcoholic lifestyle.

A Script to Drink

Ludwig (1988) presents an analysis of his own research in terms of nine basic scripts he feels predispose alcoholics to drinking. Although presented as dry drunk attitudes and reasons for relapse, the research is most interesting in the context of this chapter.

Ludwig believes nine basic thought processes exist that can occur within the alcoholic mind, enabling the alcoholic to form a script. The alcoholic becomes the essence of these thought processes, acting them out as in a movie, rationalizing both the motives and the actions. These scripts enable the alcoholic to perform in a world that becomes difficult without drinking. The following list summarizes Ludwig's scripts.

Predispositions to Drink

1. Escape script—hiding from discomfort and searching for the absence and numbness of problems
2. Relaxation script—using alcohol to unwind, refresh, relax, and reward oneself
3. Socialization script—using alcohol as an aid to socialization, releasing shyness and inhibitions
4. Improved self-image script—using alcohol to drown out low self-esteem through false feelings about oneself
5. Romance script—using alcohol to create a drug-induced state of love, romance, and flirtation to improve self-image
6. Sensual pleasure script—recollecting the physical gratification of alcohol as an abstract self-indulgence toward immediate pleasures
7. Self-control script—drinking to prove one is not alcoholic by proving one can be a controlled drinker
8. To-hell-with-it script—giving up any hope for sobriety by accepting that nothing really matters anymore
9. No-control script—enabling continued drinking through a false thought process that one simply cannot stop

Amazingly enough, the alcoholic seems capable of directing the film by using several of the scripts at the same time or by switching back and forth between them at will. As discussed earlier, we lower our standards to meet our behavior. It is imperative that we find a way in which to drink again, whether only a glass a day or a bottle under a bridge. We try anything, most often subconsciously, to give us the reasoning that allows continued use. Essentially we drown out our sorrows. The interesting thing is that until we find our own personal rock bottom, then enter recovery, we never learn that we cannot drown out our sorrows; we can only teach them how to swim.

One of the most common comments among alcoholics is that we tend to rule our minds by committee. There never seems to be a simple answer to anything, as a number of different scripts and dialogues play out in our heads prior to formulating a response to even the simplest of things. A friend in the program once stated that his mind is like a bad neighborhood, and he doesn't really want to go there alone.

When we subconsciously play out a number of scripts, looking internally for ratification of the response we feel is best for us, we also begin to believe that nearly everything going on around us will affect us in some way. Fantasies then consume our thought process. We will play out one scenario after another, until we find the script with the best perceived result for us. Sometimes, we play the same script over and over again, expecting a different result each time and becoming agitated when it always plays out the same.

Chapter 3

Alcoholics Anonymous

Alcoholics Anonymous (AA) was officially founded in 1935 in Akron, Ohio, out of the need of two individuals to stop drinking. The sole requirement of membership is the desire to stop drinking. One man who is cited as the cofounder of Alcoholics Anonymous is Bill Wilson (often referred to as "Bill W."), a stockbroker and alcoholic. The other, Dr. Bob Smith ("Dr. Bob"), an alcoholic, drug addict, and surgeon is the other cofounder of the organization. Although both men worked together in setting up a fellowship of men and women with the common goal of helping other alcoholics recover from alcoholism, Bill is often cited as the original founder and is often mistakenly thought to be the sole author of the book *Alcoholics Anonymous,* referred to as the Big Book. The main reason for this is that Bill was an extremely visible spokesperson for the fellowship during the early days, and Dr. Bob was a man of few words who often avoided the limelight. Bill did indeed write the majority of the Big Book and all of the sections that outline the AA program dealing with what came to be called the Twelve Steps, including much of what relates to recovery. Dr. William D. Silkworth, who treated Bill for alcoholism on and off prior to his sobriety, was asked to contribute the section of "The Doctor's Opinion." Other members of Alcoholics Anonymous from New York, Cleveland, and Akron contributed the remainder of the stories.

Having preceded Dr. Bob's sobriety date by barely eight

months, Bill later referred to the day of Dr. Bob's last drink, June 10, 1935, as the founding date of Alcoholics Anonymous. Another reason that Bill is better remembered as the founder of AA is that he outlived Dr. Bob, who died of cancer, by twenty-one years. These additional years also provided near a fivefold membership increase in AA from about 100,000 members at the time of Dr. Bob's death to over 475,000 members at the time of Bill's death (in 1971). Bill was the voice of AA for three decades, supposedly a name dropper who sought out friends in the rich and famous inner circles (Robertson 1988). Bill had a reputation (some of it true, and some of it false) for womanizing and adultery even during his sobriety, and at times his leadership was under question by other prominent AA members. He lived with clinical depression for years, with one bout lasting more than ten years. He was under the care of Dr. Harry Tiebout, an ardent supporter of the AA movement and later a highly regarded expert on the disease of alcoholism.

Despite his faults, Bill is the primary reason Alcoholics Anonymous is here today. Bill and his wife, Lois, lived as vagabonds for the better part of their lives, moving from one AA member's home to another and renting one-room apartments for many years during Bill's quest to get the AA message out. He relied only on monetary gifts and donations (including gifts from John D. Rockefeller Jr.) to meet his financial obligations during the early years of AA. It wasn't until the mid-1940s that royalties from the sale of the Big Book began to get him out of the enormous debt he had acquired. It is said that early in AA, Bill would threaten to quit the organization unless he could be provided with financial relief, even once asking for the purchase of a new automobile.

History

The origin of spirituality in AA is found in an earlier nondenominational spiritual movement called the Oxford Group. This fellowship harbored a radical approach—considering the year—toward a first-century Christianity-based lifestyle. Originally known as the First-Century Christian Fellowship, it was founded by a gentleman named Frank Buchman, who became a self-described evangelist and Lutheran minister. Living a sordid life, Buchman could excuse any of his questionable practices by claiming that he was guided directly by God.

During the mid-1920s Buchman's movement was focused on mainly Ivy League college campuses. His obtrusive righteousness, high-pressure tactics, and obsession with sexual sin eventually led to his being banned from Princeton University. This in itself led to the relocation of the movement to England, where again he focused on upscale universities, including Cambridge and Oxford, eventually adopting the Oxford name for his movement. Although not often discussed in Alcoholics Anonymous circles as being relevant to AA, the spiritual side of the Oxford movement can be seen clearly in the early writings of Bill Wilson. It is probably with some embarrassment that the Oxford Group was eventually ignored, as Buchman was thought by some to be a Nazi sympathizer and was, at the least, a controversial figure.

Many of the original members of Alcoholics Anonymous were members of the Oxford Group and had enormous impact on including a spiritual aspect in the recovery process. They lived by what were called the *Four Absolutes:* Absolute Honesty, Absolute Purity, Absolute Unselfishness, and Absolute Love. These later became the basis for the AA movement, as did the process of "house parties," whereby members would confess their sins and behaviors (often sexual in nature) and pledge honor to the Four Absolutes in the future (Robertson 1988). This process later became familiar as the lead stories, or "drunkologies," told by AA members in their meetings today. In fact, the name Alcoholics Anonymous wasn't even used until well into 1939 when AA formally broke away from the Oxford Group. This occurred at approximately the same time the book *Alcoholics Anonymous* was first published.

At about the same time, Sigmund Freud and his spiritually

inclined student Carl Jung were debating both the causes of and the recovery from alcoholism with seemingly conflicted opinions. While Freud leaned toward subconscious and environmental factors, Jung focused on causal attitudes and the spirituality required for sobriety. To this day there are several different opinions, all containing information helpful in understanding this disease and each presenting an interesting view from a different angle. That in itself is further proof of the complexity of both the disease and the recovery process.

The fact is, there was indeed a "spiritual awakening" prior to the Alcoholics Anonymous movement (Kurtz 1979). In 1933, Rowland Hazard ("Rowland H."), a wealthy American alcoholic, spent thirteen months in Zurich under the care of Carl Jung. Having spent the majority of this time with Jung, and a later visit back to Zurich after a relapse five years later, he became convinced that Jung's theory on the necessity of a religious conversion in recovery was paramount to a successful recovery. Rowland immediately joined the Oxford Group. It was this membership that starts the "family tree" leading to Bill Wilson and Dr. Bob. It seems that Rowland had a deep influence on an alcoholic man in the Oxford Group named Ebby Thacher, who was a childhood friend of Bill Wilson's. Sur-prisingly, Bill could not initially grasp or accept the Oxford-based religion and spirituality concept, and it is Ebby who is credited with helping Bill (through his persistence) to accept religion, using his own sobriety as an example. Sadly, well after the introduction of Alcoholics Anonymous by Bill Wilson and Dr. Bob, Ebby relapsed and later died of alcoholism. Bill's story is detailed in *Alcoholics Anonymous,* as are the words of Dr. Bob and many other early AA members.

It is said that while admitted to a New York hospital for his alcoholism, Bill experienced a spiritual awakening. Having spent many months under the care of Dr. Silkworth in the past, he at once required Silkworth's assurance that his spiritual awakening was not an indication of insanity or alcohol withdrawal but rather a true religious or spiritual experience (Rivers 1994). Bill described seeing a bright white light while standing on a mountaintop with a cool breeze, and forever referred to this moment as his introduction to a Higher Power. Silkworth noticed something truly different in Bill and told him that whatever he had found he had better hold on to it.

What is often left out of this part of the AA history is the belief that Bill may have been under the influence of certain drugs as a treatment for alcoholism. In fact, it is widely thought that years later, in 1956, Bill did in fact experiment with LSD with other members, including some clergy of AA, as a potential cure for alcoholism. This caused some controversy in Alcoholics Anonymous, even though Bill was now active more as a speaker than being involved in the daily workings of AA. Partly because of this, three years later he forever discontinued the use of all drugs. Despite all of his shortcomings, Bill Wilson gave his life to the work of AA and is undoubtedly responsible for the sobriety of millions of alcoholics and for the popularity and success of AA.

Nearly a year after having this first spiritual experience, while in a deep state of craving to drink, Bill met Dr. Bob quite by chance through the Oxford Group network. How this all happened varies from story to story, but as Bill tells it himself, he became obsessed with drinking one night when he was out of town on business. While walking past the laughter of an open bar in his hotel, he headed straight to the phone book, looking for a clergyman who might lend some help. At the moment he was stuck halfway between a church directory in the foyer and the bar at the end of the foyer. The clergyman's name he finally found was Walter Tunks, who gave Bill a list of about ten names of Oxford Group members to contact. Bill tried to call all of them but either could not connect or found that they were all busy, until the last person on the list suggested he call a lady named Henrietta Sieberling, an ardent supporter of the Oxford Group but not an admitted alcoholic. Henrietta, an influential woman married to the son of the founder of Goodyear Tires, set up a dinner meeting between a friend of hers, Dr. Bob Smith, and Bill Wilson. An interesting side note to this story is that the meeting actually had to wait until the next evening because Dr. Bob was passed out drunk when Henrietta first called to invite him for dinner.

Dr. Bob, a dear friend of Henrietta, was in the late stages of acute alcoholism. It is said that Dr. Bob and Bill sat for over six hours alone together in the study after dinner, with Dr. Bob shaking from alcohol withdrawals and Bill sweating with his cravings. It is this relationship that established the concrete premise that one alcoholic helping another is the primary path to understanding one's own alcoholism and to long-term sobriety. Dr. Bob, years later, summarized the conversation by writing, "Of far more importance was the fact that he was the first living human with whom I had ever talked, who knew what he was talking about in regard to alcoholism from actual experience. In other words, he talked my language" (Robertson 1988).

It wasn't until Bill began to express his views more publicly that alcoholism was potentially more dangerous to the public health than cancer, and long after the publication of *Alcoholics Anonymous,* that AA began to receive positive press in journals and magazines such as *The Saturday Evening Post* (in 1941) and subsequently began to attract new members. In fact, it was the owner of the *Post* who instructed the editorial staff to write a piece on the AA movement, as he personally knew two drunks in successful recovery because of the movement.

At first release in 1939, the Big Book did not sell well, and AA was in dire financial straits. Charles Bufe (1998) presents quite an unflattering, and unproven, theory about both the finances of Bill Wilson and the potential financial mismanagement of early AA donations and loans pledged for the purpose of writing the book. What Bufe doesn't mention is that for five straight years prior to the writing of the book, Bill and Dr. Bob split the sum total of all donations, less than three thousand dollars a year, between them, to keep the organization alive.

It wasn't until after many years of sacrifice that Bill and Lois began to see royalties from the book that amounted to anything. In the late 1960s they were receiving nearly $40,000 annually.

After Bill's death in 1971, Lois became quite wealthy. It is said that she received over $900,000 in 1986 from the sales of the Big Book and other Bill Wilson writings.

In 1939, New York AA member Morgan W. obtained a radio interview promoting the Big Book and the Alcoholics Anonymous program, and things slowly began to happen. The *New York Times* and *Liberty Magazine*, two very prestigious publications of the day, eventually ran favorable reviews of the book. Still, it wasn't until after *The Saturday Evening Post* article that the book began to sell well and both clergy and medical professionals slowly began to accept and recommend Alcoholics Anonymous all over the world. Currently there are an estimated two and a half million people in successful recovery through AA, and the organization has active membership chapters in approximately 150 countries.

The basic principles of Alcoholics Anonymous are said to be mainly borrowed from the fields of religion and medicine (with a primary basis derived from the Oxford Group teachings). In a letter to Bill Wilson, Carl Jung wrote, "An ordinary man, not protected by an action from above and isolated in society, cannot resist the power of evil." This was perhaps the first and last confirmation that Bill needed to grasp the concept that alcoholics need a Higher Power to recover.

It took over three years of growing pains and inner turmoil within AA for a consensus to be reached among the members as to how to present their beliefs and how to run the organizational structure appropriately. But the efforts involved in recovery through AA are conscious admissions of powerlessness and surrender.

The Big Book

Originally printed in April of 1939, the Big Book, the handbook of Alcoholics Anonymous, is read, revered, and discussed daily in Alcoholics Anonymous meetings all over the world. The fact is that through an understanding of the lead stories (or case histories) presented in this book describing the lives of alcoholics, a recovering alcoholic can find a connection to the underworld of alcoholism. It is difficult for any alcoholic to read this book and not find a parallel in many of the stories. The book itself does not explain how to stop drinking; rather, it is based on the premise that alcoholics are powerless over alcohol and require turning their lives over to some type of Higher Power to regain control. Although many alcoholics initially reject this premise, when they turn to their personal belief system to discover who or what their Higher Power is, within the guidelines of the program, they are welcomed into a program that helps millions of alcoholics across the world. The book is based upon a program of honesty and spirituality—as opposed to religion—and therefore accepts the notion that any Higher Power will do.

Although I have found it silly to listen to some recovering alcoholics describe their Higher Power as a tree or a beautiful bird, one cannot view the program in a negative light when considering the infinite possible levels of understanding one's own spirituality through a Power greater than oneself. The attraction of this concept is that it enables millions of people the world over to gently slip into a pattern of conscious connection with a Power greater than themselves, slowly breaking down the process of alcoholic, self-centered thinking.

Through this understanding of a Higher Power, most eventually come to understand a loving and forgiving God. This, in turn, allows the alcoholic to begin a journey down a road of self-acceptance and self-love. As a true means of facing oneself and the daily problems of a complex world without the need for substance use, the Big Book consistently provides the words and lessons needed to tackle life on life's terms. Part of the attraction of this concept is that AA itself seems to believe that a prospect must have hit, or be near, rock bottom to accept the program easily. Another Alcoholics Anonymous publication says, "Upon entering A.A. we soon take quite another view of this absolute humiliation. We perceive that only through utter defeat are we able to take our first steps toward liberation and strength. Our admissions of personal powerlessness finally turn out to be firm bedrock upon which happy and purposeful lives may be built." Further, "Until he so humbles himself, his sobriety—if any—will be precarious" (*Twelve Steps and Twelve Traditions* 1981). This allows those at rock bottom (and the majority of the first one hundred AA members were indeed well past rock bottom) to feel welcome and have hope for recovery, and allows those not at rock bottom to feel they have a chance for a fresh start.

The book itself is unique in its ability to avoid centering on any one particular religious belief while still being spiritually based. This provides reinforcement to the religiously trained alcoholic, hope for the atheist, and proof for the agnostic. It is more simply an instruction manual providing a means to live as a better person. Through compassion toward others, humility, tolerance, and acceptance, the alcoholic begins to build a new concept of life and a new manner in which to judge the world and himself or herself. Many recovering alcoholics can judge their behaviors today against the behavior of the past and thereby see the recovery process at work. Although not specifically geared toward the disease concept, the Alcoholics Anonymous program and the Big Book rely on the imperative notion that alcoholics are powerless over alcohol. This, in itself, provides immediate forgiveness to the relapse victim and further provides the proof of the need for the Alcoholics Anonymous program.

Ego submission to any Higher Power is a first step in understanding the world by standards set forth by a Power greater than yourself. Integrity and honesty are always part of this Higher Power, and often after the initial rejection of past religious shaming and guilt, the Higher Power takes on the form of a friendly, helpful, forgiving, and loving God.

The Big Book has been broken into many chapters specifically written to cover a vast number of alcoholic personalities and positions. Chapters have been purposefully written to relate on a personal level the experiences and the expectations of spouses, employers, families, agnostics, and many others. The journalistic manner in which the book itself was put together is not impressive. But the manner in which the book as a whole is presented has led to its becoming a sort of Bible for millions of recovering alcoholics around the world since the first printing. The book is quoted and revered by many Alcoholics Anonymous members as the written rule to a sober life.

What is most impressive in the personalized stories within the Big Book is that they make no excuse for the actions of alcoholism, make no effort to give the alcoholic a rosy picture of recovery, and are matter-of-fact about the strenuous and diligent efforts required for recovery. It is a book of lessons, tried and tested, that have worked for the authors to obtain sobriety. It often explains that these lessons may be applied differently for different people. Furthermore, it assures the reader that "rarely have we seen a person fail who has thoroughly followed our path." To look at the enormous success of the program, it would seem that they knew what they were talking about.

Additional writings from Bill Wilson in the *AA Grapevine* (the official newsletter of Alcoholics Anonymous and the predecessor to its current World Services publishing branch) discuss the intense labor and discussions that went into the original edition of the Big Book. Evidently, a roomful of alcoholics have a rough time deciding upon direction and upon content. Many stories and lessons were reviewed, rejected, or rewritten until the group agreed upon the content of the finished Twelve Steps and Twelve Traditions and the inclusion of case histories.

It has always amazed me that the Big Book, much like the Bible, has withstood the test of time. Although biased toward males, if one keeps in mind the time frame in which it was written and can ignore this innocent flaw, the Big Book provides us all with a spiritually based concept of living.

Alcoholics Anonymous is totally self-supporting through voluntary and anonymous donations from its members. There are no leaders, chairpersons, presidents, or bosses. It is an organization that is completely run by group consensus. At most meetings, the attendees put a dollar or two into a hat that may be passed around to cover the expenses of the meeting hall or refreshments. If unable to donate, one is still welcome at the meeting. To find your local AA meetings, simply look up *A A* in the phone book, call the local chapter office to obtain a list of meeting locations and times, and show up. There are always newcomers coming in and out of local meetings. Sooner or later it is hoped that after trying many meetings, a newcomer will feel comfortable at several meetings and start regular attendance.

The success of the Big Book and the Twelve Step program has been copied time and time again for many other life-affecting personality disorders and addictions. There are currently Twelve Step programs for smoking, overeating, anger, gambling, narcotics, emotions, and a host of other social issues. All have been modeled after Alcoholics Anonymous and the Twelve Step program.

Bill Wilson said it best himself in an article written for the *AA Grapevine* in 1955: "When an alcoholic applies the Twelve Steps of our recovery program to his personal life, his disintegration stops and his unification begins. The Power which now holds him together in one piece overcomes those forces which had once rent him apart."

Many reasons exist for the enormous success of Alcoholics Anonymous. It is the most successful program found to date in helping an alcoholic deal with life in sobriety. Many support the theory that the compulsive and addictive nature of the alcoholic mind is transferred to the AA recovery program, and the continued success of the alcoholic's recovery through AA replaces the past lost self-esteem. It is the compulsive nature of the alcoholic that is used in maintaining sobriety. Alcoholics Anonymous and AA-based treatment centers focus on group and peer therapy; this supports the alcoholic's need for interpersonal acceptance and reinforcement. There is little focus in A A on personalities but much focus on the problems and consequences of using alcohol. No judgments are made when one member shares experiences of being "under the influence." Rather, these lessons are viewed in the Big Book as constructive examples of the problems inherent to all alcoholics involved with continued use.

The Big Book does not present itself as the only answer or the only way. Everything is presented as "recommended" steps, and the follow-up use of therapists, physicians, and doctors is also mentioned as an appropriate post-recovery aid. The attraction of AA, and most certainly of the Big Book, is the promise of recovery through working the program and the Steps in the manner that best suits the individual. It is only newcomers' lack of control that convinces them that the Steps are the only way, because by the time they have become involved in the recovery program, they are willing to try most anything. These people are reaching out and would grasp at straws. The fact that the Alcoholics Anonymous membership consists of drunks and addicts offers the alcoholic a nonjudgmental invitation to a recovery program that has also been proven effective for millons in recovery.

Had I been told that the treatment center I entered had anything to do with Alcoholics Anonymous, or worse yet with spirituality, I would never have signed up for the program. But make no mistake about it, Alcoholics Anonymous is spiritually based. Without a firm belief in a Power greater than yourself at some point during the program, recovery in AA is impossible. It may sound amazing, but without fail, regular attendance at AA meetings and a firm understanding of the contents of the Big Book does provide the vehicle for the worst of agnostics and atheists finally to find an inner peace through spirituality.

About the Program

Alcoholics Anonymous presents a program so vague in the presentation that it allows each person to mold the program as it best suits his or her individual recovery. At the same time, it is so specific that it recommends following a stringent lifestyle through a series of Twelve Steps that provide sobriety one day at a time. The program itself stays clear of long-term focus as well as continuously dwelling on the past. At the same time, the program asks the newcomer to "keep coming back" and to look ahead to the next Step (or level) of sobriety. It also asks members eventually to review completely the past bad behavior, share it with another, and make direct amends where possible for that behavior.

AA allows members to move at their own pace, placing little emphasis on how far along in the Twelve Steps the member has gone. What is often rewarded, through applause (and, at some locations, medallions) at local AA meetings, are anniversary dates of sobriety. Whether it's the anniversary of one month or ten years, all alcoholics understand the importance behind the ceremonial aspect of recognizing these milestones. It is important to point out that this is a celebration of the program not any individual success.

All alcoholics have gone through a living hell, different from everyone else's yet so similar in pain. Great pride occurs in not only finally being accepted by a group of peers but also being admired for one's integrity in persistence and commitment to sobriety. This, in short, we find as a substitution for lost rites of passage. Alcoholics understand alcoholics, and alcoholics can help one another like no other combination of forces. In AA meetings, there are no judgments against things done, things said, or the manner in which one presents oneself. About the time an alcoholic at an AA meeting begins to believe his or her story is unique, another member will tell a similar story with twice the impact.

The program is primarily based upon regular attendance at local AA meetings and involvement at those meetings in the discussions of past lifestyles as compared to a spiritually based lifestyle. Most meetings end with a prayer and then the slogan "Keep coming back; it works if you work it," encouragement for the newcomer and a reminder to the old-timer that the program does work, or all of those alcoholics wouldn't be standing there together in sobriety.

Old-timers recommend ninety meetings in ninety days, as this is one program where too much of a good thing will not hurt you. For those without prior treatment, this is a good idea. For those entering AA fresh out of an intensive treatment center, it may seem overwhelming and unnecessary, and in fact, they may be entering AA with a false sense of knowing more than the members. An effective and professional treatment center can essentially pack the effect of hundreds of AA meetings into one short month, thereby giving the recovering alcoholic a great start when later entering the program offered by Alcoholics Anonymous. Nonetheless, nothing can take the place of an AA meeting or the counseling one can receive through the compassion of experienced members.

A simple premise for recovery is to live one day at a time, focusing on staying sober for one short day. It is said that anyone can fight the battles of just one day. Many break down that rule of thumb into "keep it simple" or "live in the moment" to shorten the time period into even smaller segments that one must focus on during sobriety. Alcoholics often have the propensity to project themselves way into the future, with all kinds of different scenarios—worrying about things that may never occur, elaborating on situations that if left alone, would probably go away, and complicating the simplest of thought processes. Living in the moment and trying to keep it simple enable the alcoholic to find a way to focus on the situation at hand. Breaking down the frustration into simple terms can also provide an answer previously hidden by false interpretations.

One part of the program is setting aside a regular daily time to meditate and pray quietly. Many begin this ritual without any knowledge of how to pray. Many also begin solely to satisfy the requirements of the program. But at some point during the program, this becomes quite natural. AA members may begin to feel naked in a day when their prayer and meditation were skipped.

Hundreds of daily meditations and short one-paragraph prayers are found in the many books available at your local bookstore or library. Hazelden offers perhaps the widest variety of daily meditation guides geared to men, women, and children. Owning a small collection of these books can enable newcomers to review the daily writings in several books each day, helping them to become familiar with many types of meditations and prayers. These books are Twelve Step–based interpretations of a recovery lifestyle necessary to any recovery program. While generic books on spirituality, religion, and personality disorders are fine, simple help with establishing a conscious contact with our Higher Power is paramount for the recovering alcoholic and addict. Any local bookstore or library will contain a section that includes basic meditation and prayer books written specifically for people in recovery and for their families.

The Twelve Steps

The Alcoholics Anonymous program is based upon twelve simple yet specific Steps for a healthy and successful recovery and sobriety. In fact, all Twelve Step programs use variations of these exact Steps. It is recommended that each Step be studied and taken slowly. A danger exists when newcomers simply read a Step, believe they have completed that Step, and move along prematurely. We must completely understand and live each Step before moving on to the next.

The Steps read so simply that they often cause the newcomer to hit a brick wall at some point during the program and then need to move back to a Step already taken. It is for this reason that the First Step is discussed often in AA meetings by even the most experienced members. The reaffirmation that one has not taken over control and is constantly turning things over to one's Higher Power is required in any program based upon submission and ego release.

Pretending to have completed any Step only fools oneself and is a major contributor to relapse. By the time newcomers are ready to start work on the Fourth and Fifth Steps, they should have spent an enormous amount of time reflecting on past behavior and listening to other members give their lead stories or give their explanations of how alcohol affected their prior lives. Newcomers must also be willing to be totally honest with themselves and with others. The Fourth and Fifth Steps are so private that they are rarely discussed in public or at AA meetings, but they always must be completed with the help and witness of another. The Eighth and Ninth Steps are more mature versions of the Fourth and Fifth Steps but have now become a repentance of sorts. The repentance, however, is focused only upon the need for recovering alcoholics to clear their conscience, not necessarily to expect forgiveness from those they may have hurt in the past. In this regard, AA members have been known to send anonymous money orders to people many years after having stolen money from them while drinking.

While making amends, the help of a sponsor or other recovering, more experienced member of AA should be enlisted. This is useful in keeping the amends in perspective and setting up proper expectations on the part of the alcoholic. It also helps the recovering alcoholic gain a sense of having a witness to this new way of life.

Under no circumstances should a recovering alcoholic try to make any amends where it might cause additional harm to another. Often making amends may simply mean not ever performing an action again, while never discussing it with anyone except perhaps a sponsor. A man who has had an affair is more likely better served by never committing adultery again. The wife may or may not need to know about the affair, but in most cases, the alcoholic in recovery feels that telling her is important. What is not important are the details. They cause no relief to either the alcoholic or the wife and probably cause pain to both and even, perhaps, to the "other woman."

By the time recovering alcoholics are into the last couple of Steps, they are trying to make amends every day for any improper actions of that one day, thereby constantly "cleaning up their side of the street." It is this continued good living, one day at a time, that provides lots of good yesterdays. It eventually produces an alcoholic who is free of alcohol and living a self-assured and spiritual life. At this point of recovery, the recovering alcoholic's attention now turns toward helping newcomers and working with alcoholics to find a spiritual and alcohol-free life.

Alcoholics are often asked why they continue to attend AA meetings years after being sober. This is a Twelve Step program that can and should be repeated over and over again. It is a program that never ends for alcoholics, as we are always "in recovery." A relapse can occur at any time with this disease, as it can with most other diseases. It is said that it is a disease of 10 percent alcohol and 90 percent attitude. Staying involved in prayer, meditation, and continued work with other alcoholics can only enhance the probability of continued recovery.

Alcoholics are frequently asked why they can't have just one drink. This question is continually asked because many people still adhere to the belief that it is willpower, not disease, that causes problems with alcohol.

Many alcoholics, in fact, believe that they could have just one drink. If the theories presented by many researchers are correct, particularly the progressiveness of the disease as pointed out by Jellinek, at some point the alcoholic would believe that she or he could again have just one drink. What starts out as innocent quickly turns into control and denial, and soon the alcoholic goes from one drink a month to one a week, to one a day, and is soon back to old habits. Just as before, the alcoholic soon believes that she or he is in control and falls back into an alcoholic mind-set.

For the few for whom this would not occur, the risk is too great to take. The saddest part of this relapse is that the alcoholic often has no clue how far the fall is until it is too late. Denial takes over, and the alcoholic falls back to where he or she was before first achieving abstinence and sobriety.

Alcoholics are generally happy, spiritual, compassionate, and tolerant people while in recovery and are unwilling to trade the self-love that stems from these feelings for the risk of what can happen in drinking again. Alcoholism is a slice of living hell, while recovery is a slice of heaven. The common thread of those who relapse is that they stopped working the program or going to meetings. If the program is worked diligently, if honesty is a naturally practiced way of life, and if the alcoholic puts sobriety above all other things, the chances of recovery are strong. Missing meetings is only the symptom of a potential relapse. The disease is the cause.

The Big Book includes chapter after chapter written explicitly to detail a new way of life that promises to be rewarding through sobriety. We could not control our disease alone, but through the teachings of those who have gone before us, we can now learn how to control it through contact with our Higher Power and through working with other alcoholics.

Following the Twelve Steps and the Twelve Traditions of Alcoholics Anonymous is the most successful program the world has ever known in combating the disease of alcoholism. More important, it can bring millions of unhappy people into a world of happiness and self-acceptance. It is important that the Steps are understood and followed, thus adding the responsibility of going to meetings and working with others. Learning from our contemporaries is a benefit that can last a lifetime.

The Twelve Steps of Alcoholics Anonymous*

1. We admitted we were powerless over alcohol—that our lives had become unmanageable.
2. Came to believe that a Power greater than ourselves could restore us to sanity.
3. Made a decision to turn our will and our lives over to the care of God *as we understood Him.*
4   Made a searching and fearless moral inventory of ourselves.
5. Admitted to God, to ourselves, and to another human being the exact nature of our wrongs.
6. Were entirely ready to have God remove all these defects of character.
7. Humbly asked Him to remove our shortcomings.
8. Made a list of all persons we had harmed, and became willing to make amends to them all.
9. Made direct amends to such people wherever possible, except when to do so would injure them or others.
10. Continued to take personal inventory and when we were wrong promptly admitted it.
11. Sought through prayer and meditation to improve our conscious contact with God *as we understood Him,* praying only for knowledge of His will for us and the power to carry that out.

* *Alcoholics Anonymous,* 1976, pages 59–60. Reprinted with permission. (See editor's note on copyright page.)

12. Having had a spiritual awakening as the result of these steps, we tried to carry this message to alcoholics, and to practice these principles in all our affairs.

The Promises

If we are painstaking about this phase of our development, we will be amazed before we are half way through. We are going to know a new freedom and a new happiness. We will not regret the past nor wish to shut the door on it. We will comprehend the word serenity and we will know peace. No matter how far down the scale we have gone, we will see how our experience can benefit others. That feeling of uselessness and self-pity will disappear. We will lose interest in selfish things and gain interest in our fellows. Self-seeking will slip away. Our whole attitude and outlook upon life will change. Fear of people and of economic insecurity will leave us. We will intuitively know how to handle situations which used to baffle us. We will suddenly realize that God is doing for us what we could not do for ourselves.

Are these extravagant promises? We think not. They are being fulfilled among us—sometimes quickly, sometimes slowly. They will always materialize if we work for them (*Alcoholics Anonymous* 1976, 83–84).

This passage is read at the opening of AA meetings all over the world to remind the alcoholic of the future. The Promises emphasize that they must be worked for and do not come freely. But it is also emphasized that they will *always* come to those who do work for them.

The Traditions

The members of Alcoholics Anonymous had an enormous problem on their hands in the beginning when formulating just how to run an organization intent on anonymity and on the grassroots efforts of one alcoholic working with another to achieve sobriety. Nearly seven years after the publication of the Big Book,

Alcoholics Anonymous had begun to grow and needed a written policy, called "Traditions," to ensure a cohesive understanding of the intentions of the program and of the organization.

The Twelve Traditions of Alcoholics Anonymous are the best answers that the experience of the membership at that time could give. In writing the final draft, one of the members asked a simple question: "How can Alcoholics Anonymous best stay whole and survive?" The Twelve Traditions are reprinted below in the "short form," condensed from the initial writings of more than five pages in length. One can see from these Traditions the importance of anonymity of the person and the organization, and the importance placed upon the general AA values.

The Twelve Traditions of Alcoholics Anonymous (Short Form)*

1. Our common welfare should come first; personal recovery depends upon A.A. unity.
2. For our group purpose there is but one ultimate authority—a loving God as He may express Himself in our group conscience. Our leaders are but trusted servants; they do not govern.
3. The only requirement for A.A. membership is a desire to stop drinking.
4. Each group should be autonomous except in matters affecting other groups or A.A. as a whole.
5. Each group has but one primary purpose—to carry its message to the alcoholic who still suffers.
6. An A.A. group ought never endorse, finance, or lend the A.A. name to any related facility or outside enterprise, lest problems of money, property, and prestige divert us from our primary purpose.
7. Every A.A. group ought to be fully self-supporting, declining outside contributions.
8. Alcoholics Anonymous should remain forever nonprofessional, but our service centers may employ special workers.

* *Twelve Steps and Twelve Traditions*, 1952, 1953, 1981. Reprinted with permission. (See editor's note on copyright page.)

9. A.A., as such, ought never be organized; but we may create service boards or committees directly responsible to those they serve.
10. Alcoholics Anonymous has no opinion on outside issues; hence the A.A. name ought never be drawn into public controversy.
11. Our public relations policy is based on attraction rather than promotion; we need always maintain personal anonymity at the level of press, radio, and films.
12. Anonymity is the spiritual foundation of all our traditions, ever reminding us to place principles before personalities.

AA Meetings

AA meetings are broken into two major categories: "open" and "closed" meetings. An open meeting is open to anyone interested in alcoholism and anyone wishing to stop drinking. Both AA members and prospects as well as researchers, teachers, therapists, and interested parties are welcome at these meetings. A closed meeting welcomes only alcoholics, or "those with a desire to stop drinking," with a strict adherence to this policy. Although one could fake an introduction to others as an alcoholic or someone wishing to stop drinking to attend a closed meeting, it wouldn't take long for the members to discover the truth.

Within these two major groups fall many separate submeetings surrounding a specific subject matter. A simple question is asked at the beginning of some meetings as to whether anybody has a specific subject or a particular problem (often referred to as a "burning desire") that may need some group insight. This is usually a member's sobriety-threatening topic. It has been said that attending an AA meeting is like getting three thousand dollars' worth of free therapy in one hour, and these group sessions certainly support that claim. Subject matters at these meetings might include powerlessness, resentments, gratitude, tolerance, or any of the basic parameters of AA. Subject matter brought up by members varies from anything as small as their local carpool to something as painful as losing a child and how to maintain sobriety through that pain. No matter the subject, each person has a time period in which to express his or her views or discuss any other important item.

Other meetings are called "beginners meetings." These meetings are usually held weekly and often at the local clubhouse. The early stages of recovery, powerlessness, and the Twelve Step program are the subjects most often discussed. Many long-term members use these meetings as a refresher course or as a Twelfth Step of sorts, so rarely are the beginners the only people in attendance. These meetings are valuable to the Alcoholics Anonymous movement in that they support the early AA recovery concepts and continue to spread the word to new prospects. The name of the meeting alone seems to welcome nervous newcomers, although the same subject matter is often discussed at many other meetings.

"Big Book (question and answer) meetings" are typically begun with a question from an Alcoholics Anonymous publication of several hundred topic questions regarding the Big Book theories and writings. An example of such a question might be "Do we need to take a fearless moral inventory to maintain sobriety?" All willing attendees would take a turn in presenting their feelings on the subject, reflecting on their own experiences while drinking and in recovery. At times, a second or third question may be read and responded to by the attendees, if time allows. One of the criticisms of these meetings is that the old-timers may use their time to "grandstand," or to promote their self-worth. Often, these comments tend to stray from the Big Book question and can cause repetition of subject matter, drawing out a meeting's length. Regardless, Big Book discussions are very educating and rewarding.

A "Big Book study meeting" is where attendees take turns reading a paragraph or two out of a particular chapter of the Big Book until the chapter has been completely read. Then the members take turns relating their own personal experiences to the chapter read.

A "Step meeting" is specifically focused on the various Steps of the Alcoholics Anonymous program. At these meetings, one or more of the basic components required of the Twelve Steps is discussed in a roundtable fashion. At one meeting, the topic may be "surrender," at the next "powerlessness," and at yet another "Higher Power." These meetings are particularly valuable as an educational tool in understanding both the Twelve Steps of Alcoholics Anonymous and the Big Book.

In a "lead meeting" members tell their version of how their drinking started and how their recovery is proceeding. This usually lasts for about twenty minutes, followed by comments and discussion from people in attendance.

The "home group" is the term AA members use for their favorite and regular meeting. This is the one meeting during a busy and hectic week that AA members find time to attend. It is the meeting in which they feel most comfortable expressing themselves. Although they may attend many other meetings at many other locations, they always "come home" to this meeting. This is also the manner in which Alcoholics Anonymous can occasionally attempt to keep track of a membership total.

As anyone can start up an AA meeting with just two people, meetings are usually initially started by core members. Those core members continue to attend, and as the membership within this group grows, the core members may seem "cultish" to the newcomers. As cliques can form in any group, it is important to these "leaders" to be careful not to alienate their newcomers. Name-dropping within these meetings is casual, with references pointing at well-known AA recovering alcoholics telling their viewpoints. As a means to exhibit their membership and closeness to the core group members, this also can cause an uncomfortableness within newcomers who at best are already feeling a sense of not belonging. Occasionally, a newcomer may feel a self-righteous attitude from long-term members. This is completely against the code of ethics the Big Book prescribes, that there are to be no leaders, celebrities, or chairpersons in AA. On the other hand, AA tells us to "take what we need and leave the rest." In this vein, if one attends any meeting with open ears, it is difficult not to hear something that can benefit a recovery program.

This name-dropping does often occur at the grassroots level. Many of the core members of a home group are sponsors and friends to other members, and most have been involved with AA along with the other core members in some form or another prior to the formation of the group. An advantage in knowing this before attending the first meeting is in recognizing who these successfully recovering people are early in the recovery process and listening closely to their words.

A home group meeting is widely thought of as a more true AA experience than the regular club meetings at the local AA chapter club or office. These members often socialize with each other outside of the meetings, an unusual occurrence within the AA club structure. It is for these reasons that the newcomer should visit many meetings at many different locations until completely comfortable in expressing complete honesty at one certain meeting. It is only through this total honesty that the newcomer can begin to take a fearless moral inventory, relying on the experiences of other members as guidelines.

A "group conscience" is a meeting within a meeting. It is simply a meeting that occurs, usually after the regular AA meeting has been terminated, to discuss group matters. Voting, how to disperse donated funds, support of the national Alcoholics Anonymous organization obtaining speakers, renewing the lease or rental agreement for the meeting hall, and local chapter events are most often discussed.

In each city, a handful of other specific types of AA meetings are also generally available. There are meetings for nonsmokers, gay men and lesbians, lawyers, doctors, Catholics, Protestants, and many other groups. There are discussion meetings for men only, women only, mentally disabled people, and those with a host of other common denominators.

To attend any AA meeting, simply show up. You will indeed be welcomed, and although the regulars will know you are there, they welcome the chance to help another recovering newcomer. Seeing the newcomer often reminds old-timers of when they came and helps their recovery process along. They also recognize that the words of the newcomer are often a refreshing change from some of the same old stories. Many have ongoing outpatient programs that also welcome newcomers at no charge. As a last resort, contact Alcoholics Anonymous at the national headquarters in New York at 1-212-870-3400. This is also the best place to obtain many pamphlets and writings with in-depth information on AA and the benefits offered.

Obtaining a Sponsor

One of the most important needs of a newcomer to AA (next to finding a home group) is to find a sponsor who will provide guidance through the recovery process and the Twelve Steps of Alcoholics Anonymous. Sponsors come in all shapes and sizes so it is important for newcomers to take time to find the sponsor who best suits their needs and allows them to become completely honest. It seems to be an unwritten rule to find a same-sex sponsor who can better relate to the specifics of the disease and one's past actions. Eventually, this is the person to whom one may reveal his or her deepest and darkest secrets when completing the Fourth and Fifth Steps. One usually tries to find someone with at least a year of solid recovery, demonstrating a thorough understanding of the AA program. Many recommend approaching one's first choice with a request of being a temporary sponsor until one can find a permanent sponsor. This gives both parties an "out" if the situation doesn't work or becomes uncomfortable. It is a good idea before the deal is final that both get together and discuss the rules. Some sponsors demand certain readings and writings, calling the newcomer often and checking on his or her progress. Some sponsors ask the newcomer to call them only in a dire emergency or a sobriety-threatening situation. For the alcoholic not too far down the scale, cravings are not the major issue at hand, and this sponsor may not be as much help as someone willing to meet for lunch every now and then to discuss the program.

Again, time should be taken before one makes a sponsorship agreement. Many alcoholics take as long as six months or a year to find the right sponsor. Sponsors have jobs, families, and other responsibilities and often are already sponsoring other newcomers, so it is not surprising if a first choice asks one politely to look elsewhere. A sponsor need not be a friend or grow into a friend, but a sponsor must be trusted and respected and have a willingness to help another into and through recovery. In addition, and most important, a sponsor must have a sound knowledge of the Alcoholics Anonymous program and Steps and must, through example not words, be an honest reflection of that program.

Lead Stories

A frequent occurrence at AA meetings is the retelling of a recovering alcoholic's experiences while drinking and throughout recovery. This is referred to as a "lead story." Occasionally, meetings that center on a lead story are referred to as "lead story meetings." Usually taking about an hour and given by someone who has been successful in recovery for some time, these stories bring reality into the lives of the newcomers and old-timers alike. At most treatment centers, each person in the group eventually shares his or her lead with the other group members. Not only does this allow an honest, nonconfrontational means to get it all out but also allows the recovering alcoholic to begin a journey of a new type of honest interaction with other people. It is also common at treatment centers and hospitals to have recovering alumni return after some successful time in recovery to give their leads to the newcomers or clients. Part of the program of Alcoholics Anonymous requires anonymity and confidentiality, and these leads are given with the knowledge that they will not be used against the person giving the lead. Usually a brief announcement is given prior to the lead: "What you see here, what we do here, when you leave here, let it stay here."

Lead stories can be fascinating and they can be boring. They can instill fear and pain, even horror, and they can bring up old painful memories of one's own past. They can cause rage and even resentment against the person talking. They can be funny and they can be "drunk-a-logs" meant to impress the listeners, stories of wild drunken behaviors, as though they were a macho badge of some sort. They can be given by people who have obtained spiritual peace and have little chance of a relapse, and they can be given by people who may relapse tomorrow. They can involve tears from the person talking or from the listeners. In short, they can amount to almost anything. But what they always have in common is solid proof that alcoholics are not terminally unique. It has all been done before, it is all forgivable in God's eyes, and it all serves as experience on which to build a new way of life in recovery.

Some have discussed the discomfort in hearing a lead story because they no longer wish to receive comfort through another's pain. It is important to remember that the people giving the lead need to give it, want to give it, and are helping themselves through recovery in giving their lead. In recovery centers and clinics alike, the group members usually go around the room sharing their feelings on the completed lead with the person who gave it. Resources and blocks to recovery are discussed, helping the lead alcoholic to see himself or herself through another's eyes, in many cases for the first time ever.

Although lead stories are shared to give the alcoholic an opportunity to discuss how drinking affected his or her life or how he or she initially sank into alcoholism, they can take on other forms. It is hoped that through a discussion of past drinking behaviors and how those behaviors have affected others, listeners can come away with some type of relation to parts of their own story. There seems to always be some type of commonality. In discussing how sobriety has improved one's life, it is further hoped that this information reinforces old-timers' recovery process and aids newcomers in beginning a new life of spirituality.

Another benefit from listening to a number of leads is recognizing again that this disease can affect virtually anyone. Over time one will hear from people in all walks of life. One will hear how alcohol has affected those near to the alcoholic, and those distant. One will listen to thousands of behaviors of people out of control. Most important, the alcoholic who recounts such behaviors will be standing there in recovery, totally sober, and in most cases exhibiting a sense of spirituality and happiness. This in itself indicates the success of the AA program as well as the possibility for change in the worst of alcoholic cases.

Criticisms of Alcoholics Anonymous

Many recovering alcoholics and addicts question the need for the anonymity required and recommended in AA. Bill Wilson described Alcoholics Anonymous as a movement based upon attraction rather than promotion. Many feel that maintaining this posture in the current environment of cyberhighways and instant information weakens the organization and leaves out in the cold many who could gain enormous help through AA, if they were aware of what the organization stood for. I myself, for example, knew nothing about AA or alcoholism prior to entering treatment and could have benefited greatly from some advertised information regarding Alcoholics Anonymous, as well as information on recovery. It is important to understand the reason, or the Tradition, behind Bill's description. It is far more important that the organization survives, through anonymity, than it is that any one person be put on a pedestal. Sobriety is the celebration of the organization, not just the individual.

Some people can point to the "just say no" antidrug program in our school systems as an example of a well-established program geared at educating our youth to the dangers of drugs. They feel this could perhaps also benefit alcoholics. Many young children chide their parents for smoking, drinking coffee, and even eating foods of low nutritional value, because of lessons learned at school. Yet no national educational program exists that explains the symptoms of alcoholism or the general effects of alcohol. This AA standard of anonymity is required to protect the reputations of recovering alcoholics, but naysayers would submit that if the public were better educated about alcoholism, this type of protection might not be required. This is not to say they necessarily propose that all alcoholics should publicly reveal their identities. What it does request is that AA take a look at providing information on a more advanced and regulated basis to the public. Another drawback to anonymity is that research into the success of Alcoholics Anonymous and other programs cannot accurately be studied and recorded. In staying anonymous, some feel the negative stigma of alcoholics is perpetuated.

The Twelve Steps have been criticized as being "holier than thou," containing reinforcements to self-centeredness and exhibitionism. Ogborne (1989) argues that strict alliance with AA tends to prevent the diagnosis of a dual disorder. Focusing only on the disease concept minimizes other existing personality and behavioral problems for a short time, while placing most of the blame on alcohol.

Some believe the spiritual nature of the AA program makes it most attractive to those with a background in Christianity, leaving out a large group of needy individuals with other religious beliefs and those without a religious understanding of any kind. Others feel that it is most attractive to middle-class members. The AA program, however, is currently being used and supported in prisons all over the world and has become successful with recovering alcoholics from virtually every religion.

There are others who view AA as some type of cult. Some critics refer to the "religiousness" of the organization. In fact, it is spiritually based, a discernible difference. These naysayers point out the tendency for AA members to perceive themselves as a chosen group. This may be true to the extent that members often feel lucky to have found something (anything) that works for them in eliminating alcohol use and alcoholic behaviors. I have never once met a member of AA who felt as though some god had plucked him or her out of obscurity and placed him or her in recovery because he or she was "chosen." What is discussed freely is that God does work in our lives on a daily basis, that God has something to do with everything that happens, and that a connectedness to a Higher Power did occur shortly before or upon entering recovery. AA has been called dogmatic as it relates to cult characteristics (Bufe 1998), but it is emphasized in the program and in the Big Book that the Steps are only recommended, giving recovering alcoholics plenty of leeway in shaping their own recovery programs. In fact, one of the most-used slogans in AA is "Take what you need and leave the rest behind."

The most understandable complaint against Alcoholics Anonymous is that it seems to be centered on group therapy and rejects the notion of recovery in isolation. Some people simply are not comfortable in groups, and some, although comfortable, are not at ease in sharing their personal lives with strangers. Trice and Roman (1970) first discussed this while ignoring that the program does support silence from individual members at AA meetings. It also supports a direct and private, one-to-one relationship with a sponsor. AA supporters further argue that it is precisely this reintegration into a mini-society that best aids the overall shedding of isolation and a self-centered alcoholic world. Successful AA or group therapy only benefits the efforts of recovering alcoholics in both learning to listen and being open and honest with others.

One last criticism implies that AA members are taught to be disrespectful of authority and, therefore, have a tendency toward rebellion. In truth, AA teaches compassion, tolerance, patience, honesty, and respect for everyone. Submitting to authority is secondary to an inner belief that one's actions are now acceptable in successful recovery. This is not an art easily mastered. Through continued involvement in Alcoholics Anonymous, one can only grow toward a respect for those who maintain a high level of integrity and spirituality. If those people placed in positions of authority do not exhibit these qualities, many alcoholics will in fact lose respect. What is more important is that AA members are taught to meditate and pray for enemies and friends alike.

The key to eliminating resentments for AA members is to pray for them. Members of Alcoholics Anonymous eventually learn that we have all been placed on earth to perform God's will. They further believe that accepting God's will and trying to the best of their abilities to be of service to God is important for sobriety and is simply nonnegotiable. That an alcoholic must place his or her sobriety with God above all else fertilizes the outsider's view of disrespect for authority. In any spiritual program, there is no authority higher than God as you understand Him. I take issue with those who support the viewpoint that following God's will, even when it goes against some authority here on earth, is disrespectful.

Chapter 4

"My Lead"

I was born in 1956, overseas in England, the son of an air force enlisted man. From the first day I entered a treatment center for alcohol addiction, I felt as though I had lived a normal and happy childhood with all the comforts and love any child could need. Yet, I never remember feeling truly connected, and most certainly, I never truly felt happy with myself. It wasn't until recovery that I had the courage to look at my life honestly, intent on finding any possible correlation between my addiction to alcohol and my childhood environment. This is not to say that I needed or wanted someone to blame for my pain or that I do not accept full responsibility for my past actions. What was important was to set the stage for my personal need to drink. Nonetheless, it remains my decision, my disease, and my life story.

It wasn't until I gave my first lead and had evaluated my personal moral inventory in writing that I began to see a correlation between my past actions and behaviors, my current belief systems, and some of the many reasons I turned to alcohol. There are many psychological, physiological, and environmental influences on alcoholism. It became my mission to find out if I was truly an alcoholic, and if so, why. I believe that all of the following influences in some way affected my predisposition to the disease.

I still find some embarrassment in telling my story, but I tell it here in hopes of providing proof that anyone can become an alcoholic—my life had not been in any way abnormal prior to my alcoholism. I would give anything to make this disease go away for good. But I know it is here to stay. I also know, through my research for this book, that I can still exhibit many of the alcoholic characteristics and many more of the historical predispositions to the disease.

Sadly, I have little recollection of my father throughout my youth. In fact, I have virtually no specific memories of him until the day he called my only brother and me into the living room and told us he was leaving for Vietnam for a couple of years. This is not to say that he was never home before then, but rather that we had a dysfunctional relationship. I was nine or ten years old when he told us he was leaving. It may have been weeks before he left, but my memory of him stops on the day he told us and begins again the day we picked him up upon his return from Vietnam, at the airport, two years later. In writing this paragraph, I can recall only one other moment of early closeness with my father. It was some years earlier when he left for Washington, D.C., with my mother, for his job in the air force, and my brother and I were left with my aunt and uncle for the summer in another state.

What is most interesting about all this is that I remember many details from the two years he was gone in Vietnam: how we lived, funny moments, school, and the normal childhood memories most of us have. I also have vivid memories of my earlier childhood that do not include him. These memories start about the time John F. Kennedy was killed, when I was in the third grade. Understand, however, that I considered my father a loving and respectable man, my best friend at the time of his death many years later. Only in reviewing my lead did I recognize that I maintained no specific memories of him and began to question how this was even possible.

Having moved from state to state after our arrival in America in about 1959 due to my father's military transfers, we didn't settle down in the suburbs of Chicago until I was in the fourth grade. I lived there through my high school years until I left for college, out of state.

Mostly because frequent moves had almost forced me to be aggressive in my continued search for new friends at each new city, I was often the class clown and began my exaggerations quite early in life to gain acceptance from others. Although I was surrounded by other neighborhood boys I considered my friends, early in school I felt that I took the brunt of many jokes and was not truly accepted. Looking back, it was probably some degree of false perception, but at the time, I recall asking my mom if we could move again. I believe that this was the start of later alcoholic tendencies to feel inferior. I still have strong recollections of just not fitting in, of being different. I remember trying hard to be "one of the gang," trying hard to be athletically talented, simply trying, as most children do, to be popular. No matter, as with most alcoholics, I simply felt as though I did not belong. This feeling stayed with me until I entered recovery.

My mother is the type who inadvertently assures you that nothing you do is quite good enough. Again, I say this without prejudice or any lack of love. In fact, it is the recovery program that has taught me that she indeed loves me with all of her heart. I believe that she simply was a product of the Dr. Spock experience and the 1950s uneducated parenting. My mother obviously had a tough time raising us without Dad. In retrospect, I feel that most of the child-rearing responsibility fell on my older brother. In that regard, quite early in my life, I was accustomed actually to raising myself. Left alone to play when I wanted, to go where I wanted, and to do what I wanted, without the firm hand of a father, I developed concepts and belief systems that best suited me. I am certain my mother would argue this, but I further assure you that it is absolutely true. In fact, upon my father's return from Vietnam, my parents bought a small boat and eventually began to go away for private weekends, leaving every Thursday or Friday afternoon and returning on Sunday. We were always invited to go, and for the first couple of years we had to go, but once we were old enough to have a choice, at about fourteen or fifteen years old, both my brother and I always stayed home in our own little private world. During that time, I went my way and my brother went his. Since he is three years older than I am, by the time I was a sophomore in high school, he was in college, so I had the house to myself for my weekend parties. And I could tell you some real stories about those parties. It was about this time that I began to gain some popularity. In retrospect, the risks I took back then were for the sole purpose of getting someone to like me. Although I can still look at this period of my life fondly, I can also recall how alone I felt there in the house, for full weekends, to do as I wanted. I felt a sense of abandonment that haunted me for years. In addition, I can remember, even at that young age, my tolerance to alcohol increasing as the years went on. I once worked part time for a man down the street, in a business in his garage making air brakes for bicycles, and was once challenged by him to a drinking contest. He would drink a shot of hard liquor, against a beer for me. Of course, he drank me under the table, but my contest with alcohol had begun.

As a younger child, I was the one always spilling my milk at the kitchen table, getting in minor but continuous trouble at school, having one less A on my report card than my brother; I grew up with the feeling that I was always letting my mother down. To this day, my mom has the uncanny ability to dish out guilt at virtually every occasion. The Christmas present is never right, I don't call as much as her friends' sons, and, most certainly, she has no concept of alcoholism as a disease. Again, I now find this all too normal, but back then I recall questioning my self-worth. I can remember wondering what I could do differently to gain the attention and love of my mother. The funny thing is that she was a good and loving mother; I always knew she was there for me if I needed help. I also knew, however, that she wished I would do things differently. When I left for college, she made a needlework sign for my dorm room that said "A man who walks to the beat of a different drummer." How right she was.

My brother and I have always joked about what we term the "Tommy Smothers" stereotypical arrangement our family had. I never had a serious discussion with my parents that I could remember and rarely spent any time around the house as I grew into adolescence.

One of the earliest signs of abandonment came when my brother and I were young. Our regular Saturday always included being dropped off at the local YMCA for a full day of scheduled activities: bowling, swimming lessons, archery, roller skating, a movie, lunch, and a host of other wonderful activities. We were dropped off at about 8 A.M. and picked up at about 4 P.M. There was little true supervision that I recall, but I do remember always wishing I could have been with my friends and wondering about why we were always left alone. I am certain my parents considered this to be a sign of their love for us and were doing what the fifties had taught them to do for their children. I am also sure that it was probably an expensive undertaking for a lieutenant in the air force in 1964, and they cut corners somewhere else to provide this for my brother and me. What no one realized was that it also caused an early thought pattern of going through life alone.

The most memorable type of punishment for our wrongdoing involved a simple statement from my mother: "I had bought you this nice present, but now that you've been bad, I am not going to give it to you." To this day my brother and I joke about some large warehouse somewhere, stuffed with all these gifts we were never given. It wasn't until my mother used this exact line on my eight-year-old daughter a couple of years ago, and my daughter broke into tears, that I remembered how much pain this caused us as children. My daughter came running to me saying, "Grandma doesn't think I am good enough for a present" and cried for ten minutes. I recalled how I, too, had always felt "not good enough."

My parents were always there for us. But in times of emotional crisis, even into early adulthood, during discussions of my problems, more time was spent on what they felt I was doing wrong. Sometimes people hear what they want to hear. In my family, you heard what my parents wanted you to hear. At about this time in my life, I can remember the exaggerations that I began to rely on to gain acceptance. The experience I gained from my mother was refined to an art where I could not only sense what people wanted to hear but also say the words in the way that most impressed them. During any problem or conflict in my youth, I can still hear my mother saying, "Tell them this" or "Tell them that" with no relation to the truth. If my mother could tell a small lie to get to the front of the line, she would. I later became an expert at this myself. To this day, my mother pushes her way through the lines at the airport, insisting her flight is about to leave, so she can check her luggage, then sit for an hour, relaxing at the gate, awaiting the real departure. As I know she will eventually read this, I feel obligated to add that she is a kind and warm mother, and my happiness is a priority to her. She doesn't even know that she does these things.

In my first year of high school, I began to drink on weekends with some regularity. Without any supervision around, it was easy to accomplish. Because of this, I now see why several of my friends' parents would not let them come to my home, especially on weekends. At the time, I tried hard to emulate Eddie Haskell on *Leave It to Beaver* without much success. Typical weekends included always getting drunk at some point, and nearly all of my gang was doing it consistently. It amazes me that we all kept this hidden from our parents for so long. My first drunk consisted of chugging a bottle of Boone's Farm strawberry wine. For several months, this became the natural thing for all of us to do. The difference between myself and my friends, however, was that they rarely finished the bottle, and I always did, as a means to gain acceptance.

Although I can't remember exactly when, it wasn't long after first drinking that we all began to smoke pot. Looking back, all of this was an excuse to change our moods and make us more secure with ourselves. Those who developed a secure sense of their own identity slowly dropped out of this routine one by one. The majority of us continued this pattern as it progressed into heavier drug use, even through four full years of active sports and good grades in high school. I recall never really liking pot but using it as a requirement to being a man. This was the "hippie" time period in our U.S. history, and our actions were being socially accepted by a larger population each year. Demonstrating against the Vietnam War also gave us an excuse to drink and smoke pot. I truly believed at the time that those fine soldiers wanted us to protest.

That I was able to make good grades without any true studying aided my disease to take firm hold of my behavior. This played a major role in my college grades at the beginning, for I had never learned how to study in high school or how much time was required to learn difficult subjects. By the time I graduated high school, I had experimented with virtually all accessible drugs. At times, my conscience kept me from swallowing the most dangerous drugs offered, but I would find something else, like alcohol, to make me high enough so those around me believed that I had taken the tougher drug. Although this amount of drug use was the norm for my gang, those outside the gang assumed our use was more than likely limited to pot and alcohol. This was most evident by our success in sports and grades.

Having grown up in the 1960s, I had all the mentality brought out at Woodstock and the 1968 Chicago Democratic Convention. At the time, I thought all of us were sexually promiscuous, as I was having the time of my life. In discussing my stories of high school sexual success with close friends some twenty years later, I realized that both this part of my life and the overuse of alcohol and drugs were frankly greater with me than with my friends. Their memories differed greatly from mine, and therefore most of my stories were taken as just stories. Many of my amends begin with this period of my life. I used anyone for anything I needed and believed simply that this was how you were supposed to live. During the last year of high school, my closest group had already completed the required courses, so our schedules included a lot of study halls and half-day schedules. Often we left campus and ended up at my house drinking or snorting THC, the chemical ingredient in marijuana. We would return to school for our last class of the day and believe that no one even noticed.

By this time in my life, I had already begun to lose control of my behaviors. I spent a lot of time covering my tracks but not truly worrying about the times I couldn't. It was also during this time that I remember making a conscious effort at organizing and looking forward to my next use, although I didn't recognize it until recently. My friends from those years whom I am still in contact with now tell me they always thought I overindulged a bit. Again, I thought it was normal and that we all were doing it at the same levels.

I can also remember the start of living in extremes. The highs were very high and the lows very low, but I accepted no mediocrity in my life whatsoever. I will avoid too much detail for reasons of confidentiality, but I can say there exist a number of happenings for which I am still hard pressed to find the proper amend. I accept that I am guilty, and I am willing to make amends. This attitude is such a complete turnaround from my past that it may be amend enough.

Upon graduation from high school, I moved away to an out-of-state college. I was the only one from my group of friends who did so. In looking back, with the knowledge of the AA program and lots of therapy, I believe that it was my "geographic fix" for my problems and subconscious insecurities. A new life seemed attractive at the time, but a continuation of the same lifestyle yielded the same results.

My first year away was spent partying with my new group of college dormitory friends, but because of my grandiosity, I was never fully connected to any particular group and gained no true friends from college. I moved from group to group until, later in my second and third year, I settled in with a regular group of drug and alcohol users. Due to a God-given natural level of intelligence, we all pulled decent grades despite a lack of any real studying. In fact, I graduated on the dean's list. The hardship of doing all the studying the night before testing took its toll on all of us, in the form of coffee, speed, and alcohol.

I was talented at convincing my friends and family back home of my success in school and pretended to have many new friends. Although I was getting decent grades with no effort, it wasn't until a professor suggested that I was in the wrong field that I had to prove my abilities and finished with a high average for the year.

This effort was more the result of an ego than of any thought of what the future might bring if I didn't apply myself. I believe that the rejection from the professor was the last straw in a long line of continued isolations and rejections. For some strange reason, another professor later took me under his wing, and I progressed in my field to the top of my class in short order. I owe this all to him and stayed in contact with him for a long time after graduation. He was a father figure to me, and without God placing him in my life at that time, I could have easily taken another road leading to complete despair.

In looking back, it seems that somebody was always there at the precise time that I needed help, and for a long time, I always seemed to be in the right place at the right time. Despite feeling alone in the world, I somehow always had a belief that someone, perhaps a Higher Power, was looking out for me. I know that there were many instances in which I was invited into a situation that could have taken my life in a direction that might have ruined it forever. Somehow, often through no effort of my own, I stayed away from those situations.

Throughout this period I worked full time, despite the financial aid I received from both my parents and the college. Most of the extra money, of course, wound up paying for my partying. I began working in restaurants at night and didn't start my evening of partying until well after all the restaurants were closed but the bars were still open. Again, because of the crowd I was involved with, it seemed normal to start an evening at ten or eleven o'clock and party until daybreak. By now cocaine was the drug of choice, and it seemed everyone I knew was using it frequently. I am amazed I didn't become totally addicted, but I stayed in touch with alcohol instead. I became good friends with a man who was one of the primary providers of coke, and later with his source. I was able to spend many a night getting high for free, using as much as I wanted. This in itself aided the progress of my alcoholic disease, as I never experienced the financial burden that usually goes hand in hand with expensive drug use; I could continue my drinking and drugging at will. The drug itself also provided a high that allowed an increase in my use of alcohol without the alcoholic drunken effects. By the time I had graduated from college, I was up to using well over an eighth of an ounce of cocaine every few days. All this, and I managed to hide my secret life from nearly everyone and to graduate with a 3.5 grade point average.

At this point at my particular college, it is true that the use of cocaine, marijuana, and alcohol were generally accepted by most of the local society. I was hanging out with the high rollers, frequenting the best bars, discos, clubs, and restaurants in town. At one particular four-star restaurant we frequented, we were provided a table behind a privacy curtain, and after dinner, we were brought the ceremonial bottle of complimentary Grand Marnier, a small mirror, and a straw for our cocaine. Even earlier on campus, the National Organization for the Reformation of Marijuana Laws (NORML) was active, and for a couple of years the punishment for on-campus use of marijuana was a twenty-five-dollar fine. I reflect on these facts only as an indication of how easy it was in my case to progress deeper and deeper into my addictions. The ego I was building at this point has taken years to tear down, and to this day, it occasionally gets in my way.

For my graduation, my parents came a thousand miles, only to have me tell them that I was opening a restaurant with a friend instead of pursuing my profession. Of course, their reaction was not one of support at first. But once they realized I was serious, they did lend me two thousand dollars to help keep me financially afloat. Again, this allowed me to increase my use of alcohol, as required of a man of my stature. Many a night after all the local bars were closed we would go back to the restaurant, and I would play "Mr. Big," opening our bar for the continuation of the festivities. The people I hurt through satisfying my own needs during this time is something I still think about. As each day went on, I seemed to think more and more about myself. At the time, of course, I truly believed that I was not hurting anybody else and what I did was therefore nobody's business but my own.

At this time, I was dating a lovely woman for a short period. We spent most of our evenings after getting off work late at night, drinking, retiring to the bedroom at morning's first light. I do not remember ever doing anything else with her. We had dated only a short time and had been broken up for a couple of months when I found out that she was pregnant. She didn't believe in abortion, and she had the child. We agreed to give our child up for adoption. I believed deeply that it was the best thing for the child. At the time, it was truly the right thing to do, as I was deeply involved in myself and drugs and could have only caused pain in any child's life. When we decided to give our daughter up for adoption, the agency assured us of the new parents' credentials and income, but it wasn't until years later that any of this truly mattered to me. Not a day goes by that I don't think of my lost daughter, and I still often find myself in tears. At that time, however, I remember feeling a sense of being in a fog. I remember being mad at the woman I had dated for getting pregnant and for not telling me until it was too late. When I first was told, I believed it had to be another man's child.

I just started my own family eight years ago and can't imagine how bad a father I would have been in those days. Nonetheless, not only do I owe enormous amends to this lovely lady but also hope someday to find and meet the daughter I have never met. Not a day goes by that I don't take this secret to bed with me. It would take an entirely different book to deal with the pain of this subject. But I must add that I feel love deep inside for that daughter. I have hired an investigator (or intermediator) to locate her once she turns eighteen, but until then there is nothing more I can do. This will eat at me until the day I know she is all right. Despite my current wonderful lifestyle, not knowing if my own daughter needs any help provides a sense of overwhelming guilt each time I think about it, even in full recovery. Again, I know it was the right thing to do so many years ago. I know she may not want to ever meet me, and I know I may be perceived as an intruder by the family that has raised her. Nonetheless, my desire is much more centered on making sure she is safe and happy than on interrupting her life. I have supplied the county adoption agency with a letter to her, in hopes that she may someday feel the need to meet and perhaps know me. In needing to make this amend, I must focus on the possibility that everyone involved could be hurt by what I do and how I handle the amend. I must go forward carefully, with compassion for others, without regard for my own feelings.

Eventually, while working at the restaurant, one of the regulars offered me a "real" job in my studied and chosen field. I jumped at the chance and left the restaurant after a year and a half. Again, someone was watching out for me, as evidenced by the job I eventually obtained. I went into the interview thinking I was applying for an entry-level position. I brought my college portfolio, lied through my teeth, and somehow left that office with the department manager's position—in charge of seven other professionals with much more experience than myself. It seems the company was also looking to fill the manager's position, and the man who hired me thought I was applying for it. In short, the right place at the right time. The funny thing about it was that I actually did a good job of it. When asked a question by one of my employees who was far smarter than I, somehow I would delay my answer "to think about it" for a day and would spend that evening in the library or at home studying to find the correct response. The next morning I would address the problem with my staff, impressing them all with my experience and knowledge. After some time, I had crammed my missed college studying into a year or two of professional work and became successful and respected.

All through this time period, around 1981, I would occasionally go out to lunch with my boss and have a three-beer meal and even smoke a joint once in a while on the way back to the office. Once in a while we might visit a bar that served pizza and beer for lunch. It was amazing that together we ran such a successful company. I remember one time flying out of state to one of our divisions, only to find out that the franchisee lived in a dry county. After a nice dinner with his family, I was dropped off at my hotel room to turn in. I then called a cab and drove about an hour to get to a bar still open. I came back to the hotel completely drunk, waking up with an enormous hangover, and tried to complete another day of meetings with our division manager. And I didn't have a problem?

After leaving my first real job, I switched jobs about every three or four years, always moving up, always with great financial rewards. If I wasn't promoted every year or two, I would simply resign and move on. I moved up swiftly through the ranks of my chosen field and was virtually always the one to be promoted. At every company my numbers were the best ever, our quality and scheduling improved, sales increased—and my alcohol use also secretly increased. I had been a functioning alcoholic at twenty-three years old. By this time, my use of cocaine had stopped, only because my friends were changing and I didn't know where to buy it any longer. But when I did find it, a weekend bender was in order, usually with a beautiful woman whom I fell in love with, then never called again. I am not trying to be cute. I truly fell in love, felt guilty about the relationship or my actions, hid from the possibility that she might actually get to know the real me, and ran. It was about this time that I developed a part-time relationship with a beautiful college girl who occasionally worked as a stripper. I kept the relationship a secret from everyone, friends and professionals alike. I felt secure being myself with her solely because of what she did for a living, while I went off every morning pretending to be someone else. To me, she was in a position lower than mine, so I could be myself around her. She was also in law school and is now a respected attorney.

I began to win both local and national awards from my industry. I was the youngest person ever invited on the industry and advisory board of the local university. I was also the youngest person ever to serve on my industry's local board of directors. And I was now drinking heavily on a nightly basis. Despite my professional success, I felt like a failure. Nothing was good enough, and I always wanted more. I was conscious that my goals came easily and had feelings of guilt because of that fact. Every time I achieved a particular professional goal, I immediately placed the pressure of a new goal upon my shoulders and treated my accomplishment as unimportant. I thought to myself that if I achieved it so easily, it couldn't have been a difficult task in the first place. My low self-worth could not allow me to accept my accomplishments but reminded me every day of my failures. At this time in my life, I had no personal or spiritual goals whatsoever. Everything centered on my career. Many of my supervisors also were heavy drinkers at the time. Much time was spent supposedly talking business, in bars across town, late into the evenings.

The companies that I worked for had their best years and best profits, and no one could stand in the way of my career. It was at this point in my life that I learned I could judge my self-worth by my income instead of my actions. I forgot how to keep score. A valet parking receipt was probably more valuable than any good deed. For the first time in my life, I felt as though I was important. This fueled a belief that I was also more valuable to the world than the average Joe, and I acted with more grandiosity with each passing day. My days were spent working twelve to fourteen hours, and the world owed me my nights out. It wasn't until I entered recovery that I realized I was not spending time with any of my true peers, as I surrounded myself with people at different, yet impressionable, financial and professional levels. I spent my after-hours time with those willing to provide support or stay up all night at local bars with me or with women willing to feed my ego. All this to make me feel like I was somebody, when in fact I already had the world at my fingertips and didn't know it.

It was at one of these bars that I met my first wife, a local Realtor and a regular at most of the fancier clubs. We met, dated briefly, and were married within six months. Two weeks after we were married, she decided to spend the balance of another drunken night with another man and did not return home. I should have seen that something was wrong in her life when her own family refused to come to the wedding. The pain I felt convinced me once again of my lack of personal value in the world and provided the ammunition I needed to assure myself I would never be hurt again. I withdrew further into isolation, despite my outwardly friendly and playful demeanor, and once again found that alcohol could numb the pain. Our divorce was expensive and nasty, which is amusing, as we really didn't have much to fight over except our egos. I haven't heard a word about her or seen her since the divorce. During this period, I satisfied myself through extensive drinking. I wonder now whether I experienced periods of blackouts. I am certain I made an enormous fool out of myself on many occasions with many people. I just can't remember the details.

To bring my parents back into the picture, it was during this time that I received a letter from my father telling me I had been disowned and not to contact my mother or him ever again. He said it was over something mean I had said to Mom on the phone. I have never found out what it was. As I explained earlier, years later my father and I made up, and at the time of his death, we were best friends. He forgave me for my past behaviors based primarily upon his respect for my professional success, but I will never understand how we both looked past each other's faults and found love for each other at the end. At the time I received the letter, I had a recollection of never feeling a part of the family anyway, so it was no big loss. These were my alcoholic thoughts, not necessarily the truth. The point, however, is that the disease allowed, or forced, me to believe these thoughts as complete truth.

Years later, out at a local bar after a drinking night at a professional basketball game, I saw the most beautiful woman I had ever seen in my entire life. The whole world slowed to a stop when I saw her across the room. Without sounding corny, I was actually breathless for some time. Eventually, I was lucky enough to spend a few moments and one dance with her. I will spare the story of how, with only her first name and a rough idea of where she worked, I spent about a month trying to find her. After all, she was too respectable to give out her phone number and was seeing someone else at the time. Interestingly enough, I found out some time later that she did not frequent bars. She was the first "straight" woman I had ever known, let alone fallen in love with. Once I finally found her, it took another month of phone calls to talk her into meeting me for lunch, and quite slowly we began to date. Despite it all, this woman is still my wife today, and since recovery, my heart still flutters when our eyes meet across a crowded room. She is the most beautiful, honest, patient, sensitive, and caring person one could ever hope to meet; yet, as I will explain, I spent the next ten years breaking her heart over and over again.

The first experience came just before we were married, when I was accused of flirting with a woman at work and asked to re-sign. Remembering that this lead is supposed to be totally hon-est, I must add that I had rejected her advances many times at the office but did indeed flirt with her to an extent not acceptable for a manager. I also did the best I could to welcome and encourage her advances and hide the fact that I was engaged. She filed the complaint after learning that I was getting married in a couple of months. Nonetheless, this was only the first hint of what became a normal state of promiscuity that caused my beloved wife pain and distrust for years.

At my next position with a new company over a thousand miles away, with my caring and forgiving wife following the career of her husband, leaving her own career behind, my drinking was again party to me leaving the company. I was a company hero in terms of performance, but my personal actions outside of the office were cause of possible embarrassment to the company. I negotiated a settlement whereby I would resign. This was after three years of soaring through the ranks to the position of executive vice presi-dent and later senior vice president. I was driving a company Cadillac, living in a half-million-dollar house, making six figures, raising a newborn daughter, and risking my life through alco-holism, only to satisfy my insecurity and ego.

At the time, I had uncovered a scheme by one of the owners of the company to hide income and perform accounting irregulari-ties to benefit himself and his family. Without going into details, it was only this information that gave me a "golden parachute" upon my departure. It was at this same time that my father passed away and, I believe to this day, the exact moment that I no longer cared about things of a spiritual nature. I wore my "religion" on my chest, as a friend later told me, yet I had virtually no understanding or involvement in spiritual things. I had given up the need to be responsible to anybody but myself. The death of my father was not a traumatic, alcoholism-causing event. I do feel, however, that it provided a further sense of isolation that fueled the need as time went on to find a way to numb the pain.

My wife and I did have some problems in the bedroom, and we had little communication between us, but that is her story to tell, not mine. What I do know is that I lost an enormous amount of time with her and my children, in searching for someone or something false to feed my ego and help hide my fear. I spent time with anybody willing to drink, to nod their head as I discussed my success, and to allow me to run wild in my imaginary second life. I was so successful and so afraid of failure that I had to numb the joy and the worry at the same time. Even in early marriage, to a woman who would have done nearly anything I asked, I felt rejected and totally alone. As an alcoholic, I would subconsciously blame her for my happiness and would find fault in her actions to make me feel in control.

It is now evident that I was searching for recognition or acceptance from others to satisfy my insecurity and low self-esteem. I believed I was not getting the things I deserved from my wife, so I sought them elsewhere. I believed that it was her responsibility to make me happy. The manner in which this disease can affect our loved ones enabled her also to believe I was responsible for her happiness. I then spent my personal time as I felt I needed and as the world owed to me. I did what I wanted, when I wanted it, and how I wanted it, without regard for how my actions affected others. Through it all, my wife stayed with me and showed me respect and full support through all of her own doubts. Frankly, my entire nature was self-serving and often promiscuous at this point. My jokes and my language at home and in public were geared to some type of sexual expression. Most of it seemed innocent from my perspective back then, but it was obviously repulsive to many who feared me enough to force any awareness on my part. I had lowered my standards to match my actions. The friends I had, the time frame in our history, and the drinking all allowed me simply to act as I wanted, without any tolerance for others.

Again, we relocated to a new state, as I took a position with a company in need of a professional to grow with the company, eventually taking over control of all operations. After nearly three years, while I held the position of executive vice president, my ego got in the way of what was becoming a great relationship with the owner, and I resigned. At the time, I truly believed that I had outgrown the company and was having difficulty because all my hard work was going to line the pocketbook of the owner and his family. He was paying me well. I don't believe I have equaled the amount of money in a year I made there. Sadly enough, the owner and I have never talked since, and I truly miss his genius and his integrity. At times, I miss the relationship we might have had and all I could have learned from him. His company has flourished without me, and mine has slid along, year after year, sometimes good and sometimes not so good. He believed that I was a traitor and had planned my departure for some time. The truth is, I was at a stage of insecurity that needed a few compliments every now and then, and the owner didn't have the capacity to give them. Furthermore, had he given them, I probably wouldn't have heard them. I left a wonderful position with a wonderful company, solely out of fear of failure. In looking back, I was probably intelligent enough to know that the company was beginning to outgrow *me*.

Eventually I started my own business. On the surface, I looked extremely successful as I fell deeper and deeper into alcoholism and isolation. I was the best actor in the area, outspending, outpartying, outliving, and outworking them all. It was about this time I began to feel I was straightening out, however, and I began to negotiate with God. I would go to bed every night praying for forgiveness for my actions that day and asking for help. Inside I was alone, scared, and isolated from everyone near me. It wasn't that I was "doing" so many bad things, but that I was "thinking" them. Resentments toward others could linger for months and often years. I was going out with "the boys" at every occasion and missed a large part of my oldest daughter's infancy. Still, I began to believe that there must be something wrong with me. This was the last couple of years of living in an alcoholic hell. The harder I tried to make people like me, the further I pushed them away. I began frequently to say and do embarrassing things when I drank, straightening up just in time for the next day of work.

In a sad way, my drinking and alcoholism probably provided me with the desire to excel at work. It was the only place I could engulf myself in something that gave me some external satisfaction. My clients received the benefit of my perfectionism, yet several of them also turned against me near the end of the project, due to my alcoholic personality, not the results of their job. It was the alcoholic, self-centered, never-wrong, always-perfect mind-set that beget negative feelings against me and my company, not the performance of the company. I would have done anything for my clients to avoid losing money on a job and to gain their affection and approval. The problem was how I shoved it in their faces when I was right and they were wrong.

Both my wife and I started to believe that leading separate lives was a normal part of American life. We had the country club membership and a new half-million-dollar house; we ate out whenever we wanted and always had new fancy cars—the best of everything. Frankly, most of the people and clients we knew at the time lived this way also. Both of us got caught up in it while falling deeper and deeper into a mutual depression and state of insecurity and unhappiness. Through it all, we never truly talked, seldom made love, and ignored the way our marriage was falling apart due mostly to my drinking. Most certainly we wouldn't share any feelings like fear, insecurity, and distrust. We hid those deep within to avoid the potential of losing the only security blanket each of us had come to know. My drinking had increased to regular nightly episodes and weekend drunks. We manipulated and controlled each other as a means of self-acceptance, by making the other person less. She through using my drinking against me, and me through using a perceived lack of sexuality and understanding against her. I never became violent but the perception of my ability to be violent should I so decide was enough to keep our household in turmoil. Most of my hard drinking at this point occurred out of the house or in the late evening, after everyone else would be in bed. It became the only way I could fall asleep and get a good night's sleep, then return to a full fifteen hours of hard work the next day.

I am taking painstaking efforts to write the truth as I know it. It is important that my lead be vigorously honest without promoting my identity. Keeping this in mind, I must add a few words for the codependent reader. I am guilty of actions I will never forget. The guilt may never go away, but my Higher Power, God, as I prefer to call Him, is a forgiving God. I know that He has forgiven me, and I am comfortable with that. We alcoholics are much harder on ourselves than anyone else could ever be. Nonetheless, it still pains me to hear the rumors, to get the judgmental looks, and to remember some of what I did. This is a disease that took over the fiber of my being. Without my work, I would most probably be dead. And, as I'll soon explain, without my family, I would have died a long time ago. It is important to recognize, however, the absorption of the disease and the actions resulting from the disease that also took over a large part of my wife. Codependents have the need to blame the alcoholic in order to find innocence in their own behaviors. After all we put them through and tried to hide, no wonder they feel no need to look at their own thoughts and behaviors. I assure you, however, that the perpetuation of the disease is helped along by the enabler and the controller. The problem is, all marriages can take a turn for the worse through hard times, whatever they may be. Alcoholics simply do not have the tools to work on the problems without alcohol. That, in turn, creates a mind-set unable to work through life on life's terms.

We attended marriage counseling for some time. I faked my way through it the best I could. During our separation, I was drinking a twelve-pack a day when I wasn't working, a bottle of cognac in shots, and additional drinks in the bar at my hotel until closing. Again, this behavior was acceptable and normal to me at the time. I simply needed a couple of drinks to calm my nerves. Every minute not drinking was spent working. The only thing I had left in my life was my work, and I became a tyrant and a perfectionist. Nothing was ever good enough, and I now believe that I also inadvertently taught my clients to believe that nothing was ever good enough, causing or allowing them to demand perfection also, an impossible request.

If you had asked me then how much I drank, I probably would have said three or four beers a day and absolutely believed it. Treating an alcoholic has to be one of the most difficult jobs in the world. Not only are we seasoned and professional liars when it comes to our drinking, but we don't even always know when we are lying about drinking. Many alcoholics have extremely high levels of integrity and honesty in all matters not related to drinking. It makes up for the continued denial surrounding the drinking. At the same time my drinking was at its worst, my integrity at work was above reproach (the only place I was willing to judge myself). Everything was black and white; there existed no gray areas. This caused me to take a stand against a client solely to point out that I was right on a trivial issue. I subconsciously refused to see another position or how someone else might perceive a certain situation. I can remember other times that I took a hard stance, causing resentments on both ends, with friends and family, clients and employees, for no apparent benefit. If it was a battle that I knew I could win, I would fight until the end. If I didn't have the ammo ready to win, I would give up quickly, as I simply couldn't stand to lose.

Eventually, my wife and I began marriage counseling again. Through this counseling, we decided to try our marriage again. She now had to work on her sexuality, as I forced this issue at every turn with the therapist, so I also felt vindicated. I was asked to give up alcohol for six months. Although my wife still says I didn't make it, I insist I did. That doesn't matter. I believed I quit for six months, and the belief gave me the proof and right to drink freely, as surely I wasn't an alcoholic after all. A small period of abstinence gave me a license to drink as much as I wanted forever. As soon as the marriage seemed to be back to what we thought was normal, we quit therapy altogether. The problem was, our "normal" was only a road to failure.

My drinking behavior slowly began to sink to a new level. I was proud that, as a business owner, I could damn well have a beer or two in the afternoon at work if I desired. My clients frequently joined me for an afternoon beer in the office during a meeting. I'm sure now that it was a special occasion for them, but it was becoming my normal work habit. I had custom ordered a briefcase with a holder for four beers on the lower level—but I didn't have a problem. A mentor of mine, an extremely wealthy individual successful in the same business, also drank at his office during the day, so I tried to emulate him. The problem was, I couldn't handle it, for I was an alcoholic. I didn't get drunk; I worked as effectively as most. I just didn't like myself.

At this time, I became friends with a gentleman who was an associate to my company. We began to meet weekly for a Friday beer. It wasn't long before we would polish off five or six before going home, not thinking a thing about it. I still maintained my nightly allotment at home as well. Shortly, we were calling each other after every hectic day and setting up a late-afternoon meeting at "our" bar. After I came home and my family all went to bed, I would stay up until one or two in the morning drinking cognac. But because I did it while I was working in my home office, I told myself I deserved it and I wasn't hurting anybody. I complained that a lack of sex was my wife's fault, yet I was going to bed drunk and rude almost every night. I would often go out with the boys, then have problems understanding why, when I came home drunk, rude, obnoxious, and arrogant, my wife wasn't turned on.

At this same time, I began to exhibit many of the symptoms of alcoholism on other occasions when out with my wife. I became verbally abusive toward most anyone when drinking. I refused to let her drive after I had had too much to drink. And all of our entertainment centered on my drinking. I would even sneak alcohol into a movie theater to add to my soda. My wife began to make regular demands that I give up at least hard liquor, giving me all the more reason to drink without her. Eventually, I was meeting my friend at a bar every night, leaving work at about five o'clock so that I would have enough time to drink five or six beers and still arrive home on time. I could then walk in the door expecting that no one knew I was drinking and pretend to have my first drink at home. My temperament during this period was one of absolute righteousness, causing my family to run around picking up the house and straightening everything perfectly before I walked in the door. I still always found something wrong and made sure it was addressed. Even my youngest daughter ran from my temper when I had been drinking and tells me now "how much nicer" I am since I stopped. I can't seem ever to forgive myself for the pain I caused not only my wife but also my own children through this period of my life.

It was during this time, I now know, that I began to experience blackouts. I acted perfectly normal but did not remember what I had said or done the night before. Even my regular drinking partner began to question my behaviors and attitudes. I began to convince my wife that she was imagining things I had said because I was certain I could never say something so mean. I could not admit that I might have a problem with alcohol, yet I remember private thoughts that perhaps I should cut back a little. The blackouts occurred after work when I was drinking, so I believed that I was functioning normally. I could only judge myself by what I had left—my work. Remember, I was now praying to God every single night to help me with my loneliness, insecurity, total unhappiness, and behavior, but I didn't think I had any problem with alcohol.

I was convinced that all my problems were everyone else's fault, particularly my wife's. She wasn't making me happy, and that was her job, after all. I worked hard for all the things we had, and I deserved a clean house, wonderful sex at will, and perfectly trained children. I deserved the world to revolve around me, and she wasn't doing it right!

I now started thinking about drinking early in the day but

hadn't got to the point where I actually took a morning drink. My work was too important to me, so I always made sure I planned my drinking, leaving plenty of time to do what was needed at work. I would never begin to drink until I had fulfilled the requirements of my job. This planning is an early indication of alcoholism. This time away from work and family, lost while drinking, also caused me to work seven days a week.

I would often lie in bed and stare at my beautiful wife, with tears running down my face while she slept. I would silently ask her for forgiveness and promise to become a better husband and father. My wife and I would go out for dinner often but always with other couples, probably subconsciously to avoid being alone together. I was at the point in which I would say I had to use the restroom and sneak to the bar for a quick shot of hard liquor. I would joke with the bartender and waitress, all the while believing that they fully understood how unfair it was that I couldn't do this at my own table. One particular couple who were friends of ours gave me the most enjoyment, as the man was the only person who could keep up with my drinking of cognac and still order one more. Their actual company was not enjoyable, as they always argued with each other as the night progressed. But it was worth having someone with us who supported my habit through a similar action. Believe it or not, I used to take my entire family to this little local Mexican restaurant and sneak into the bar to a waiting shot of liquor. I snuck out into the bar so often under the pretense of using the restroom that when they saw me enter with my family, they would be prepared for me in the bar. Like Norm in the comedy sitcom *Cheers*, many bartenders knew my name— but I didn't have a problem.

In these, the last days of my drinking, I subconsciously knew that my life was spinning out of control. I did try to reach out to several people with hints of needing help, but as an alcoholic, I had to protect my insecurities and despair from being shown. There was no way anyone could read into my comments a true need. In addition, those close to me knew well that they had better not question me or my actions. Like most people, I would present my case to as many people as it took to find someone in agreement with me; then I was certain that I was once again proved to have the right opinion. Like a drug dealer stealing some of his friend's share, I was now sneaking out to other bars, in addition to the times with my drinking friend from work, so that even he wouldn't know I was drinking more than he knew about. I would set a meeting at five after work with him, but I would leave work at four and stop somewhere else for an hour first, then meet him for a few more drinks.

The "rock bottom" for me and my family started innocently enough with a young woman that my entire family knew quite well. Frankly, even though a young woman, she was experienced well beyond her years. I think my wife would admit this woman was experienced even beyond her own years. Slowly, this woman began flirting with me (or we began with each other), and like a hungry fish, I went after it hook, line, and sinker. As usual, I really only needed the reinforcement and acceptance of having a young and pretty woman interested enough in me to flirt. Even now, in telling this story, I feel as though I am making excuses for my actions, so I assure you that only I am responsible for what I did. My wife was out of town visiting her family, and this young woman spent days at our home and stayed late into the evenings after the kids went to bed. I was working nearly all the time and in my active alcoholic state believed that I certainly didn't have the time to raise my own children, so we all appreciated her help. I thought nothing about this at the time, as it made me feel as though I was still young at heart, but in looking back, I probably knew where it was going. It seemed perfectly normal to me, and to my wife, that the young woman would hang around, but I, of course, always secretly wondered if she had another motive. I tell this part of the story only to show a glimpse of how an alcoholic thinks during excessive use.

One of these nights, very late, as the young woman was leaving, she made a pass at me (or I thought she did) as she left. I actually turned away from it. You see, it actually made me so proud that I had done this out of respect for my wife while she was away. Some weeks later, when my wife was in town, it was okay to go ahead with it. It wasn't cheap then and most certainly not the same as adultery—and I didn't have a problem.

It all happened in about two minutes, and I was sick to my stomach for hours afterward, throwing up, but I still didn't have a problem. The guilt was tearing me apart for days, and I was searching for a way to tell my wife without losing her. Every second of every day was spent with enormous fear and despair, and I was drinking full time, almost all day long. I truly do not know whether the incident was a blackout or not and refuse to use that as an excuse of any kind. But I cannot remember any of my actions before, during, or immediately after the incident. I had drunk ten or twelve beers and a dozen cognacs or so and remember only that I didn't think I was drunk. I was sick to my stomach because of what I had done, not because of the liquor. The first recollection I have is throwing up in the bathroom at home much later that evening. I somehow knew what I had done, or the extent of how wrong it was, but it felt more like a bad dream than any sense of reality. I cannot, no matter how hard I try, remember a large part of that evening. I can, however, remember virtually every single ounce of guilt and shame, some of which will never leave me.

Eventually my wife confronted me and without batting an eye, I admitted it. I still don't understand why, but I do recall a deep relief, despite all the pain, in finally telling the truth. In retrospect, I believe that I wanted to be found out, and I was somehow crying out for help. I felt so alone, so scared, and most certainly had fallen to the point in which I didn't trust myself. Much worse, I had fallen to the point in which I hated myself and what I had become. Despite it all, I held extremely high levels of morality and integrity, and I couldn't understand why or how I had let myself down again. I must also admit that I remember hoping that my wife would know what to do to help me. Imagine that.

This time I had taken my wife and my children to the darkest point I had ever taken them. She left me and took my children a thousand miles away. The day she left, I drank three bottles of cognac and a case of beer and did not get drunk. Alcohol was frankly never mentioned as having any role in my behavior initially, as both of us were now convinced I had much deeper problems. It was easier to accept the possibility of deep-rooted psychological problems than it was to accept a problem with alcohol. I would have much rather been put in a psych ward and given shock treatment than admit I had a problem with alcohol. My wife wanted a divorce, and for the first time in my life, I found myself needing someone else. Still, at this particular point, I had not accepted that alcohol had anything to do with it.

Probably for the first time in our relationship in many years, I realized that I truly loved my wife. I was now aware that I had ruined my life. My business was being ignored, my family in ruin, and the world as I knew it would be forever different. After she left, around the second week, I loaded a double-barrel twelve-gauge shotgun, sat down at the breakfast table, and drank. I had written a good-bye note and an honest apology for all the pain I had caused this dear and lonely woman. She had stayed with me through it all, and I knew this time it was really over. I had nothing to live for. Better stated, I was simply tired of living. I assured myself that my children would be better off without me and even imagined them in the arms of a substitute daddy. I was crying daily, with complete lack of control. The phone rang as I sat staring at the shotgun.

By the grace of God, my wife called and told me she would agree to meet with the marriage counselor one last time, with no commitment to our relationship, but only to decide what to tell our children. Then, for the first time in a week or so, my oldest daughter got on the other end of the phone. She will never know it, until and unless she reads this book, but she might have saved my life that night. She said these words to me that I will remember as long as I live: "Daddy, if you loved yourself, Mommy would love you too." At this point, I did something truly "stupid," something that to this day I cannot explain. I dropped to my knees and I prayed. I said four simple but eternal words: "God, please help me." And it was the last time that liquor has touched my lips.

I called our marriage counselor, and she asked a couple of

simple questions that changed my life forever. She asked, "Do these types of actions usually occur after you have been drinking?" "Would you consider going somewhere just to find out?" Obviously, at this point I would consider anything, and a light-bulb went on in my head that was brighter than any light I had ever "seen" before. The Big Book refers to the need for some type of spiritual experience. I can tell you that I am not one to admit to this type of nonsense, but at that exact moment, I felt the presence of a divine being fill my soul for just one split second. In that precise moment, I knew that if I worked hard, things could be better for me. I can't explain it any better than that. Somehow, that one split second gave me a glimpse of a peace I had never experienced. I knew then, although I didn't know what to call it, that my Higher Power was giving me a chance finally to end the pain. It was like spending a split second in the presence of God. It was a feeling that today I would do anything in the world to feel again, and all I have to do to find it is stay sober.

My wife (who was now living out of state with our children) flew in for one day to meet with our therapist, and I then told her and our therapist of my decision to leave for Hazelden, in Minnesota, in a few days. Before she came to town, I spent virtually all of my time calling many of the leading treatment centers and clinics in the country. If it were not for the professionalism exhibited by the woman who later became my personal case manager, Lisa Reynolds, I would have never proceeded to the facility. I thank her now for her compassion, direction, and caring manner in which she helped me to help myself. To this day, I consider her one of my closest friends, yet I know little about her. She did all this without lying to me or exaggerating the program. She never mentioned spirituality, God, or Alcoholics Anonymous. Had I thought for a moment that this was about alcoholism, I wouldn't have signed up. I could admit that I might have a problem with drinking a little too much, but my denial was far too strong even to consider the alcoholism. And I most certainly didn't need three or four weeks involved with some "holy roller" cult. Most of my questioning at all of the centers I contacted involved how much control I would have while there, how often I could have visitors, and whether or not I could walk out if I wanted to. I believed that I could go to the center, take a pill or something, and then be able to manage controlled drinking. I still didn't believe that I needed to quit drinking completely, although my life had become totally unmanageable due to my drinking.

When I left for treatment, my wife was still intent on divorce and probably was for many months after my return from Hazelden, nearly four weeks later. If there can be any way to prove the program does work, I am that proof. My wife saw immediate changes in me—real changes. It is the only thing that kept her around another day, one day at a time. Even I didn't see the changes she saw in me, as I was focused solely on my recovery at that time. I had finally come to recognize my past behaviors, accepted responsibility for them, and knew it was a place I never wanted to go again. I saw a light at the end of the tunnel. I don't want to underemphasize or place some false heroic angle on my recovery, but it takes work, hard work. Simply stated, it is a miracle. I am thoroughly convinced that, should the day ever come when I stop working on my recovery, I will relapse. This is a lifelong process of working toward growth every day.

Part of recovery is the pride involved that comes with your own personal success. It is the hardest thing I have ever done in my life, and it is all mine. Rather, it is all God's, for without His guidance and love, it would not have been possible. I have completely changed my belief system, my lifestyle, my attitudes, and my relationship with God. You *can* teach an old dog new tricks. If someone like me could find success in recovery, anyone can. I lived my entire life on my terms, often with success. It is still unimaginable to me and to my friends that I have truly become a caring individual. Many people now tell me what a jerk I had been while drinking. I can't help but wonder why they maintained a relationship with me at all in the past. My wife tells me now that through it all, she could still see the good in me. I can only thank God for that. One thing I would like to add at this point is my disdain for those who perform awful actions and then, as an excuse for forgiveness, say that they have now found religion. Many people use religion and God as a means to prove falsely to other people that they have changed, that the action was by another person. How then can I describe alcoholism in the same vein without feeling fake myself? All I can say is I truly believe that alcoholism has been shown to take over the mind of an alcoholic. Without alcohol, I believe in different things now. Without alcohol, I do things differently now. And every day I thank God for what He has done for me.

My experiences at Hazelden are better left for the chapter on recovery, but I cannot close my lead without expressing my love and respect for that organization. We were all always treated with the utmost respect. The program allows for a slow growth of knowledge and acceptance of the disease. I rapidly became convinced that I was an alcoholic, but I still refused to believe that it was the only cause for my past actions. It took weeks to convince me that they were indeed actions common to alcoholics. Hearing the histories of my peer group enabled me to see this much more clearly every day. My last week was mostly meetings and more meetings, counseling and more counseling. It seems that word had been shared by my case manager, or counselor, that I now believed that I was an alcoholic, but I was also not sure if that was the cause of all of my actions. I was interviewed and counseled by a therapist, a psychiatrist, the chaplain, the unit managing counselor, my counselor, two other counselors, a psychotherapist, and a grief counselor before I began to accept that I was possibly a good person with a bad disease. To convince me that they were right has taken many instances in which I could have repeated my past behaviors or thoughts and didn't.

Many people enter recovery without attending a treatment center, and many others hold treatment centers in disrespect as some kind of "spin dry." I believe this is a result of the early 1980s rush toward treatment and the many sham and failed centers throughout the country. I have been told by many AA old-timers to hide my affiliation with a treatment center, but I simply cannot. I am proud that I was given a chance. I am proud that there are places to go to learn how to live a spiritual life. And I am proud to know those with a much more successful recovery program than I, who never went to treatment. God helps us all go our own way, and this was mine. No better or worse than anyone else's, just mine.

I now awake every single morning and spend a half hour with my family in meditation and prayer. I have a conscious connection with my Higher Power, God, and feel Him in my life throughout the day. I rarely have to ask for forgiveness and spend most of my prayer time in gratitude or in asking for help with tolerance and compassion toward others. I pray for the happiness of those whom I may not like, and I try hard to see their position. I pray on and off quite naturally throughout a normal day, and things that used to baffle me I handle with ease. The Promises of the Big Book are indeed coming true.

My marriage is stronger than ever, and my wife and I have fallen in love all over again as new people. I no longer find many other women attractive, and with those I may, I have never even had the thought of pursuing a flirtatious relationship. Our sexual relationship is for the first time based on satisfying the other, not ourselves.

I admit that we still have problems, just as most marriages come across. The difference now is that we don't hold the issues back, and we are more intent on working things out than in winning. I don't work her program, and she doesn't work my program. We have learned we cannot control each other. We have also learned what true intimacy involves and are beginning to learn how to communicate.

My company is running professionally, but I do not worry about finances, as I trust that my God's will shall be done. I am doing the best that I can and the best that I know how, and I know that satisfies my Higher Power. I am closer to my children than most other parents I know and now spend almost all of my free time with my family, enjoying every minute of it.

Our youngest daughter and I actually have a great relationship, and I feel as though I know her well. Prior to recovery, the relationship I shared with my children was on my terms. Now the relationship is on our terms. My other children comment often about how much they like Daddy since he went away to school to learn how to take better care of himself. I can honestly say that my children are now my friends. I am involved in a regular exercise program that has taken almost thirty pounds off of my beer drinker's frame, and I feel mentally healthier than I had thought could be possible. Stress levels have dropped considerably, and the emotional extremes have nearly vanished. I can now tell my clients no when it is deserved, without the need to give in to their demands solely to make up for personal behavior. In fact, there is no giving in at all. Relationships with clients are now mainly handled with professionalism, with decisions made on the merits of the facts surrounding the topic.

I laugh at funny things when I am all alone, and I am working on becoming incapable of telling a lie. I enjoy my regular recovery meetings and feel naked throughout the day when I miss one. I still make lots of mistakes, but I accept the fact that we all make mistakes. I also expect and accept the mistakes of others. I can still be angry occasionally, but I direct it toward the item, not the person, and generally harbor no resentments. I realize that where resentments occur, I have a responsibility in them. It is true that many of my old friends have deserted me, particularly my drinking friends. The new people I have met, however, like me for who I am, not for what I have achieved. And the friends I have made in the program live their lives by example, with as few words as possible.

I am secure in my faults and I am secure in my talents. I feel as if I belong to this world and am here to serve God as He wishes. For the first time in my entire life, I have found just a little slice of peace, serenity, and happiness. For the first time in my life, I like myself.

Chapter 5

Recovery

I regard recovery as a slow process that involves every fiber of one's mind and body. One cannot expect success through a treatment program alone. Recovery is an ongoing process of replacing bad behaviors, habits, attitudes, and thoughts with new ones. Recovery takes work, or it will not occur.

Abstinence from alcohol is just the beginning of any recovery program. I have always enjoyed thinking about recovery as though my past consists of a large bucket of dirty water. As each day in recovery passes, with new behaviors that include tolerance, compassion toward others, acceptance of my faults, and, above all, spirituality, a drop of fresh, clean water falls into my bucket. The disease of alcoholism is said to be 10 percent alcohol and 90 percent attitude. In other words, the disease is about what is going on in the mind. Recovery is about working on the mind-set that was numbed through the use of alcohol. Alcohol use is the symptom of much larger and more important issues.

Eventually, the dirty water has been diluted by clean water, and I find myself doing anything to protect it and keep it clean. As they say in AA, it takes a lot of good days, one day at a time, to provide one with a lot of good yesterdays—and a lot of clean water. The further we move into recovery, the harder it is for us to accept a step backward, or even a drop of dirty water. Others have described recovery in just that manner. Recovery is like walking up a slippery and icy hill. As long as you keep moving forward, you can make it, but the second you stop moving, there is the chance you may slip backward. Gorski and Miller (1986) more appropriately refer to it as walking up a down escalator. John Niehaus (1997) coined the phrase "The recovering alcoholic is similar to a wire stripped of its insulation." To me, this best describes the sensitivities of the alcoholic while in early recovery and emphasizes the importance of a slow recovery process.

How one enters abstinence and recovery is unimportant. Which program or method of treatment is also unimportant. Whether one enters an outpatient program or a treatment center, joins friends at Alcoholics Anonymous or any other program, is also of little importance. What must occur is that the alcoholic finds a way, any way, to stop drinking. I hope this book has laid forth some concrete evidence of successfully proven methods to consider. More important, I hope that this book has provided some basic understanding that alcoholism must be treated as a disease.

The Process

Recovery takes on many forms and occurs in various stages of the disease for different people. But recovery is possible for virtually anyone willing to undertake the proper amount of work and guidance. Many different programs and processes are available for the recovering alcoholic, and many people are successful in recovery for various reasons. Ludwig (1988) reaffirms that alcoholics are more likely to strive for recovery through a glimpse of heaven only after having lived through hell. The process has been referred to by a number of sources as "uncovery, discovery, recovery."

Many therapists argue that the focus of recovery should be to elevate the self-esteem and morale of the alcoholic. This assumes that the alcoholic has already undergone the process of "deflation of ego" as described by Bill Wilson. Others seem to support Alcoholics Anonymous's Fourth and Fifth Steps which convey that this attitudinal change can occur through a confession of sins to another.

Gorski and Miller (1986) identify a development model of recovery. It is best described as the completion of specific recovery-related tasks in a correct order (similar to the concept presented in the Big Book and AA) to properly facilitate recovery. It is interesting to learn that they believe the increase in self-esteem begins to occur in the late stages of recovery.

A quick look at the concept of recovery can benefit those trying to understand the formula. First and foremost, there must exist within the alcoholic a desire to stop drinking, or recovery is impossible. Once this has occurred, the alcoholic must realize the consequences of drinking. A direct correlation between the bad thoughts and behaviors and the drinking must also be accepted. The alcoholic can then begin to accept powerlessness over alcohol and understand the disease concept. This enables an understanding of the total lack of control and the need for outside help from peers and a Higher Power.

Once this has occurred, the alcoholic can begin to work on a new belief system and new behaviors. This work will stabilize thought processes, providing assurance that a new life is underway. Again, after many successfully lived yesterdays, the alcoholic will begin to grow, develop self-esteem, and become a different person.

Gorski and Miller's Developmental Model of Recovery

- The Pretreatment Period—Learning by the consequences that one cannot safely use addictive chemicals.
- The Stabilization Period—Regaining control of thought processes, emotional processes, memory, judgment, and behavior.
- The Early Recovery Period—Accepting the disease of addiction and learning to function without drugs and alcohol.
- The Middle Period—Developing a normal, balanced lifestyle.
- Late Recovery—Developing healthy self-esteem, spiritual growth, intimacy, and meaningful living.
- Maintenance—Staying sober and living productively.

Brown (1995) reviews another standard model of recovery that is widely accepted in therapeutic circles. The stages in this model are described as the transition stage, the early recovery stage, and the ongoing recovery stage. In the transition stage, the alcoholic is taught the fundamentals of recovery, behavioral modifications, and abstinence. In the early recovery stage, after a period of abstinence, the alcoholic is taught about relapse, obtaining an awareness of the fundamental relapse signals. In the ongoing recovery stage, the needs of involvement in AA and reinforcement of recovery benefits are discussed.

Other people are absolutely necessary in any recovery program. After years of internal isolation, alcoholics have learned to judge themselves through their own set of belief systems and, as mentioned earlier, often lower those standards to fit their needs. Group therapy has long been shown to be of the utmost importance in helping alcoholics finally see the pain that they have caused others, and in accepting alcoholism as their primary problem. Alcoholics Anonymous provides one of the many forums to share with and listen to other alcoholics without judgment. This allows the alcoholic to describe, analyze, and surrender.

Regular attendance at AA meetings as an aftercare treatment provides a context in which to grow continually in recovery. One would be foolish to attempt sobriety without involvement in Alcoholics Anonymous, the most successful program for alcoholics. This practice expands the potential of a model recovery process and continually reminds us that others are with us in our fight for sobriety. The term *others* in this context includes AA members, group therapy members, friends, and family members. The last group poses the most difficulty when alcoholics first enter recovery. After years of feeling the pain caused by one close to them, the friends and family members are rarely ready to be a primary support group. These people are often in need of therapy or a codependent-based peer support group themselves. They often want restitution, either emotional, physical, or monetary. The amends process of Alcoholics Anonymous is truly meant for the benefit of the alcoholic, not as restitution for the codependent.

As Vaillant (1983) suggests, no evidence exists that recovery and abstinence from alcohol has ever harmed the alcoholic. With this thought in mind, most alcoholics have now lost yet another reason for refusal of a recovery program. In studying the Twelve Steps of Alcoholics Anonymous, I have become convinced that the entire world could benefit from these same Steps, regardless of people's disposition regarding alcohol.

Milam and Ketcham (1981) lay out a formula for a successful treatment program that includes a minimum four-week inpatient treatment with mandatory medical detoxification, educational programs that stress the disease concept, nutritional therapy, emphasis on Alcoholics Anonymous, and follow-up care. They also stress involvement of family members when possible and strict discipline to work the program. Many people have their own recommendations on just how a recovery-based lifestyle should be run.

All people are different, and all will require a program tailored to their own needs. Only the alcoholic can truly know what those needs may be or what the true issues are that most affect the attitude and behavior. I am honored to know people in recovery who have had only the benefit of Alcoholics Anonymous and others who have attended outpatient or inpatient treatment centers. One or the other has no greater proven success rate. What is evident, however, is that those who do not work the program will relapse. Bill Wilson says that there are alcoholics who are simply constitutionally incapable of following the steps required for sobriety.

Mark L., in his tape *An Evening of Twelve Step Humor*, tells a story of a man in recovery lost in the world of sober living. He wonders to himself if it is possible for someone to quit drinking just one day too late. A sign I saw recently on a church bulletin board stated "Those waiting for the twelfth hour to find God may die at 11:30."

Rock Bottom

Bill Wilson writes that alcoholics need to be "softened up," or hit "rock bottom." They must accept a complete dependence on anything that may help them achieve sobriety. In the Big Book,

Bill refers to this as deflation of ego. He also believes that prior to any religious or spiritual conversion, an understanding and acceptance of humility must occur. This is typically easily accepted by alcoholics due to the extreme sense of sin they have carried with them for so long.

Milam and Ketcham (1981), on the other hand, write, "The widely accepted belief that alcoholics have to hit rock bottom before they can be helped has been completely discredited in recent years." I believe that this thought depends on the description of what rock bottom is, rather than on a belief that an alcoholic must enter a problem stage before he or she will be willing even to consider abstinence. Bill Wilson credits William James, author of *The Varieties of Religious Experience,* with the concept of the need for deflation of ego. This is the onset of a problematic state that will allow the ego to become deflated due to the problems surrounding and confusing it.

Over 50 percent of alcoholics seeking treatment are forced into it in one way or another. They often will say that some "certain crisis in their lives backed them into a corner and forced them to seek help." Ludwig (1988), on the other hand, believes that alcoholics are continually experiencing major traumas in their lives but only refer to the last one as hitting a bottom. As Ludwig states, "The designation of bottom serves as a convenient, retrospective label for a turning point." Although I do agree with the idea behind that statement, I further believe that regardless of past problems, due to the continuation of pain and problems in an alcoholic's life, the problems themselves seem to get worse on every occasion.

For an active alcoholic to lie, control, and manipulate and to skirt around and out of yet another crisis is tiring and painful at the least. Eventually, as the disease progresses, a crisis that is truly less extreme than a prior episode is *perceived* as being much worse. If it is a repeat episode, such as having a wife stating that she is this time leaving for good, the threat begins to sound more truthful, and the crisis becomes real. Alcoholics will find their own rock bottom, and the bottom is completely different for each person.

Litman (1982) describes these crisis points, or bottoms, as a time when the alcoholic has to make a conscious choice between an immediate change in behavior or continued alcohol use with the possibility of a completely ruined life. Jellinek (1960) further states, "In a large portion of alcoholics . . . pre-alcoholic, highly psychological vulnerability is essential."

Symptoms to Expect

Anyone entering recovery should expect a wide variety of symptoms. All recovering alcoholics and addicts can also be assured that they will probably experience additional symptoms unique to themselves. This section explains the symptoms that may occur during successful recovery, as opposed to the symptoms for relapse, in hopes of forewarning recovering alcoholics that simply entering treatment does not guarantee a life of happiness. While in the early stages of recovery, we will not hear angels singing. Sobriety is a new and completely foreign way of life, and an alcoholic must learn entirely new responses and behavioral patterns to succeed. The changes do not come easily and take a lot of hard work. Nearly all of the past thoughts and responses must be essentially thrown out. New responses to life must be learned, one day at a time. It is a process that can take time and works at different speeds for different people. It is said that good thinking does not provide good actions, but good actions do provide good thinking. Once this type of transformation begins to occur, the alcoholic will begin to find a peace never felt before.

Prior to entering a recovery program, one of the most important things to know is that all of our problems will not go away. What we may gain is the ability to deal with those problems better than ever before. Many people who frequent AA meetings describe still having confusion over their current problems. In fact, part of the role of AA meetings is to discuss any particular member's problems. In talking with these people, usually newcomers, it seems that their expectations of recovery include the thought that if they did not drink, their problems would go away. Kolb

(1973) believes that few well-adapted and psychologically healthy recovering alcoholics are found among those in the initial stages of recovery. Life is simply not that kind to any of us. Through an effective recovery program, one can only hope to learn that everyone has crises and problems in life.

Learning how to accept these problems as part of life can provide a strength throughout recovery that enables us to tackle the problems straight on—without alcohol or drugs. Eliminating the extremes in emotions through recovery provides a thought process that eventually yields a subconscious understanding of dealing with life on life's terms.

It is normal for the recovering alcoholic to come upon a number of negative psychological and physical responses to the elimination of alcohol. As the alcoholic mind is continually and slowly removed from the individual, many changes occur that cause an uncomfortable beginning in sobriety. For alcoholics in recovery, these are signs of recovery and should be taken as positive steps toward a new spiritual life. They may not always be the most pleasurable symptoms and are not necessarily the final stage of thought processes for the alcoholic, but they are movements toward a future life of spirituality. It is my opinion that the worst of these symptoms are less painful than the best of the active alcoholic symptoms to both the alcoholic and the codependent. The following list is paraphrased from Parham (1987).

Initial Negative Symptoms of Recovery

- Insomnia—As the brain chemistry begins to revert to a normal level, many alcoholics experience a period of sleep deprivation and a lack of the REM, or "dream stage," of sleep. Drunk dreams can occur at this level.
- Agitation—Continued and confusing changes in lifestyle cause regular periods of agitation and verbal aggressiveness.
- Confusion—Virtually all alcoholics go through a period of confusion as they strive to find themselves, then have problems recognizing the new self.
- Sober Isolation—As the AA program is a "me" program, focusing on sobriety as the most important thing in the world, many

alcoholics can easily revert back to a state of isolation in sobriety. As this can be one of the danger signs for relapse, it is imperative that Alcoholics Anonymous or other support group meetings address group connectedness.

- Sober Guilt—As opposed to the guilt realized through the first five Steps of Alcoholics Anonymous, the recovering alcoholic may begin to remember additional past behaviors that can cause additional guilt while in recovery. About the time one begins to feel cleansed by addressing past behaviors, new memories will surface to be addressed. It is important to note that this occurrence is guilt centered and is healthy to recovery, as opposed to shame-based feelings.

- Sober Righteousness—Although usually healthy in the initial stages of sobriety, the self-righteousness that can come with a life that now includes a Higher Power can lead to a dangerous belief that sobriety is now secured and no further work is required.

- Loss of Control—It is common for recovering alcoholics to experience some loss of control over their emotions. As they begin to "feel" again, the recognition of foreign feelings and emotions can be upsetting and confusing. How to deal with these feelings takes time and work.

- Partial Recovery—Through regular attendance at three to five AA meetings a week, many recovering alcoholics can equate abstinence or sobriety alone with a successful recovery program. Sobriety is only the beginning to serenity and peace in one's life. All twelve of the Steps must be followed, completed, and started again. Similar to the dry drunk syndrome, many alcoholics stop at a particularly difficult point in recovery, then move back to the previous Step or stay at the point of recovery where they are. This can be evident in people who have ten or more years in recovery but still carry resentments, fears, and egos around with them on a daily basis. Holding on to control means a lack of surrender, and without surrender, recovery is impossible. These are also the people one most often sees relapse, even after extended periods of abstinence.

- Complacency—Similar to partial recovery, complacency includes not working the program. These alcoholics are prone to missing meetings, eliminating prayer and meditation over time, and falling into a general feeling of false security about their recovery.

- Loss of Appetite—Part of the physical nature of alcoholism is substitution of the alcohol for food. It is common that an initial loss of appetite may occur or continue for several weeks or months.
- Impairment of Memory—As the neurons of the brain bounce around in a frenzy during initial abstinence, short-term memory can be affected. In fact, all phases of memory can be affected. One will lose thoughts of years gone by for a short period of time or lose thoughts of yesterday and, conversely, remember old thoughts that have been tucked away for years.
- Anger—In recovery we are cautioned about anger. There is no doubt in the world that anger can be a problem. It can also be a blessing. Anger can move us; it can stir us up and get us stimulated into action. Its energy has great power. When anger agitates us, we act. Yet the problem is not the energy of anger, it's how it is expressed and put into action.

Treatment Centers

Having had the luxury (and pain) of attending one of the most prestigious treatment facilities in the world, I admire and respect those recovering alcoholics who have achieved sobriety and serenity through AA or an outpatient program as their primary means of therapy. I do not believe that my recovery would have been successful without the use of a full inpatient treatment center. It should be noted that scientific research (Institute of Medicine 1979; Lindstrom 1992; Chapman and Huygens 1988) shows no discernible difference in the recovery success rates of an outpatient-only program, a full four-week or longer inpatient-only program, or a combination of both. Milam and Ketcham (1981) take issue with this and argue that inpatient treatment offers better recovery rates. There are published records of differences in recovery rates between treatment facilities, and even the different units within a particular treatment facility. No data exists to show that one particular type of (length of stay) program is more beneficial than another. If one were to evaluate the published rates of outpatient programs against inpatient programs, one would find that the majority of inpatient centers provide or recommend the most follow-up and aftercare and, therefore, have the better published recovery rates.

After a brief stay in the detoxification unit, a typical day at a typical inpatient treatment facility starts early, around 7 A.M. The patients are expected to rise in time to make their beds, often attend a volunteer prayer or meditation period, and join their peers for breakfast at 8 A.M. The day is filled with group discussions of alcohol- and drug-related topics, listening to peers discuss how their use has affected their lives, sharing one's own story, and various types of therapy. Meetings with therapists, psychologists, psychiatrists, and even clergy can become part of a daily regimen to understand the disease concept. Lectures are usually given three or four times a day, revolving around the many subjects found in this book. Minigroups are formed, breaking apart from the entire group to evaluate any one of a list of roadblocks to recovery. Often alumni come back for a discussion of their ruined lives prior to recovery. As an example to the patients that anyone can be successful in recovery, they offer a brief review of their lives in recovery.

Treatments are and should be tailored to each patient's needs and problems, with a focus on the psychological baggage that may best be addressed behind closed doors during the initial stages. Treatments present both short-term and long-term goals, with an emphasis on a realistic set of expectations that the patient can fulfill.

Group therapy is the emphasis for the day, with participation nearly forced by both peers and counselor. Isolation is not tolerated, and the "senior peers" will see to it that the "newcomers" are helped along until they become involved in the process on their own. Usually visitors are allowed only on weekends or holidays, and fraternization with members outside the peer group is not allowed, particularly with the opposite sex. This allows for easier bonding within the peer group, establishing a degree of trust that will enable the sharing of private moments and issues during group therapy sessions. The day will usually end around 8 or 9 P.M. with some peer members engaging on their own in further discussions on the process of recovery. Often, television or music is not allowed on the unit until around this time.

Morris Chafetz, founder of the National Institute on Alcohol Abuse and Alcoholism, states that alcohol research and treatment are complex, affecting all classes and age groups in all geographic locations. A brief stay in a treatment center will confirm this statement, as one will find a diverse population within each individual unit.

The first few days or the first week are focused on eliminating the alcoholic's or addict's need to control, and to help the patient to see a past pattern of unacceptable behavior. This nearly always includes an in-depth analysis of past alcohol or other drug use. This period takes different amounts of time for different individuals but must occur for the alcoholic and addict to see that they have lost control over their lives and are powerless over their drug of choice—the prerequisite to entering a Twelve Step program. Once this has occurred, the treatment program is focused on the various alcoholic traits upon which the patient may require the most work. At the same time, the patient begins to work on the individual Twelve Steps, one at a time, under the direction of a therapist or counselor.

All professional treatment programs should also include a recommended outpatient follow-up program including involvement in Alcoholics Anonymous and contact with other alcoholics. In my case, I was referred to a therapist, weekly outpatient hospital program, AA, an exercise program, and tai chi, an ancient form of slow-motion martial arts, used mainly for relaxation therapy. Again, I cannot imagine my recovery moving forward without all these ingredients and feel blessed when I watch newcomers enter one of my weekly AA meetings as their only source of recovery.

Surrender versus Compliance

First discussed in 1953 by Dr. Harry Tiebout in the *Quarterly Journal of Studies on Alcohol,* the difference between surrender and compliance is as nebulous as the difference between religion and spirituality. Tiebout believed that the difference between benefit and no benefit in the treatment of alcoholics relates directly to a distinction between surrender and compliance (Vaillant 1983). Menninger was interested in what he referred to as the actual "conversion point" at which surrender might occur. Ivan P. Pavlov called it the "ultraparadoxical phase of transmarginal inhibition," similar to the rock bottom previously discussed. This is simply the state of mind preceding therapeutic surrender. Furthermore, it is the state of mind by which previously conditioned responses change from negative to positive. Pavlov spent a lot of time on this subject in his research on induced stress on animals, particularly dogs. As dogs had more and more stress placed upon them, invariably they would change personalities. This would often occur to the extent that a previously aggressive dog would become docile toward his handler. Certain statements describe the point of true surrender: "I give up," "I can't do it myself," "I am not God."

Tiebout continued his research and writing on this subject as he discussed the concept of the "big ego." He believed that this unconscious, second inner personality was a "state of feeling" from persisting elements of dysfunctional childhood. This ego included omnipotence, intolerance, and impatience, or a deep-rooted desire to control. He once stated that humans need divine help to conquer the big ego. The Big Book says that this ego is the root of trouble for the alcoholic, being strongly supported by the alcoholic's simple selfishness and self-centeredness. The process of ego reduction, first described by Freud, is relative to the size of the original ego. It has been said to be a painful procedure, and one that is never complete.

Surrender is the full and complete submission to a Higher Power and a release of the big ego. Surrender is the point in which all the stress and tensions begin to be released and reality begins to take over. Compliance is the conscious ability to hide the big ego in a fashion that is acceptable to oneself and the AA program or other therapeutic assistors.

Withdrawal

A complete book could be written about the various components of alcoholic withdrawal. The withdrawal process varies as much as the disease itself. Depending upon the level, stage, or typology of alcoholism, the psychological and physical symptoms unwind at drastically different levels. All alcoholics will, however, experience some type of withdrawal as the brain and body fight their way back to sanity. Removal of depressants, such as alcohol, from the central nervous system triggers a release of a substance called norepinephrine from deep within the center of the brain. This can eventually cause extreme anxiety and dependence tremors.

Usually found only in the most progressive alcoholics, delirium tremens (D.T.'s) are perhaps the worst and most dangerous withdrawal symptoms. As the serotonin and norepinephrine brain amines begin to change and the acetaldehyde levels drop, the alcoholic's brain goes haywire. Chemical and electrical activities are agitated. Due to the past adaptation of the brain to the presence of alcohol, many abnormalities begin to occur when it is removed. As these feelings of discomfort are discovered, cravings will try to motivate the alcoholic into continued use. This can be cause for loss of memory, hallucinations, paranoia, and, at times, violent behavior. This is the hallucination stage, most often described as "bugs are crawling all over the body."

These symptoms vary mainly in response to prior consumption levels and at times can be as serious as unconscious epileptic seizures. Milam and Ketcham (1981) remind us that the mortality rate among untreated alcoholics going through D.T.'s is some forty times higher than that of heroin addicts. Another reason to recommend a full detoxification in an inpatient treatment center is that D.T.'s can be virtually eliminated with proper professional medication.

The "protracted withdrawal syndrome" (common in one form or another to most recovering alcoholics) is known to last much longer than expected in most alcoholics. In this withdrawal, the alcoholic simply doesn't feel right but doesn't know why. The syndrome includes nausea, agitation, anxiety, insomnia, restlessness, and depression. The alcoholic searches for reasons for these feelings and begins to blame everyone but himself or herself (Ludwig 1988). At this stage, the alcoholic may begin to question whether or not sobriety is worth all the work and all the pain. Having not yet found any true serenity through recovery, the alcoholic wonders if he or she was better off while drinking (Milam and Ketcham 1981).

Prevention

The National Institute on Alcohol Abuse and Alcoholism (NIAAA) listed thirty-eight sources for various prevention measures (NIAAA 1996, no. 34). Among them, listed together in groups, is the need for prealcoholic prevention and education. Another interesting commonality is the server and supplier educational programs. If a nonalcoholic bartender were better educated about the disease, for example, perhaps many an alcoholic would benefit from the compassion and understanding in being refused one last drink and in receiving a taxi ride home. Several of these sources follow in hopes of exemplifying the many programs in use and the many more that are needed. The NIAAA has left out numerous programs of recovery as they also relate to prevention, such as Turning Point in Minneapolis, a program that focuses on the family aspect of education for the codependent, most particularly the children.

NIAAA-Listed Prevention Measures

Policy Interventions

1. Alcohol taxes
2. Raising minimum legal drinking age
3. Zero-tolerance laws (blood alcohol concentration, or BAC)
4. License revocation laws

5.   Server liability

6.   Warning labels

Community and Educational Interventions

1.   The Saving Lives Program—A partnership among media, businesses, schools, and colleges in Massachusetts; yielded a 25 percent reduction in fatal car crashes.

2.   Life Skills Training (LST)—Educational program for grades seven through nine to enhance self-esteem, increase knowledge of drinking, and honestly promote realistic consequences of drinking.

3.   Project Northland—A multicomponent school- and community-based intervention program to delay, prevent, and reduce alcohol use.

4.   Alcohol Misuse Prevention Study (AMPS)—For students in grades five through eight, focusing on peer resistance skills.

5.   Project STAR—Involves schools, media, parents, and community to reduce, decrease, and delay alcohol use in children above sixth grade.

6.   Drug Abuse Resistance Education (DARE)—Taught to ten- and eleven-year-olds, aiming to inform about alcohol and other drugs and to teach decision-making skills to help resist use.

7.   Server Training—The education of professional alcoholic servers about underage consumption, liability laws, and recognizing customers with intoxication.

Relapse and Roadblocks

There are many reasons that alcoholics and addicts relapse. But, as Bill Wilson says in the Big Book on page 58, "Rarely have we seen a person fail who has thoroughly followed our path." Gorski and Miller (1986) wrote, "Once you abandon a recovery program, it is only a matter of time until the symptoms of post acute withdrawal appear." They believe that this loss of control (called *relapse syndrome*) will eventually lead to relapse.

Roadblocks to recovery include a number of attitudes in the alcoholic that can lead to relapse. Some researchers have called alcoholism an allergy of the body. Marlatt and Gordon (1985) found that relapse is often caused by an alcoholic's setting up of unrealistic expectations, then feeling failure when they are not met. One such expectation is that having one drink constitutes a failure and it will then lead to another drink or "I have now failed at sobriety, I might as well have another drink". Several drinks later the alcoholic is in relapse. This holds true not only for the goal of abstinence but also for setting unrealistic expectations with a loved one, a job, or a variety of important things. The fact is, sobriety must be the most important thing in life for an alcoholic. The other things will follow.

Anger leads to frustration, frustration leads to resentments, resentments lead to self-pity, and self-pity can lead to drinking. Many of the roadblocks fall within these primary feelings. Others look at this concept more clinically: change in virtually any form can produce stress; stress then conjures up many dangerous emotions and roadblocks that can cause drinking.

The continuous setting oneself up with expectations is often cause for failure, anger, and resentments. For example, if I arrive at the office in the morning expecting that coffee is made and anticipating having a cup as soon as I walk through the door, I have set myself up. Something as simple, and as silly, as expecting to have a cup of coffee first thing in the morning can lead to anger. If I arrive at work to find that someone has had the last cup of coffee, because of my expectations, I can, and have, become angry. Perhaps that same person was ready to start another pot of coffee and then the phone rang, and he or she became distracted and never finished starting the new pot to brew. Without knowing the facts or living in the moment, I have become angry over virtually nothing. Something so ridiculous as wanting a cup of coffee has the potential to threaten my sobriety? I have found that if I try hard to live in the moment, to fight back the natural urge to project or to set expectations, I have minimized the potential for anger and resentments. I now enter the office not projecting, not caring, and not expecting to have my way or to have me as the focus of everyone else's life. In fact, I sometimes find myself entering the office believing that I will make a fresh pot of coffee for the benefit of all the employees and am pleasantly surprised when I find that there is a full pot. I realize that this is a small example, but it is real and it is a wonderful case of how the simplest things can upset the alcoholic in recovery. Charlie N., a friend in my Saturday morning meeting, once used an example that will stay with me for life. He said that, instead of projecting yourself, imagine that your Higher Power is watching your behavior. How would you then act? When people are asked if they believe in God, they may say, "Well, yes, of course I do." When asked if they believe God can see all: "Why, yes, I believe that too." When asked if they would act differently if God were in the room, and again, "Yes." Well, if God can see all, why do we have to believe God is in the room at all. Why can't we "act as if"?

In my recovery process, every time I experience an uncontrollable resentment, even uncontrollable through prayer, I come closer to a relapse. Dealing with clients who, for reasons of their own insecurity, personally attack me or my past, I cannot help but fall into some of the old feelings of inadequacy and a need to control. The difference is, I now deal with these internal feelings without the use of alcohol. I can truly look at this person with compassionate and understanding eyes. I deal with many alcoholics who have no knowledge of their disease, full of anger, ego, and self-centeredness. When faced with people who attack me, I see myself, where I came from, and, despite their attacks on me, my family, and my business. I look to my Higher Power for strength. Eventually, I find it. It is with compassion that I see that their words result from their own inner conflicts, because spiritual people do not attack other people to make themselves feel more important.

The list of potential roadblocks to recovery is virtually unending. The following list is provided only to exemplify the many areas of our being and the emotions that can be red flags to the person in recovery.

Roadblocks to Recovery

Resentments	Self-pity
Exhaustion	Complacency
Dishonesty	Arrogance
Suspicion	Frustration
Depression	Impatience
Family problems	Financial problems
Anger	Negative attitudes
Minimizing	Maximizing
Lack of gratitude	Unrealistic expectations
Guilt	Shame
Isolation	Not asking for help
Blame avoidance	Blaming others
Overdemandingness	Physical pain
Hunger	Revisiting old drinking places
Boredom	Denial of past behaviors
Grandiosity	Oversensitivity
False pride	Overreactions
Gossip	Ego
Social pressure	Peer pressure

Of gossip, resentments, and anger as potential roadblocks, Abraham Lincoln once said, "If I were to try to read, much less answer, all the attacks made on me, this shop might as well be closed for any other business. I do the very best I know how—the very best I can; and I mean to keep doing so until the end. If this end brings me out all right, what is said against me won't amount to anything. If the end brings me out wrong, 10 angels swearing I was right would make no difference."

It is important to add here that most alcoholics are not the type of late-stage alcoholics who cannot stop drinking once they have had one drink. This misconception is one of the reasons that alcoholism is misunderstood by the general public and one of the reasons for some of the improper counseling and therapy that occurs.

When answering the question "Can't you have just one drink?" I tend to explain it all a little differently. I honestly believe that I could have a drink right now, as I write these words, and not have another for a year or longer—no problem. I also believe that upon this success, the same thought will enter my mind again at some point, and due to my previous success, I will have another drink. Soon it will be okay to celebrate only special occasions, such as birthdays or holidays, with alcohol. Not long after, I am sure that I would feel safe and have a drink "just once in a while." Maybe one night I might deserve to have three or four. I do not know how far this would lead, and I do not know if Jellinek and others are correct in their positions on the progressiveness of the disease, but I do know it is not worth the chance. I have been there, done that—and I do not want to go there ever again. The pain I have caused others and myself is no longer part of who I am or who I want to be, and it is most certainly not what my Higher Power wants of me. I would not give away my peace for anything in the world, and I surely will not risk it (Lord willing) for another drink.

A much more extreme example was offered by a gentleman I spent time with at Hazelden. This man was one of the most intelligent, thoughtful, helpful, and caring members of my peer group. He certainly seemed to have it all together, and until I heard his lead story, I was convinced he was one who could teach me to stay sober. He knew the AA program as well as anyone. He was probably the most intent of all of us on finding sobriety, and he seemed to have relinquished all denial. He also seemed tolerant and compassionate toward others and was, by far, the most experienced in fighting off cravings. He had also been in and out of nine full-term treatment centers, a couple of psych wards, jail, and a host of other situations because of his drinking. In my nonclinical and nonprofessional opinion, the only problem he had was his sense of failure and resulting depression. One of the only reasons why he could not imagine that he could successfully enter full-term recovery was that he had failed so many times before.

The other problem was a sense that God had failed him before, and he therefore could not establish a relationship in such a short period of time with any Higher Power. He had been in perpetual treatment for almost eight full years and had all but been disowned by everyone who knew him. I can't recall how many times he said, "I've never made it before, why should I believe it will work this time?" Once a professional engineer, he had nowhere to go, in his opinion, even if sobriety were to be achieved. His sense of failure overwhelmed everyone in our peer group, as he was one of the most liked and respected group members. I have recently lost touch with him and pray that this book will find its way into his hands someday, so that I may thank him for all the advice and all the times he sat and listened to my problems, so that he may realize how important he is in this world to so many of us.

Alcoholics Anonymous recognizes two sides of the issue of relapse. One is that a "slip" is a failure of sorts and extremely dangerous. Having to go back to the First Step all over again is like failing a test. On the other side of the issue, Father Martin was intent on describing alcoholism as a far-reaching disease similar to cancer. Cancer victims have relapses. Why then shouldn't we expect relapses in recovery of alcoholism as a disease? Many of the people I look to at AA meetings for advice, through their words or examples, have relapsed in the past, some more than once. Whether it took a rock bottom or whether it is simply the nature of the disease is irrelevant. It is of the utmost importance that if a relapse should occur, the alcoholic try again for sobriety through whatever means available. The program works if you work it.

The "90-10 rule" sometimes discussed in Alcoholics Anonymous circles holds that 10 percent of life is what happens to you and 90 percent of life is how you handle it. Recovery programs provide the means whereby one can learn how most effectively to handle new situations with a greater ease than while drinking. The Big Book says, "We will intuitively know how to handle situations which used to baffle us." Understanding the various roadblocks and warning signs in advance can aid most alcoholics through the entire recovery process.

Gorski offers perhaps the best and most detailed research regarding warning signs of relapse. Some thirteen years after first describing the thirty-seven warning signs, he shortened the list by categorizing the signs into ten distinct phases (1989). They are listed below in order of occurrence, leading eventually to alcohol or other drug use as well as readdiction.

Most alcoholics in recovery have already tried abstinence in one form or another. Without the use of a peer group, formal treatment, a sponsor, or other form of outside help, they have no ability to recognize the various signs of relapse. As is true with alcoholism as a disease, denial seems to be the alcoholic's worst enemy. It comes swiftly and invisibly. Once it takes hold, the progressive nature of the alcoholic mind-set seems to take control again.

Gorski's Relapse Signs

1. Internal change
2. Denial
3. Avoidance and defensiveness
4. Crisis building
5. Immobilization
6. Confusion and overreaction
7. Depression
8. Behavioral loss of control
9. Recognition loss of control
10. Option reduction

Stephanie Brown writes in her book *Treating Alcoholism* (1995) that there are seven basic categories in which common issues that can lead to relapse often occur. The total list includes virtually every sign of relapse imaginable, each falling within one of the seven basic categories.

This is the most complete list and review of the various components of relapse and alcoholic therapy. In fact, I hope someday to have an opportunity to talk with Brown, as I find her book a complete and accurate guide for the professional therapist in any way involved in alcoholism.

The bottom line is to lead a good life, focus on this new way of living one day at a time, and stay in conscious contact with your Higher Power, and many of the relapse signs may never occur.

Brown's Common Issues That Can Lead to Relapse

1. Behavioral issues—Acting, being, and behaving in a world in ways that may endanger one's sobriety.
2. Cognitive issues—Thinking and viewing the world in ways that may signal danger.
3. Social and interpersonal issues—Various situations revolving around relationships.
4. Affective issues—The range of feelings and emotions that can trigger a drinking episode.
5. Psychological issues—The various mind functions such as defenses, coping, and attitudes.
6. Physiological issues—Issues dealing with physical, biological, and medical factors that may contribute to drinking.
7. Spiritual issues—A disconnection from a Higher Power or loss of faith.

Alcoholics Anonymous as Aftercare

Many people use AA as their only recovery program, but it is not a treatment program. Remember spending all that time in college, then truly learning whatever it was you studied much later when out in the real world after college? This is similar to a treatment center versus Alcoholics Anonymous. I hope that, through this book, the alcoholic will recognize the importance and benefit of becoming and staying involved in Alcoholics Anonymous. Without this program and following the Twelve Steps, sobriety would have been impossible for me.

The advantages of this jump start into society in sobriety are numerous, but worthless without follow-up care. Old-timers recommend ninety meetings in ninety days as a way of getting quickly involved and knowledgeable in the AA way of life and as a way of keeping one's mind busy and active. Alcoholics

Anonymous has been proven the most successful follow-up and aftercare program for alcoholism. Period.

Spirituality versus Religion

The importance of gaining a spiritual understanding of the world around us reaches much further than alcoholism. It is this necessity of Alcoholics Anonymous and recovery that contributes to the opinion that the AA program would also be beneficial to many nonalcoholics. Until we can find ourselves and how we relate to this world and the afterworld, we cannot be at peace. This concept can easily be accepted by alcoholics and other drug users alike. In an alcoholic state, even the worst of us can understand the need for an understanding Higher Power (as you know God) to progress and grow. What can happen quite accidentally is that once an understanding of a Higher Power occurs, an equal willingness to submit to this Higher Power can occur. Once this happens, most believe that their Higher Power wants a better life for them than they are living, and this life does not include alcohol or other drugs.

Spirituality has little to do with religion as we know it. Over time, however, recovering alcoholics will find many similarities between their religious education and their current spirituality. Some may never again attend church, using AA meetings as their "church of choice." Others will eventually find themselves deeply involved in a church program that they had once shunned. What's important is that, through a Higher Power of our own understanding, we can move slowly toward a personal relationship with this Higher Power. Furthermore, at least an attempt is being made to become more sensitive to the moral, ethical, and spiritual side of living. I haven't yet met anyone who, while working the program, maintained an evil Higher Power. Everyone's Higher Power is kind, considerate, tolerant, and compassionate. Most of us desire to be more like that individual. Some have pretended to be like this for so long, that this true introduction is quite refreshing.

Statements about spirituality from an earth person may include "I go to church every Sunday," or "I believe in God." Listening to the concept of spirituality as described by a recovering alcoholic, one will not hear self-promotions. One will hear words like *caring, helping, meditation, prayer, acceptance, gratitude,* and *understanding.* An alcoholic in recovery will usually talk about how, without a Higher Power, he or she would still be drinking. Spirituality is an attempt to become a better person through the removal of character defects by the grace of God.

The Disney God

One of the concepts I have grown to find both common and amusing is the "Disney God." After years of being taught about Old Testament wrath brought down on sinners, we were taught to fear God. An image of a giant Zeus-type character sitting high up on a throne throwing lightning bolts at all the bad people comes to mind. God, as some describe, is a punishing God. This couldn't be further from the truth. Although church taught me about forgiveness and confession, it also provided, to some degree, a belief that the bad things that happened to me were the result of God punishing me. Some religions teach us that even thinking a bad thought is a sin. I was taught to fear God, to be afraid of the wrath. In my home, God was mentioned in terms of shame. For example, in times of misbehavior, God's name might have been used: "God wouldn't like that." Never was His name used like this: "God would be proud of you for doing that nice thing." A church in downtown Cincinnati has a slogan etched in granite above the door that exemplifies this: "Bring Forth Your Children to Learn the Fear of God."

With all the guilt and shame we have carried with us for so long, a wrathful God was easy to accept. I used to pray every night before I went to bed for forgiveness of my sins and behavior. I had this warped understanding of God and sin, that if I could pray for forgiveness quickly after each episode of sin, resentment, and self-centered living, I would be safe from hell for the time being. The time periods between prayers, particularly when I was drinking, therefore became quite dangerous, further contributing to my guilt and fear. Most everyone I have shared this with who are also in recovery completely understood or once followed the same attempts at redemption.

Laurie Beth Jones, in her book *Jesus in Blue Jeans* (1997), opens her prologue with a dream she once had. Jesus came to her wearing blue jeans and said that he had come to others in robes because they wore robes; he comes to her in blue jeans because she wears blue jeans. It was the first reading experience I have ever had about a familiar Jesus, one I might be able to get to know. I was also impressed by George Burns's portrayal of God in the movie *Oh God*. I found it so refreshing to have my image of the Disney God finally broken down to find a Higher Power to whom I could relate.

Through my personal recovery program, I have finally found a God who is loving and forgiving but demanding in that He wants the very best for me—but I need to work for it. My relationship with my Higher Power has become the most important thing in my life. I think about Him often, what His will might be and how thankful I am. This in itself is medicine enough to keep me growing as a better person every day. I make mistakes, perhaps more than ever, but through His love, I can now accept them as part of who I am.

Feel Good—Feel Bad

This phrase comes from an AA meeting when a friend (Steve W.) answered the Big Book question "Is prayer needed for recovery?" He described that most of us tend to pray naturally when we are experiencing problems and need help. Then when our prayers are answered and we begin to feel good again, we forget to pray. Then sooner or later, we are having problems and feeling bad again. Feel good—don't pray; feel bad—pray. I thought that this best exemplifies the need for continued and daily prayer and meditation that includes gratitude during the good and the bad times.

Over time I have come to believe that God answers every single prayer. He says yes, or He says no, and sometimes He says wait.

Norman Vincent Peale relives the memories of his mother with this same attitude regarding prayer. Garth Brooks plays a twist on prayer with his hit song "Unanswered Prayers." After years of holding on to feelings for an old girlfriend, a man happens upon her one day with his beautiful and caring wife at his side. His old girlfriend, for whom he had prayed to God to have as his own in years gone by, had become quite ugly and nasty. It was then, when he saw her again after many years, that he thanked God for unanswered prayers. Perhaps he didn't hear God say wait when he had prayed those many years before.

It is most important for recovering alcoholics not to expect a phone call from their Higher Power with the daily agenda. God gave us a mind. It is up to us to use it. Through daily prayer and meditation, it is easy to learn how to pray and learn the directions and teachings of our Higher Power. These directions are already within us. He gave them to us a long time ago. Through recovery, it is simply up to us to ask Him to help us understand His will. God will do for us only what we cannot do for ourselves.

Many people say that they do not know how to pray and therefore become uncomfortable with this part of recovery. As stated before, many books are available for daily use in prayer and meditation, some explicitly written for recovery. What most have in common is a simple and nonthreatening approach to prayer. I have included some of my favorites in the last chapter of this book.

Prayer can begin (and last for years) as simple silence, an inner focus. Over time it can evolve into a personal and nonformal talk with a Higher Power. My time with my Higher Power is now devoid of formality, as I feel I am talking with my best friend. Although I don't start my prayers with "Hey, bud," I'm certain God wouldn't mind. I try to begin and end the day with thanks, with gratitude for all He has given me and allowed me to experience and learn. This must also include thanks for the worry, as it is an experience from which I hope to learn. I then force myself to pray for others rather than myself. This is still a difficult thing to do. Only after this can I talk with God about the things that are troubling me or the things in which I feel I need a direction. It is difficult sometimes to pray about the little things in life, particularly when I remember that there are starving people and those much worse off than myself. But when approached on a personal basis, as my Father, or my friend, I know He wants to hear about whatever is troubling me, and I feel comfortable wherever my thoughts and prayers take me.

Dealin' with Feelin'

Looking ahead to recovery, one should expect to encounter new feelings for old dealings. In other words, things that were once believed to be understood are now absorbed and thought about differently. This experience can be uncomfortable at times, despite being recognized as a better way of living. For example, after a lengthy period of recovery, one friend described his dismay and discomfort at watching another friend slip slowly into drunkenness one evening when out with their wives for dinner. He described himself as being detached from the situation and saw so much of his past self, as the friend moved from friendliness to unfriendliness to grandiosity to rudeness. This continued with each drink to the point where he and his wife had a fight over who would drive home. Dealing with new feelings or dealing with feelings for the first time (versus dealing with emotions) is indeed new to an alcoholic. Many formulas exist for getting a handle on these feelings and keeping them in perspective. Among the best is simply to enjoy the moment, accept it as God's will, and take it easy.

During early recovery, a counselor at Hazelden calmed my worried ways daily with her tender reminder, "Take it easy." Expect to be confused and often overinterested in your feelings during early recovery. Expect the feelings to be absorbed without the emotional extremes of the past. But also expect them often to provide a new twist on life. Once they are understood and accepted, expect a more peaceful existence.

Stinking Thinking

I have always loved this phrase. It is so descriptive of what happens in an alcoholic mind, particularly during recovery. Take a bunch of brain cells and short circuit them, take away alcohol for the first time in years, add to the recipe the onset of brand-new feelings, a life and family in disarray, a job on the edge, and the rumbling of rumors—and you have "stinking thinking." The alcoholic now wants to hold on to the past behaviors and attitudes that protected him or her so effectively. How does one suddenly deal with life straight on? This jumbled thought process, stinking thinking, provides the alcoholic with a shield from the truth. It must be addressed immediately and must be recognized to be addressed. Without an active treatment program and proper follow-up care that includes the advice of others, stinking thinking can quickly take over and reopen the door to alcohol use. Gorski and Miller (1986) call this thinking a "setup" for relapse, as it often involves the belief that abstinence is the only component of recovery, similar to late-stage alcoholic denial.

HALT

Hungry, Angry, Lonely, Tired. These emotions and conditions are completely under our control and should be halted as soon as they appear, as they easily allow the onset of stinking thinking, as well as relapse. In recovery we should experiment with all of the positives and resources we can and not risk losing sobriety over one of these items. The tools listed in this book may not be for everybody. If one or two work for the alcoholic or codependent reader, I am happy. However, the alcoholic owes it only to herself or himself to learn how to prevent relapse. So many of the emotions and feelings during recovery cannot be controlled. It is only beneficial, therefore, to follow a program in which one takes full control of everything possible. Each one of the HALT items can introduce the recovering alcoholic to self-pity that will allow the loss of will and eventually lead to drinking. There is simply no excuse for this to be a reason to lose sobriety.

Upside Down

Most researchers point to the need for a complete change in belief systems during recovery to provide continued success. Hardly anyone truly lives by the morality and spirituality of the Twelve Steps, and the Steps therefore inspire a radical change for most anyone, including alcoholics. This was most apparent, in my case, by the number of priests and other "normal" people within my peer group at Hazelden. Hoffer (1951) believes that alcoholics, as "extremists," find it much easier to switch from the extreme of using to the extreme of abstinence and spiritual behavior than to succeed in drinking moderately. One extreme (an addiction) simply changes place with the other (an acceptable adaptation).

Madsen (1974), on the other hand, makes a much simpler point. He believes that one cannot hold two distinctly different concepts at the same time, such as trust and mistrust, or drunkenness and sobriety. He refers to this as a desire for simplicity. The AA slogans "Take it easy" and "Easy does it" support this view. It is so important for the recovering alcoholic to keep things simple and not become involved with the emotions of years gone by. Life often presents things in a new color—gray. No longer can alcoholics think only in terms of black and white. They must exercise the ability to see the good that can come from virtually any situation through trust in their Higher Power.

Phil Kavanaugh, managing counselor for the Shoemaker unit at Hazelden, presents what I feel to be the best example of a complete upside-down change in beliefs as required for successful recovery. He separates the de facto (active alcoholic) priority system from the principle-based (recovery) priority system. Essentially, this is the total reconstruction of our belief system, with spirituality becoming paramount in a successful recovery program. The entire manner in which we have judged our success in life is now turned around as we find we have not been keeping score the right way.

Kavanaugh's system places spiritual and personal needs first as a means, through new actions, to put our spirituality and our sobriety first. Nearly everyone—alcoholics and nonalcoholics alike—has said that this concept could help anyone caught up in the rat race that has become our normal way of life. In my case, I simply forgot how to keep score. I believe that this new system of keeping score can also lead to a happier way of life.

When I first took a look at the de facto priority system, I saw my life flash before my eyes. It described the manner in which I had lived for as long as I could remember. Like many of my clients, I kept score by what I had, not by who I was. To this day, I find myself feeling an ugly pride when I think of the things I have, rather than the way in which I live. The only way I have found to release this pattern of thought is through gratitude. The easiest way to build gratitude, for me, is to give thanks to my Higher Power.

After only a few weeks of treatment, the principle-based priority system began to make sense to me. My whole world came crashing down. It was like awakening one morning to find that I had been living my life the wrong way. I believe now that, back then, I subconsciously believed that even God kept score through what I had achieved. I believed that God was probably prouder of me than of some poor alcoholic under a bridge.

A complete reversal in one's belief system is perhaps the most disheartening process one could ever undertake. Couple this with vigorously honest Fourth and Fifth Steps of Alcoholics Anonymous, a complete moral inventory, and an alcoholic is sure to have difficulty in dealing with enormous self-doubt, guilt, and, in some cases, shame.

The process itself, however, comes quite naturally to the recovering alcoholic. We all want happiness and, most certainly, peace. Once we alcoholics can accept that our way of living must be changed, we can finally do something about it. If an alcoholic reads the de facto priority system and still believes that something is more important than sobriety, the alcoholic has not accepted powerlessness.

Only at this point can an alcoholic begin a life without feeling a responsibility for people and things, and move to a life of being responsible to people. We cannot control another's actions. While becoming responsible for our own actions, we can indeed find responsibility to our loved ones through our example, through living a life centered on spirituality.

De Facto Priority System

1. Money—I must have money to live; money is a concrete measurement of my value and worth as a person.
2. Work—I have to work. Work provides the money I must have. Work gives me a role; being successful at work is easier than at the job of being a human being.
3. Family—I should be responsible for the people in my life. I should be able to provide for them as well as make them happy emotionally.
4. Self—I want to be happy. But I have given so much of myself away for the above priorities that I have nothing left except self-indulgent wants—alcohol, drugs, sex, etc. "I deserve to have fun."
5. Spirituality—I can't believe or trust spirituality. It isn't practical in the real world. God isn't going to write a check.

Principle-Based Priority System

1. Spirituality—I must live my life based on spirituality and principles to find sobriety or real personal satisfaction in my life.
2. Self—I have to take care of myself, to try to please myself rather than others. I need self-respect to have any true serenity and contentment in the here and now, which is all I truly have.
3. Family—My family are the friends I didn't choose and relationships more complex than I imagined, so I still operate by *shoulds*. However, I now realize that I need to be responsible *to* the people in my life rather than *for* them.
4. Work—I want to work. I want it to be in an area of satisfaction rather than drudgery to meet an imagined

goal. I want to be constructive in this life, to make a
contribution and best utilize my abilities.

5.   Money—I can't let money control my life. I realize I
need money to live but I need to keep it in perspective.
If two priorities compete, I must follow the higher
value to have self-respect and balance in my life.

Intervention

Most alcoholics are forced into recovery or treatment in one way
or another. For some, it's as simple as hitting rock bottom. For
others, it can be a court-ordered treatment. For many others, the
threat of losing something important to them (a spouse, a job)
causes a movement toward recovery. One way this threat may be
made plain is with an intervention.

Intervention is the planned interruption of the drinking
process through involvement by someone who cares deeply
enough for the alcoholic to want to help. After reading the previous chapters, it should be evident that this is a most difficult, at
times impossible, process. Although success can be had in helping an alcoholic into a recovery program, if the alcoholic does
not want to change and does not see the pain she or he is causing
self and others, the alcoholic is capable only of completing a
treatment program as a dry drunk.

Completion of a treatment program has little to do with full-
term recovery. Aftercare must be included within the recovery
process. In fact, what is referred to as aftercare (often Alcoholics
Anonymous) is frequently used as primary care for many recovering alcoholics. The majority of relapse victims will admit
that their relapse occurred because they stopped working the
aftercare program and held on to the alcoholic mind. A dry
drunk can hold this belief system for years. It is for this reason
that the first priority of intervention is to force the alcoholic
into seeing (and believing) the pain being caused to self and
others.

An intervention should always include a professional who is well acquainted with alcoholism, the alcoholic mind, outpatient and full-term treatment centers, and relapse. Interventions with clergy or family alone, though well intended, are often unsuccessful. Many alcoholics will reject the initial notion of a Higher Power, religion, and spirituality. They will certainly scoff at the idea that a priest or minister can or should provide advice. The Big Book, in fact, is based on the premise that an alcoholic needs another alcoholic to explain the facts, to relate and educate through example, not words. If possible, a recovering alcoholic should be included in the intervention team.

A typical intervention includes some deceit at the start, making it uncomfortable for all involved. The alcoholic will probably become defensive, perhaps abusive, depending upon length and amount of prior alcohol or other drug use. A team should be put together with the sole intention of convincing the alcoholic of having a major problem that needs to be addressed. This may occur through concrete examples of problems related to the use of alcohol or drugs. Getting DUIs and other legal problems are cases in point. Losing a job or experiencing financial difficulties, if spelled out clearly, may provide acceptable examples.

A written list is often required for the intervention, because the alcoholic will have an excuse for every item on the list and deserves time to speak. It is only after a lengthy dialogue, with continuous excuses, that the alcoholic may begin to see that there might be a problem. The list is best presented by someone close to the alcoholic, hopefully with compassion and understanding. The alcoholic will probably have the thought on his or her mind of walking out of the meeting, so patience and timing are crucial during this discussion. It is critical that the members of the intervention team work together in a noncombative manner, constantly reinforcing the inner child of the alcoholic, allowing him or her to keep what little self-esteem is left. This point cannot be emphasized enough. Some may want to take on some of the excuses and lies during this meeting. They should wait. There will be ample time for that later. It's important to remember the purpose of the meeting. One should not assume that by reading a few basic paragraphs, he or she could perform an intervention without first consulting professionals who have been involved in one successfully beforehand.

The most effective and important part of an intervention is the inclusion of family members and loved ones. Their purpose is to list fully and explain how they have been hurt by the alcoholic's behavior. This list should be short but completely honest. Loved ones should say what they mean but not in a mean way. A typical comment might include, "Before you drank so much, everyone said how kind and happy you were, but now some of us are concerned about your happiness." The family members should take turns, itemizing their pain and their love for the individual, offering full support if the alcoholic agrees to treatment.

Although it is an issue often debated, it is important at this meeting also to lay out the ground rules only as they are true. Threats or promises shouldn't be made unless they can be kept, or they will provide future excuses should the alcoholic not enter treatment. For example, a wife may say, " I love you, Bob, but the pain you are causing me and our children cannot continue. We have had enough, and we all deserve better." The wife had better plan on truly leaving if he does not stop drinking and enter treatment. It would be important for her to add, "But, if you enter a treatment program, we will support you all the way." Again, each person present must include a personal version of the pain he or she has felt and how he or she sees the alcohol use affecting the alcoholic's life. Sometimes it has helped to say, "If you don't need the treatment, it still won't hurt you." A wife of an alcoholic in recovery recently called me. She had demanded that her husband rent his own apartment away from her and the children once he returned from the treatment facility. At first I applauded her decision to detach with love. Then I heard her conditions for his return. The alcoholic had not worked for a couple of years, as he was battling his disease. But he had a master's degree and plenty of experience in chemical sales. His wife wanted to tell him that he could return home once he had found a good job. She asked me what I thought about this. I had to take a deep breath before I answered. This demand had absolutely nothing to do with his sobriety and in my opinion would have placed enormous pressure on him to work toward achieving something that might have been cause for relapse. When I told her I wasn't an expert but recommended against it, she asked what I would have done. I simply told her that if she loved him as much as she said, I would tell him he could come home when he was truly sober. This example shows that during intervention, we all may say and do things, with the best intentions, that may not be best for the alcoholic.

One reason for including an intervention and alcoholism professional is to have an outsider who is familiar with alcoholism as a disease provide this concrete proof. Any reading materials that may help the alcoholic see the error of his or her ways should also be included. Another reason for a professional's presence is to have someone to answer the question "What do I have to do next?" (Lord willing, the question will be asked.) This professional can also act as a facilitator, as opposed to an intermediator. This professional will help to keep the meeting on the correct line of discussion, or it could well get out of hand and lose effectiveness. An alcoholic will make several attempts to turn this meeting against those present. A facilitator will not let that happen. If accepted by the alcoholic as a fair judge, the facilitator can say and do things that family members and loved ones cannot.

Including a recovering alcoholic or offering a meeting with a recovering alcoholic (and going straight there) can only help the active alcoholic see that he or she is not alone, that other alcoholics recover, and, more important, that others understand. The alcoholic probably will not read the Big Book until talking with someone else about it first. It would benefit all present to read at least the chapter on intervention, if not the entire book.

The actual intervention should be well rehearsed by everyone involved. Plans should be made, even to the extent of packing a suitcase to take the individual directly into treatment if the chance presents itself. A professional facilitator can provide the names of various agencies and treatment centers to contact well in advance. Most often, the alcoholic is tricked into attending this meeting through false pretenses. A "dinner party," "stopping by Mom's house," or any excuse will do. Contact the local Alcoholics Anonymous office, hospital, or treatment center for information on intervention.

The Pink Cloud

Recovering alcoholics may grow quickly to a point of overconfidence and complacency called the "pink cloud." By recovering, I mean even those who have many years of sobriety. The pink cloud is particularly dangerous to sobriety, promoting an unconscious self-righteousness that can block further growth within the recovery program. That the alcoholic notices changes in his or her own life and behavior is evidence for success at recovery. It is important for the recovering alcoholic to remember that the success is only to date and only at the first stage of recovery. Recovery occurs one day at a time. Projecting into the future has been our worst enemy in the past and should be avoided during recovery.

The pink cloud can be seen in recovering alcoholics who slowly begin to miss meetings, cut back on prayer and meditation, and drift occasionally into the stinking thinking and the dry drunk attitudes so dangerous to recovery. There is no free ride in recovery. It takes work. If the work stops, the recovery stops. A pink cloud above the head of an alcoholic is opposed to the teachings of AA and to proper spiritual growth.

Along with helping work the Steps of Alcoholics Anonymous, a sponsor is most helpful in bringing the alcoholic back down to earth when riding a pink cloud. A close working relationship with a sponsor and other friends in the program is the largest benefit to an alcoholic who forgets the true purpose of the program—to be of maximum service to God. It is ironic that an alcoholic works so hard during recovery to find an inner peace never felt before. The program is a selfish one in that sense. It demands that we alcoholics put our sobriety first and that we establish a connection and friendship with our Higher Power. Once that seems to have been achieved, an alcoholic finds a new way of life that includes self-esteem and self-acceptance—the exact same things that can lead to a belief that can occasionally bring back our old ego. With daily prayer and meditation, and with a relationship with others in the program, we can fight this natural tendency, through humility and gratitude.

Chapter 6

Tools for Success

Anything that proves to be a tool for successful recovery should be examined and used, if possible. It is important, however, that recovering alcoholics select the tools that best work for them. Every individual reacts differently to different stimuli. Not all tools work for all people. Needing the reinforcement that can come with successful initial recovery, alcoholics should not grab at every tool. That may risk failure. Upon entering recovery, each alcoholic will find special issues to be dealt with to facilitate recovery. Many of the available tools, both psychological and physical, have been touched on in these pages. The most important tools are people, listening, and involvement. You get out of it what you put into it. Many of the available tools will not work for certain people, but others may find themselves using to great success tools not mentioned.

Change Not the Pattern

Despite the need to change virtually every behavioral pattern—not to frequent old drinking haunts and friends, to change self-centeredness into compassion for others, and all of the other changes required for a successful recovery—there are things that should not be changed. An alcoholic in recovery is going through an awful lot and should not be overwhelmed by other major life decisions. The focus should and must be on the recovery process.

Having finally found a new way of life, the recovering alcoholic may make decisions that will later be regretted unless a full understanding of his or her emotions occurs. Belief systems are changing every day, as the alcoholic is finding his or her true self. Until they are understood and solidified into a steady, unchanging set of beliefs, major decisions should be avoided. These include decisions regarding a divorce or a new relationship, a job change or a move to a new area, and financial decisions; such decisions would be better decided after an established period of recovery. There is no need to add to the burden of recovery until recovery has been established. Many decisions made during the initial recovery stages may well be thought about completely differently a year later. For this reason, a recovering alcoholic should wait a year or longer before making major decisions.

"Act as If"

In 1954, the Reverend Samuel M. Shoemaker wrote a story about an unfortunate who came to him admitting that he didn't believe in God and certainly didn't know how to pray. Shoemaker asked him to "try an experiment," as he had nothing to lose. He asked him to get down on his knees and say anything at all that came to his mind, addressing his thoughts to "The Unknown." He then asked if the man could read just one chapter from the Bible, from the book of John. Solely out of respect for Shoemaker, the man obliged, but fighting every step of the way. This went on for some time, until one day the man actually began praying to God and reading the Bible and other works on his own. The man eventually became a spiritual leader within his church. Shoemaker believed that this was possible because the man "acted as if he had faith" until faith came by accident, or "until there was an opening for God to come through."

The slogan "act as if" has been used in AA circles ever since. It enables newcomers to grasp the concept that spirituality won't come easily or quickly, but if you give it a try, it will eventually come. Another way of saying it is "Fake it till you make it." Not to be confused with a dry drunk, this recovering alcoholic wants to succeed, and through trying to find a conscious contact with a Higher Power, a contact will indeed come.

The *Twelve Steps and Twelve Traditions* says, "We of A.A. do obey spiritual principles, first because we must, and ultimately because we love the kind of life such obedience brings."

Separation of Thoughts

It is important for the alcoholic to separate the many thoughts and feelings while in recovery. Many individuals have written about the processes whereby one can benefit through psychoanalytical focus on one thing at a time. It is easier to explain by saying, "Take it easy." Don't try to do too much at one time. Learn the difference between an alcoholic mind-set and a recovering mind-set. Reflect upon past behavior to realize that the new behavior is refreshing. Eventually, one will learn to slow down and enjoy the moment. Carlson and Bailey (1997) say that during active thinking, one's mind recalls events from memory. During passive thinking, one's mind is free-flowing, not really thinking at all. This natural state, they believe, "constantly bring[s] you fresh, harmonious thoughts."

Behavioral Imagery

Ludwig (1988) discusses how one might use the thought process to avoid drinking. Rather than think about what you are *not* going to do, he suggests thinking about what you *are* going to do. The premise behind this is twofold. First, this imagery is positive, allowing reinforcement upon success. Second, it provides a pattern of positive thinking that establishes itself as habitual. For an alcoholic, this might mean thinking about going for a workout instead of thinking about not going for a drink. It means going forward into an unpleasant situation with thoughts of being compassionate and tolerant rather than thinking about all the negatives that may develop. One of the major problems during initial recovery is setting expectations incorrectly. For example, in the beginning, I would enter a meeting at the office with thoughts of what was going to happen. If I was to meet a disgruntled client, I would be fully prepared to do battle. I had expectations based on my need to still hold on to control, even during recovery. Once I "let go and let God," my expectations vanished and I could begin to enjoy even the most uncomfortable situations as a matter of life. Now, my own behavioral imagery includes being a spiritually based person. Although I may still fail at this, I now find that the meetings go much more smoothly, and I enjoy my time at work in a completely different light.

Humility

The need for humility cannot be stressed enough to the recovering alcoholic (or anyone else for that matter). Humility is the understanding that everyone is equal, that we are no better or no worse than anyone else—quite a departure from the alcoholic mind. Humility alone will eventually eliminate the majority of the alcoholic thought processes, the pain of insecurity, and the need to control. Recovering alcoholics with humility are successful in their recovery programs and most likely are of the most help to newcomers. If compassion and understanding of others' positions are tools for recovery, humility is the toolbox.

Recently, I bought my sponsor what I thought to be a comical and perfectly acceptable present. It was an all-white shirt with the words *Relentless Sponsor* printed across the front. Although he was quite happy with the present, he added a few words to his thank you. They once again helped me to remember the program. He simply asked me how he could wear the shirt in humility. I said that of course it was a joke. He answered that for something to be a joke, one had to assume that the reader would understand it. Thank you, Rob, for always keeping me on the straight and narrow.

Spirituality and Faith

A conscious connection to a Higher Power provides a foundation for understanding who you are and who you are supposed to be. This does not come easily and is foreign to most of us, particularly alcoholics. Many of us profess to have regular contact with "our God" of choice. But a spiritual "connection" involves much more than words; it involves deeds. As stated earlier, good thinking does not provide good deeds, but good deeds do provide good thinking. Spirituality is a way of life that recognizes our powerlessness and allows us to surrender to the will of our Higher Power.

Living a life intent on satisfying a set of spiritual principles will yield a life that can bring a serenity never realized before. Faith in one's Higher Power provides faith in oneself, the single most important aspect of self-esteem. Self-esteem eliminates the need to pretend, to control, and to hide. With a spiritual life we eliminate the need for excuses and lies. We learn to accept our mistakes and learn from them. Eventually, normal daily routines and things that were boring when we drank become acceptable, if not enjoyable. The need for extremes diminishes, allowing a stable environment in which to succeed in recovery.

Peg Thompson, in her delightful book *Finding Your Own Spiritual Path*, states, "In all enduring spiritual traditions, it is given that compassion and service are an integral part of walking a spiritual path." Bill Wilson (1967) refers to an earlier letter in which he says, "A clear light seems to fall upon us all—when we open our eyes. Since our blindness was caused by our own defects, we must first deeply realize what they are. Constructive meditation is the first requirement for each new step in our spiritual growth."

Norman Vincent Peale (1993) writes, "Saturate your thoughts with peaceful experiences, peaceful words and ideas, and ultimately you will have a storehouse of peace producing experience to which you may turn for refreshment and renewal of your spirit."

Deepak Chopra (1994), a popular contemporary author and spiritualist who blends physics and the laws of nature with philosophy and practicality, has laid down seven spiritual laws of success in his book of the same name:

Chopra's Seven Spiritual Laws of Success

1. The Law of Pure Potentiality—We all have the ability to achieve any dream.
2. The Law of Giving—The more we give, the more we will receive back.
3. The Law of Cause and Effect ("Karma")—Every action causes a force that will return the same action back to us.
4. The Law of Least Effort—The principle of least action and therefore least resistance.
5. The Law of Intention and Desire—Your true potential is affected by your true intentions and desires.
6. The Law of Detachment—One must give up physical attachment to the results of one's intentions and desires.
7. The Law of Purpose of Life ("Dharma")—Our Higher Power, or God, has given us a purpose here in our lives.

Eye Movement Desensitization and Reprocessing

Used often in California but rarely known in most therapeutic circles, Eye Movement Desensitization Reprocessing (EMDR) was first developed by psychologist Francine Shapiro in 1988. It is said to accelerate the treatment for low self-esteem, shame, anger, and guilt issues. It is said that one day while on a walk to a meeting, with distressing thoughts in her head, Shapiro began to watch and count the lines on the sidewalk. At the end of her walk, she felt comfortable with the issues that were troubling her and realized the rapid eye movement while walking may have helped her in this regard. Upon further research into the possibility that this might work on others, she founded the principle of EMDR.

It has long been understood that our brains support the inner child through our dreams, particularly those that occur during the REM, or rapid eye movement, state of sleep. EMDR involves conscious rapid eye movement as the individual thinks about past events affecting the unhappiness of the inner child. The therapist assists only in facilitating the eye movement and processing the information that may surface.

The therapist does not suggest any methods for resolution of the issues. Resolution comes solely from within the individual as the negative feelings become conscious. It is said that the negative feelings can be greatly reduced with just one treatment, particularly when dealing with traumatic events such as abuse, abandonment, and, possibly, alcoholism. Some therapists believe that regular treatment may aid in the elimination of vivid recollections related to past traumatic event.

Adjustment to Acceptance

Contrary to popular belief, the notion that full and complete support and recognition to a recovering alcoholic provides the self-esteem required for sobriety is not true. Major inner turmoil develops during recovery involving the understanding of acceptance. Having perceived for so long that they are less than others and having behaved to protect themselves from the pain of rejection, alcoholics find acceptance to be a new and misunderstood feeling. It takes time to change behavioral patterns and even longer to accept that these new behaviors are now accepted by others. Recovering alcoholics not only challenge their own actions and belief systems, as mentioned earlier, but they also question the actions of others around them. Acceptance is wanting what you have, as opposed to having what you want.

The alcoholic mind doesn't leave overnight. Insecurities can still engulf the thought process, even after extended periods of sobriety. Acceptance is the ability to think consciously about what we have done in the past and relate it to what we have changed, and are doing, in the present. Working a Twelve Step program is therapeutic to this acceptance and aids in the elimination of shame and guilt.

Recovering alcoholics must come to this understanding on

their own. In recovery they develop new belief systems, rules, and goals and judge themselves against these standards. Although the support of others close to them is welcomed, if not demanded, it is certainly not the only reinforcement that must occur. Relating themselves to the standards of a Higher Power as He is understood is the basic premise for any judgment of spiritual performance. Learning to be of service to a Higher Power and fellow humans is paramount in feeling reinforced and accepted in recovery. This type of acceptance is at times painful due to failures, but over time it can yield a person who is content with the knowledge that she or he is accepted, despite the shortcomings, and therefore becomes acceptable to self.

Positive Addictions

William Glasser (1976) is perhaps best known for his beliefs that include the successful use of "positive addictions." The nature of an addictive personality can be used to benefit the recovery process. Those who criticize the workings of Alcoholics Anonymous point out that many alcoholics simply change addictions, becoming addicted to recovery instead of active alcoholism. Glasser makes the point that the very nature of an addictive personality provides persistence and often supports an uncompromising balance to achieve the necessary goals. Glasser feels that love and worth are the requirements that make people strong. A desire to succeed that does not recognize failure provides the ability to keep going through the roughest of times. Without alcohol affecting the ability to reason and plan, a recovering alcoholic can change addictions to his or her benefit. These new addictions, Glasser believes, are found through loving and being loved or by doing something worthwhile.

Positive addictions are, therefore, healthy and noncompetitive replacements for the addiction of alcohol. Both "healthy" and "noncompetitive" are desirable, particularly in recovery. In his book *Positive Addictions*, Glasser enlists the support of a marathon runner in his research to evaluate the positive addiction to running. What he finds is that the actual addiction does not occur quickly. It takes success and practiced endurance (as it does in alcoholism, music, physical fitness, the arts, and every other form of addiction).

Using a hobby, charitable work, physical exercise, or any other positive addiction to promote self-worth will benefit the entire recovery process. This positive addiction is not assumed to work solely through repetitive efforts. It must be something that the recovering alcoholic enjoys doing. It may be an old, forgotten pastime such as gardening, or a completely new one. But most important, spirituality, work, family, friends, hobbies, and recovery must at all times be kept in balance.

Another criticism of Alcoholics Anonymous is that many in AA become the essence of the written program, rather than an example of the outcome of *following* the program. In other words, rarely do people with a disease believe themselves to be only the symptoms of that disease. Diabetics do not spend all day judging themselves only by the boundaries and the required treatment of that disease. Healthy individuals maintain a balance in life that includes also having a disease. Likewise, alcoholics are not the symptoms of the disease. They must work to provide a sense of balance that includes interests other than alcoholism or Alcoholics Anonymous. Many in recovery can be occasionally found quoting the Big Book as scripture yet living an internal life of a dry drunk. When the focus is on only the program and not the results of it, the recovery has become unhealthy.

Touchstones: A Book of Daily Meditations for Men provides a meditation for balance:

> We seek balance in our lives. The greatest sign of unmanageability in our past was the unbalanced lives we led. This is no easy lesson to learn. We are inclined to grasp for a single answer, thinking we now have the key insight to a happier way of life. As men, many of us have pursued our happiness in work with little time for anything else. Perhaps, for some, the singing and playing we have done were part of

our addiction or participating with someone else in their addiction. This makes it feel dangerous or frightening now to be playful in recovery.

We can find ways to have more balance in our lives. Spiritual vitality grows when we make room in our day for lighthearted play as well as serious tasks.

AA stresses that working with and helping another suffering alcoholic (the Twelfth Step) is most beneficial as a positive addiction. From the first positive publicity of Alcoholics Anonymous this was pointed out. A writer for *Liberty* magazine (September 1939) stated his opinion of the AA program from a review of the Big Book: "Recovering alcoholics were experiencing a psychic change. Their so-called compulsion neurosis was being altered— transferred from liquor to something else . . . a psychological necessity to rescue his fellow victims from the plight that made them so miserable."

Communication

Learning how to communicate will lead to a new type of intimacy that surpasses any past relationship. Communication involves, however, the willingness to be vulnerable. Sharing one's feelings can be cause for rejection, a dangerous proposition to the initially recovering alcoholic. Becoming involved in AA and AA meetings benefits the recovering alcoholic. Here, the initial sharing is practically guaranteed to be accepted nonjudgmentally. AA sharing is the expressing of an idea or thought that does not require a response.

Many books about communication exist, and many therapists make a good living teaching it. They start with the need to begin sentences with, "I feel" or, "I believe" rather than, "You." Over time clients are taught to eliminate the words *shoulda, coulda* and *woulda.*

The majority of marital problems center on the lack of communication. Our society, having grown into a "me" society, has compelled many of us to focus on our own feelings, rather than honestly sharing them with others. Recovery is a time for true honesty, vulnerability, and the sharing of feelings, to grow and mature into a new spiritual person.

Richard S. (1988), a recovering alcoholic, wrote a pamphlet entitled *Communication Skills* in which he lists several tools for effective communication that I have always found interesting.

Communication Tools

1. Listening to others
2. Speaking up and asking for time to talk
3. Reaffirming that you heard it the way the speaker meant it
4. Reaffirming that the listener heard it the way you meant it
5. Asking sincere questions with respect and kindness
6. Agreeing to disagree
7. Complimenting the listener
8. Not attacking the way others communicate
9. Not judging others' communication skills
10. Not taking another person's inventory
11. Owning your own behavior

Refusal Skills

It is imperative that one's refusal skills, or "avoidance," grow throughout the recovery process. Nancy Reagan, perhaps best known for her involvement in the "Just Say No" program during her term as first lady, helped the world to realize the necessity of refusal skills when dealing with drugs and alcohol. More than just saying no to continued use, refusal skills can also help one to cope with the overwhelming stress of the drastic changes involved in recovery. Refusal skills help minimize addictive thinking. On the other hand, an alcoholic not prepared for the guaranteed necessity of refusal skills will fail in recovery.

During recovery, many occasions will arise that test our refusal skills. Events, thoughts, questions from friends, places, and a vast variety of triggers cause the need for a predetermined—and preferably well-practiced—refusal skill. Refusal may mean simply leaving a potentially hazardous situation. Refusal skills may require out-and-out rudeness, if that is the only manner in which to protect the sobriety. They may be needed because of another's action or may be required to combat an internalized thought. Whatever the cause, a recovering alcoholic must have the knowledge and ability to work refusal, using all means necessary to continue a program of abstinence.

At a time when many outside factors are influencing the recovery rate, the recovering alcoholic must focus on the difference between needs and wants. Learning to refuse the wants and work for the needs can provide a foundation of strength to say no to a variety of situations, behaviors, and, of course, alcohol use. The first step in this process is to prioritize the most important things in your life. Listing recovery, along with spirituality, as the most important issue is the basis for the first three Steps of Alcoholics Anonymous. Then all other decisions must be based upon a domino effect of the higher value taking precedence over all decisions. One must evaluate and weigh the options, knowing that drinking is not the solution to any problem. At all times, the recovering alcoholic must place sobriety above all other values in life. An abstinent, recovering alcoholic following the Steps of Alcoholics Anonymous, even with no particular additional effort, often takes care of many of the other troubling issues associated with alcoholism. You can't drown out your sorrows; you can only teach them how to swim.

Physical Fitness

One of the positive addictions I have become involved with is getting my beer-battered frame back into shape. It came to me only recently that a sound mind and a sound body go well together. Physical fitness helps to relieve stress. It is something that you can see the results of quickly, and it can fill a void of time left from the periods you no longer use to drink. It is also beneficial to the recovering alcoholic as it is noncompetitive. In my case, I made a commitment to myself that I would use—for my recovery—all of the past time I spent in bars drinking. Over time this included about 25 percent for working out, 25 percent for my family, 25 percent for spirituality, meditation, and praying, and 25 percent for the AA program in some way. What became evident over a short period of time was that I still had more free time than I ever had before. I no longer require rejuvenation from binges; I no longer wish to spend time alone so that I can drink more; and I no longer spend time covering my tracks.

When visiting AA meetings it is easy to see that (as in the real world) most people do not focus on their physical fitness needs. That is not to say that I, or anyone else, needs to be a workout junkie, but it does provide a sense of recovery for me. The physical toll that drinking has on any alcoholic is obvious. For that precise reason I believe that physical fitness should become a necessity for anyone in recovery. Walking, bowling, or any source of activity is a welcome sign that a new life is beginning. As a noncompetitive activity, not dependent on others, physical fitness can even provide some spiritual benefit.

In the average alcoholic, nearly 25 percent of the body's total energy needs can be satisfied simply through the consumption of alcohol. This is one of the reasons a recovering alcoholic may take some time to develop regular eating habits after abstinence. Treatment centers stress the need for a daily meal program to benefit both mind and body. The removal of alcohol alone does not in itself rebuild the damaged cells. In recovery, we must provide nutrients, vitamins, proteins, and fats as well as carbohydrates. The more balanced the diet, the quicker the body can recover. Sadly enough, most alcoholics do not realize the physical damage that has occurred, and proper diet is often left unattended throughout the recovery process. Continued poor diet can cause physical sickness and pain, major roadblocks to recovery. Low blood sugar, prevalent in recovering alcoholics, results from possible liver damage and should be attended to immediately by a qualified physician.

Another component of fitness is the need for proper sleep and rest. Not only does relaxation provide a time frame for conscious contact with a Higher Power or for prayer, but it can also be used simply for reflection. Often referred to as a trigger or relapse sign, becoming overly tired does affect the mind and the ability to decide. The importance of proper rest cannot be overstressed, but is most difficult to achieve during early recovery.

Therapy, et al.

Many of the psychological disorders discussed in this book can be best addressed by a professional. As mentioned earlier, the AA program has been called three thousand dollars' worth of free therapy at every meeting. Basically, the recovering alcoholic needs a sounding board. For some this is a professional therapist, psychologist, or counselor; for others it's an AA sponsor or a close friend or loved one. For still others it's a combination. In my opinion, one should make use of all the tools available to aid recovery. A therapist is qualified to work on a number of issues that cannot be addressed in AA, and a professional psychologist can quickly find dual disorders and depression.

At times, different medications can be prescribed to help the recovery process. If an alcoholic is also suffering from depression, for example, a number of medications including Prozac, Paxil, and Zoloft are available to minimize this roadblock to recovery. Occasionally disulfiram (Antabuse) is still prescribed, providing violent reactions to alcohol consumption. If the recovery program is honestly worked and a spiritual program is in effect, disulfiram is rarely prescribed by professionals involved in the treatment of alcoholism.

One of the dangers of therapy, particularly when it is covered by health insurance, is the current position of the health care crisis. As insurance carriers demand quicker turnarounds for all types of physical and mental impairments, the rush is on to find a quick fix or evidence of a perceived rapid recovery. This forces some therapists into a mode of focusing on and promoting only abstinence as the highest priority for alcoholics (Brown 1995).

This book has focused on the need for absolute abstinence in any recovery program. But I hope the reader has also been left with the feeling that recovery may involve work and focus on a vast array of other personality disorders and problems. If, for a short-term abstinence, the therapist is forced into ignoring what may be basic to the onset of alcoholism and the continuation of the use and dependency, the client is cheated and headed for a relapse. Recovery is a long and sometimes never-ending process. It may not always require therapy, but when it does, it should be left up to the therapist, not the insurance industry, as to when it shall conclude.

Because most alcoholics have left a wake of pain behind them, therapy is recommended to help them and codependents alike. Working through their issues separately but concurrently can act as a Fifth Step of sorts. It can also provide previously hidden Fourth Step items and help to teach communication techniques—all of which aid recovery.

Enjoy the Moment

Our experiences in life are directly related to how we believe they affect us. In other words, we tend to think about the consequences of each moment before we subconsciously decide if we are enjoying it or enjoying our perceived outcome of the moment. We can look at life as a glass half full or half empty of water. Knowing the difference between what Carlson and Bailey (1997) call healthy versus unhealthy thinking can be most beneficial to the recovering alcoholic.

In recovery, one must learn to interpret each moment differently than before. More important is to learn not to interpret at all. If we interpret the moment as a learning process, nearly every moment can provide some type of benefit to us all. This requires the learned ability to listen with an open mind. Even the most difficult of situations can be a learning experience if it is perceived in the context of the recovery process. Carlson and Bailey refer to this as "the speed of life."

Alcoholics Anonymous persuades us to live one day at a time, but full recovery can teach us to live one moment at a time. One must work at seeing the benefit in every moment, fighting back the natural tendencies for impatience and frustration. This practice will eventually lead to a responsive versus a reactive life. Taking control of our lives, being responsive rather than reactive to our needs and those of our loved ones puts us recovering alcoholics in the front position. It allows us to surrender all control of others while at the same time maintaining control of how we perceive the moment.

Gratitude

The magic of a thankful spirit is that it has the power to replace anger with love, resentment with happiness, fear with faith, worry with peace, the desire to dominate with the wish to play on a team, self-preoccupation with concern for the needs of others, guilt with an open door to forgiveness, sexual impurity with honor and respect, jealousy with joy at another's success, lack of creativity with inspired productivity, inferiorities with dignity, a lack of love with an abundance of self-sharing (*Men's Devotional Bible* 1993).

One of the benefits of attending AA meetings is that we alcoholics finally learn that we are not terminally unique. The process of hearing the stories and problems of other recovering alcoholics provides both humility and gratitude. No matter how bad things seem for us, there is always someone in AA with a story much worse. That fact alone can help us to see the good things in life and fertilize gratitude for the blessings we possess. For some, this may mean the mere fact of sobriety and abstinence. But even this small benefit to a recovering alcoholic is a whole new world filled with blessings. The founders of AA wrote a whole book filled with proof that gratitude for the blessings all of us have provides us with the ability to move forward toward a spiritual and happy life. This does not come easily, or overnight, but it is practically guaranteed that it will come.

Expectations

Happiness in recovery is in part tied to how we believe things should or will be. The need for control has become such a large part of the alcoholic mind-set that this is a difficult personality trait to minimize. Even when in recovery, alcoholics can fall prey to believing that they are or should be in control of their own sobriety and recovery. This belief encourages the denial of powerlessness and rejects the notion of a Higher Power altogether. After all, one cannot *play* God and at the same time *surrender* to God. Not requiring the assistance of a Higher Power further promotes isolation, as we begin fully to believe that we are handling our sobriety on our own. The fact is, we are the ones who have handled our lives—right into the mess we are in. How in the world could we believe that we could handle recovery alone?

This continued need for control, and more important, for the answer, sets up a chain of cause and effect. What actually occurs, especially during early recovery, is that we believe things should happen our way and then become disappointed when they don't. We are not aware of this thought process. It is the result of years of alcoholism. This is a behavioral attribute present in virtually all people in one way or another.

What needs to occur is for us to fight off the propensity to expect whatever first enters our mind. For example, if it is snowing outside in the morning before we head off to work, it would be quite normal for us to expect the roads to be slippery. Or would it? How can we be sure that the roads haven't been plowed and salted or sanded? Perhaps the highways are perfectly clear. We can't be absolutely certain. We simply cannot know what God's will is for the moment. We harbor a high degree of arrogance if we believe that we might.

Playing God and believing that we know what our spouse will or should do is a sure sign that we are failing in our program of recovery. The tool we must use is an open and loving mind. We must work hard to eliminate expectations and the need for control, taking everything slowly and easily, one day at a time. We must be willing to accept the results of every situation as God's will, looking only for the understanding of His will, not for the control of it. In recovery, acceptance of ourselves, acceptance of what happens to us on a daily basis, and acceptance of others are sure signs of a successful and long-lasting recovery.

In looking at life with this viewpoint, we can always find those who almost always feel that they have been wronged by another. Even when it is obvious that whatever caused them the discomfort was not done to them, it simply happened, they still feel that they have been wronged. The late pizza delivery person is not given a tip, even though the cook cut his hand badly back at the pizza parlor, requiring a hospital visit and stitches, sending the entire restaurant into a delay. Contempt prior to investigation is the result of faulty and selfish expectations.

One couple I know recently built a beautiful custom home. It was approximately six thousand square feet, custom finished throughout. These people had demanded and expected that the home should be complete in six months. Their entire expectation of quality and customer service then revolved only around this fact, as they ignored the basic construction of the home. The builder made no promises for a specific finish date and could only promise to do his best. Due to several factors outside the control of the builder, including both late payments and late selections from the homeowner, the home ended up being about three weeks late. The framer went bankrupt and left the job; his replacement was arrested off the job; and the builder absorbed nearly ten thousand dollars in additional framing labor because of this. Not once did the couple show any gratitude for his efforts. I know that the list of defects was small despite an early move-in under threat of a lawsuit, and the home is absolutely gorgeous. This particular couple will now, and I quote, "make it our mission to ruin the builder," through gossip and misleading statements. They feel as though they have been wronged. They had a false level of expectations and now need someone to blame. This couple has no gratitude for the God-given ability to afford such a home, for the additional effort taken by the builder and his staff, working at times until three in the morning trying to make the date. They probably have no gratitude for anything else in their life. These people are, in my opinion, without judgment, devoid of spirituality, and have let ego, greed, self-centeredness, and a lack of tolerance now control their lives.

The Christian apostle Paul once listed three important attributes of humans: hope, faith, and love. These traits, he believed, held the key to a happy and purposeful life. Surprisingly enough, he lists love as the most important of the three and goes so far as to suggest that hope and faith are the result of love. Faith is called the chain that holds the three together. Paul's discussion of the nine attributes of love is strikingly similar to the basis of a successful recovery program: patience, kindness, generosity, sincerity, humility, guilelessness, courteousness, usefulness, and good temperedness. With these attributes, even the most hardened of all alcoholics would have a difficult time forcing his or her will on others.

False expectations in recovery also revolve around projecting what will happen in the future with our friends. We have had years with drinking friends and drug friends. Not surprisingly, many turn out not to be friends at all once we are abstinent and enter recovery. Although I have been lucky enough to keep a couple of my old friends, the majority of those still drinking, and perhaps questioning their own use, have disappeared. One gentleman, a friend and attorney I had asked to be trustee of my daughter's trust fund for college, truly surprised me. I didn't find out what exactly had taken place with our relationship until recently, but I had been questioning his departure from my life for some time. He was the first person I called to tell I was leaving for the treatment center for over four weeks. He used to call me nearly once a week just to talk or tell a joke, prior to the time I left for treatment. He is also the one who told me that he always knew I had a problem with drinking. Surprisingly enough, since I have been in recovery, we have spoken only two times. He never calls anymore and takes effort to avoid me.

I believed that his behavior was due to my sobriety, my alcoholism, or another topic related to my actions and past behavior.

What I found recently was that during my first week away from home in the treatment facility, my wife had called him because she needed someone to talk to. He was, at the time, her most respected adviser, our family attorney. He came to her office, listened, offered his advice, spoke of all the bad things he knew I had done, and upon leaving, while giving her a groping hug behind closed doors, whispered to her that she had always been his fantasy and made a pass at her.

Only during our mutual recovery was my wife able to tell me this. I believe it shows that we have come a long way in being able to communicate honestly. I finally knew why he hadn't called. My wife was afraid that I would be mad at her, at him, or at myself, and had held off on telling me for some time. The interesting thing is, I wasn't mad.

Despite the inappropriateness of his actions, as an alcoholic, I understood. As an alcoholic in recovery, I can pray for him and forgive. He will never be a friend to either my wife or me again, but I am okay with that. The bottom line is that my expectations were wrong. Because of those false expectations, I had set myself up to be hurt, which I was and still am. I had expected his full support, his integrity as an attorney and as a friend. I had expected that I could control what he should have done and said from a thousand miles away. I was wrong. I now accept his actions as God's will, perhaps as a reminder of my past behavior, perhaps as an indication of human mistakes, perhaps as a reminder as to just how beautiful my wife truly is and how lucky I am to have her in my life. Perhaps God just doesn't want me to know why, yet.

Rational-Emotive Therapy

Quite simply, Rational-Emotive Therapy (RET), created by Albert Ellis, is a means by which the alcoholic can begin to learn to rationalize some of the emotions affecting the negative mindset. Shame, for example, can be easily turned to guilt, once reviewed with a conscious effort at evaluating the impact of the circumstance. Guilt can be dealt with, turned into feelings rather than emotions. Far better, shame can often be eliminated through this process. The alcoholic takes a moment to ask himself or herself, "Did I have anything to do with what happened to me?" or, "Am I responsible for what others have said or done?" When the alcoholic takes the time to evaluate the emotions taking control of his or her thought process, those emotions can be felt, then understood rationally. When emotions are left unattended, they can reinforce the low self-esteem and the belief that the thoughts are true indications of self-worth. Emotions must be recognized as improper responses for protecting our inner pain.

For example, a person sexually abused as a child had no choice in the matter, no control over the situation. By rationalizing the experience as a terrible mistake made by someone else, there is no self-blame. As difficult as it may seem, the act may lead to tolerance and understanding and calm. Eliminating the anger and replacing it with forgiveness may provide the first step in healing the damaged inner child.

An alcoholic must take the time to consciously question these damaging thoughts in hopes of minimizing the extremes presented by deep emotions. Recognizing that drinking was the cause of many past actions and behaviors helps the alcoholic to rationalize the disease concept of alcoholism and accept the possibility that the actions would not have occurred if drink or drug was not involved. Rationalizing the reasons behind resentments may lead to an understanding that the alcoholic may have had some part in causing the action that triggered the resentment in the first place. Believing that he or she might be partially responsible gives the alcoholic an opportunity to include the resentment in prayer and meditation as a means to forgive and forget. Finding compassion for others through this exercise is a benefit that anyone would surely enjoy.

Chapter 7

Shameoboros

In ancient Eastern mythologies there exists a large snakelike creature that lives by devouring its own tail. The snake became a God of sorts over the years and over time was called "Ouroboros." Since early in recovery I have used this image to understand alcoholism and the vicious circle that seems to perpetuate itself year after year and generation after generation.

The information provided within this book shows the many viewpoints as to the causes and treatment of alcoholism. Genetics and heredity, chemical imbalances and influences, psychological and physiological disorders, and various combinations of the above have been shown to play a part in this disease. All have been presented as a means to prove further that no research exists to end the speculation and diversity of opinions.

For the record, as an alcoholic, I believe in most if not all of the many scenarios and concepts presented here. That is how differently this disease can affect different people, and how very different are the many people with alcoholism. Furthermore, the results of alcoholism, including the concepts of the alcoholic mind, vary as drastically as the disease itself.

The concept of "Shameoboros" is an attempt to link the various pieces together, providing a synopsis of the unending ruthlessness of this disease. This is nothing new, perhaps just a new name for a lot of old theories jumbled together. What it allows us to see is how many different factors influence the alcoholic's use, reuse, recovery, and relapse. There are reasons all of these things happen. There are commonalities among all of us who experience these things. I believe that, somewhere in our lives, something has happened to cause us to believe that we are simply not connected to our world. Whether the event was triggered by us, caused by us, or has happened to us is irrelevant. The perception that somehow we were slighted, made less than other people, and possibly shamed into believing that we were not equal is one of the doors that allows alcoholism to enter. This act was probably inadvertent. Furthermore, it was probably overexaggerated by our own self-doubt and insecurities. Nonetheless, it was real, and it stayed with us our entire lives. The introduction of alcohol only allowed us finally to find a way to numb the feeling. Add to this the possible predisposition to alcoholism, including genetics, heredity, environment, and psychological and physiological symptoms, and one was surely well down the road to alcoholism long before having that first drink.

The Scar That Will Not Heal

I have yet to meet an alcoholic who has not suffered emotional scars from something in the past. Placing blame for alcoholism might support a purely Freudian theory, while taking issue with Goodwin and others. Is it possible that all the theories are correct? The deep-rooted scarring that has burned within our big ego and inner child can be the door that later opens on a world of alcoholism. This pain may be imagined or real, or both. That is frankly unimportant. Our own truth provides the basis for our individual existence. For us alcoholics, the attack on our self-esteem throughout the early years tends to be reaffirmed and continued.

In reviewing the preliminary draft of this book, one very perceptive individual pointed out that this may be a limited view of a predisposition to alcoholism. Nonetheless, I hold that the emotional scarring present in most if not all alcoholics is absolutely a predisposition to many of the self-guarding actions that can be a seed at least for the future growth of alcoholism. Alcoholics address emotional scars in ignorance of a correct and healthy way for their personal growth. The scars are hidden away, ignored, or pushed deep within our subconscious whenever possible. If alcohol can numb the pain or the memory of emotional scars, it provides one more impetus for continued use.

Many types of scarring can be so damaging (often unconsciously) that the scars are never forgotten or let go. This scar is never allowed to heal. For many, the emotional turmoil resulting from the inner pain and the subsequent covering up of these true emotions becomes the essence of the being. The scars can be inflicted by an unending list of persons, situations, and thoughts. Often, the scars can be misconceptions of what really might have occurred, indicating that the alcoholic has not effectively dealt with the feelings and emotions surrounding the scarring event. Only once the feelings are dealt with can the shame associated with the subconscious scars be removed. I have broken several scarring issues down to help the reader understand how many ways we might harbor scars as part of who we are.

Scarring

- Parental criticism or abuse
- Parental abandonment
- Sexual or physical abuse
- Religious guilt
- Physical imperfections or deformities
- Embarrassment
- Excessive punishment or critique from others
- Educational and learning problems
- Nonacceptance by family or peers
- Misinterpretations of others
- Perception of not being wanted
- Peer rejection
- Rumors and gossip
- Sibling rivalries
- Nonperformance and failure issues

Left unattended, these scars are like a seed that grows a little bigger every time it is reaffirmed through any event that may give validity to the feeling of low self-worth. No matter how many beautiful compliments or flowers are planted around these feelings, the weed keeps coming back and taking over the garden. Even when a specific effort is made to completely cut out the weed from the garden, the weed will eventually resurface unless the entire root is pulled.

It is unfortunate that the alcoholic treats these scars differently from the way normal earth people do. Obviously, many nonalcoholics have also been hurt and scarred early in their lives. Perhaps it is the predisposition of genetics and physiological impairments in alcoholics' brains that take these scars and abandon any chance of dealing with them. Regardless, we alcoholics do not have the tools necessary to focus on and evaluate our feelings and emotions rationally.

Reaffirmation of Trauma

Throughout our lives, many occasions occur that reaffirm how we perceive ourselves. For some, a nurturing parent or loved one reinforces the good person we know we are. For others, something as small as not making the cut for the school play or basketball team will lead to confirmation that we are not worthy. To have a parent continuously tell us we are not good enough or to have a priest or minister scare us with thoughts of hell without at the same time confirming a loving and forgiving God enables us to fall deeper into this lonely world of shame and low self-esteem. A healthy person, reared in a strong, loving family, with a good environment and a strong sense of self-esteem, does not become an alcoholic. Note the words *healthy person* in the preceding sentence.

Having been told no since birth, coupled with reaffirmation of isolation and rejection by family and peers throughout adolescence, and possible psychological disorders lay the groundwork for a life of alcoholism. Add to this the possible brain chemistry disorders and personality characteristics that have grown around the internal isolations and it is understandable why someone would want to use a mood-altering substance. That is exactly what alcohol is—a mood-altering substance. Now add to this the possibility of decreased serotonin levels, or many of the other possibilities previously discussed, and again we could possibly understand how a person becomes an alcoholic. What other avenue would our fragile mind take when engulfed by such a cunning, baffling, and powerful disease?

For many, the reaffirmation may come only internally. Alcoholics may have an A average at school but, due to the perfectionism instilled since childhood to do better, they may beat themselves up to do even better. These alcoholics have not learned to accept their mistakes and must now find ways to hide them from both themselves and others.

Let the Games Begin

As each day passes, the alcoholic requires a new trick or game to play, protecting against the possibility of additional pain. Often at this point, not knowing any problem exists, we alcoholics pick up new character defects as quickly as we are introduced to them or need them. This is the beginning of the alcoholic mind. A smorgasbord of personality traits, classified as "character defects," begins to build up. At times, one results from another, or one actually supports the other. Once again, the alcoholic creates a need for recovery that, in essence, becomes the problem. Character defects are common in virtually everyone. What is uncommon is a conscious effort to eliminate them. The games involved in protecting one from oneself can provide an impetus for additional character defects. Elimination of game playing as a substitute for self-protection provides an honest basis for communication and intimacy.

*Examples of Character Defects in Alcoholism**

- Dishonesty
- Exhibitionism

* See also chapter 5.

- Withdrawal and isolation
- Pretending
- "Must win"
- Arrogance
- Infidelity
- Self-centeredness
- Revenge
- Gossip
- Grandiosity

As each character defect grows (similar to the same type of be-havior-related roadblock to recovery), it causes further reaffir-mation that all is well. The ability of an alcoholic to hide from the true self and inner child is uncanny. What now occurs is the de-velopment of the fuel to support the emotional turmoil inside.

As early as the first insult to our inner self-worth, various emo-tional components begin development. Shame develops as we feel low self-worth. Denial grows, not only for the disease and be-havioral attributes, but also for the inner feelings of shame. Rage, anger, resentments, and frustrations are all emotions geared to provide ourselves with some type of self-worth. As the character defects take over our personalities, our personalities develop and respond to emotions rather than to feelings. These emotions, often hidden deep from our consciousness, begin to behave like feelings as they become the essence of our actions.

As we begin to act upon these emotions—getting even, for ex-ample, for something someone has said to or about us—we de-velop an additional sense of guilt. We are shamed by what we think about ourselves and shamed by what we believe others think about us. We act irrationally to combat the feelings of shame, and then we feel guilty for acting the way we do. With ad-ditional shame come additional defects of character and addi-tional gamesmanship—a never-ending cycle. Eventually, the only way we can find to numb the pain and hell of living as an alco-holic is to do the exact thing that allows the alcoholic mind to flourish—drink more alcohol. The shame, however, does not leave us. We find no forgiveness from ourselves and have no true connection to a Higher Power that can provide a sense of love and forgiveness. We feel lost in a world full of normal people and withdraw further into our denial.

The Compulsivity of It All

What next? The only thing left for the alcoholic is to surrender to the compulsivity of it all. There is no true decision-making left, no real right or wrong. All that is left is the means by which to try and shelter ourselves from the pain that we don't even know we have. We believe, of course, that we are perfectly normal; everyone else has problems. We have lost the ability to decide. Relying on a fallback to the numerous emotional images and personality defects, we reinforce the ability to keep going as though our standards are correct, providing a life of integrity. After all, it is easy to meet one's own standards, particularly when one has the right to lower them as the need arises.

At this stage, the compulsivity and addictions have taken complete control. Our compulsivity compels us into a variety of behavioral patterns that propel us into further alcohol use, which reaffirms our low self-worth. It is as though an alcoholic's sole existence revolves around the very thing that is killing him or her. The continued use causes the many behavioral patterns described in this book. The alcoholic mind takes further control through fear, opening the door to the unending character defects that support the problem.

Sound complicated? It is. The bottom line is that we have now lost control, and we now act compulsively, often against our own standards and most often without knowledge that our actions and thoughts are causing us, or anyone near us, pain.

The Circle Jerk

All alcoholics want to be accepted by themselves and those around them. Yet most of the actions of the alcoholic cause exactly the opposite result. As a result of this continued failure, an alcoholic subconsciously searches for a mood-altering substance or event. The pattern then repeats itself, accidentally nurturing the very scars present in the inner child through reaffirmation of rejection because of poor behaviors. Living in a state of emotional extremes, yet rarely touching on any true feelings, the alcoholic is now ready to pass the pain inadvertently along to another.

In dysfunctional families, this is most obvious through the passing of the torch to a codependent or child. As mentioned earlier, many researchers believe that both heredity and environment play a part in alcoholism. Here we, the active alcoholics, pass along the worst nightmare possible to our own loved ones. While we may buy the best of everything for our children, thinking we are providing the best life possible, we are at the same time nurturing the potential for them to become alcoholics. An alcoholic learns from an alcoholic. Perhaps it would be hard to prove a direct correlation, but indirectly, through our mistaken parenting and the scarring of our children (because of our own alcoholism), we indeed pass along at least the potential for them to become alcoholics. The best of our parents, friends, and mentors have made mistakes that have caused us pain in our lives and affected our self-esteem. It stands to reason that a distorted alcoholic mind can provide the torment of the building and tearing down of the self-esteem of our children.

How can we live by standards we would not approve for our own children yet not expect that they would follow in our footsteps? This is called denial. Children learn by copying and by example, not by word alone. Alcoholics have the uncanny ability to force their lack of realness on others. Children are extremely resilient, as we all know. Nevertheless, they are still formulating their take on the world and how they fit in, so the simplest of things can cause great joy or sorrow. Parham (1987), in *Letting God*, provides a short story to emphasize this point:

> Three generations of women—a grandmother,
> a mother and a little girl—went to a restaurant. The
> waitress took the grandmother's order, then the
> mother's, and then she asked the little girl, "What

would you like honey?" The mother immediately interrupted and said, "Oh, I'll order for her." Politely ignoring the mother, the waitress repeated her question, "Just what would you like to eat dear?" Glancing over her shoulder to see how her mother was reacting, she answered, "A hamburger." "How would you like your hamburger, with mustard, catsup, pickles, and the works?" asked the waitress. With glee she answered, clapping her hands, "The works!" The waitress then shouted out grandmother's and mother's orders, then bellowed, "And a hamburger deluxe with all the works!" The little girl turned to her mother in utter amazement and said, "Mommy, she thinks I'm real."

Again, this is the same old stereotypical, alcoholic scenario. The alcoholic gets a reprimand at work from the boss. He or she stops at the bar on the way home for a few quick drinks to calm down. Arriving home, he or she yells at the spouse for a late dinner and messy house. The spouse yells at the older daughter for not finishing her homework. The older daughter yells at her little sister for going into her room, and the little sister kicks the dog. It is a plain fact that alcoholism goes around and around, affecting everybody in its path. For every alcoholic, between five to seven other people are affected by the disease.

The Recipe

Let us step back a moment, putting the pieces of the puzzle together: children are reared by parents who have the best of intentions. Throughout childhood, events occur that for some reason are forever recorded as shameful experiences. In addition, these children, growing into adolescence, provide themselves with feelings of guilt due to what we will for the moment call normal improper behaviors. Throughout this period, these young adults now have many other rejections, reaffirmation of not being good enough, and confusion about just who they are and how they fit in the world. Quite possibly, they have been inadvertently taught alcoholic traits and use by their own parents and friends. This is the basis of psychological studies in developmental learning presented in virtually all fields of the social and therapeutic sciences. Let's stop for a moment. If we take for granted the widely held viewpoint that approximately 10 percent of our current population is afflicted with alcoholism, we must also assume that the children of this 10 percent are directly experiencing alcoholism in one way or another.

In hopes of finding our self-esteem and working toward the acceptance that we all need, alcoholics develop many personality traits deep within the soul to protect the pain and shame seldom recognized consciously. Alcohol becomes a means to be somebody. Use at this point is intended only to be a part of a social group. The theories regarding the onset of brain chemistry changes and continued use may be credible.

These children become adults. The inner turmoil increases as the sense of identity is centered around alcoholic behavior and use. Continued confirmation of low self-worth becomes more frequent as the behaviors become more inappropriate. Character defects spring up at every turn and compulsive behaviors take over. We can assume that continued use of alcohol seemingly provides the only means for escape. And the cycle continues.

These alcoholics now have children and begin to teach them alcoholism through actions. Remember, too, that most researchers now feel that the genetics of the disease have already been passed along to the children. The alcoholics have at least provided them some level of shame to harbor for years to come as a result of their self-centered and selfish actions. The cycle is now complete. Another alcoholic is born.

Breaking the Cycle

Obviously, abstinence and recovery are the means to end this vicious cycle. What may sound like a simple solution is probably the most difficult of things to accomplish. We must remember that we are dealing with a disease. It has control of the victims, not the other way around. I believe with all of my heart that the surrender to a Higher Power will open a door of spirituality. This will yield a long list of psychological benefits to the recovering alcoholic through a lifestyle of integrity and honesty. At the least, this type of lifestyle will benefit our children's future. A spiritual and honesty-based lifestyle will only benefit all those close to this recovering person, regardless of the effects on alcoholism and continued use.

The making of amends to those we have harmed further provides us recovering alcoholics with the eraser required to put behind us the actions that are causing guilt and stress. This process in itself will enable us to look beyond ourselves, and the recognition of others' needs begins to surface in our day-to-day life. Some (particularly Bufe 1998) have questioned what in the world making amends or conducting a moral inventory has to do with alcoholism. This astounds me. If one were to spend only a day or two talking with recovering alcoholics, regardless of where or how they achieved abstinence, one would come away with a sound understanding of the fact that alcoholics cause pain for themselves and other people.

The overuse and extended use of alcohol causes us all to do things of which we are not proud. How often have we heard people explain away their alcohol-related actions of the night before, even if with humor? It would take an evil mind not to feel some level of guilt for those bad actions once a person becomes involved in a recovery program. Most people are not evil. Why in the world would anyone then suggest that an alcoholic in recovery not apologize for inappropriate actions?

A friend I know well gets a lot of laughs year after year for his drunken actions. Once, he got drunk, got into a fishing boat, pushed himself out into the lake while a bunch of people looked on, and fell overboard when he tried to stand up. Many people told me about the story and how funny he was. Not one person mentioned a possibility of a drinking problem. Another time, this same friend got drunk at a country club after a day of golf. He lived on the golf course and was driving his golf cart home while drunk at the end of the night. Evidently, he overturned it and became stuck under it. As the story goes, the police arrived and finally freed him. Again, the story was told all over town as a funny and acceptable story with no mention of the possibility of a drinking problem. One last story about the same person, again while coming home from a day of golf: As he turned a sharp corner on the golf cart path next to another home, he lost control of the cart. This event happened where two little girls were selling lemonade to the other golfers. He ran into the little table, spilling the lemonade, breaking a lawn chair, and scaring the little girls so badly, they won't sell lemonade on the course ever again. I have spoken to him about it, and he does not remember any of these events, except for losing control of the cart and talking with the little girls. The other people in his foursome also talk about it with humor.

I tell this story without judgment. I include it only as an example of how we, as a society, easily ignore the possibility of drinking problems in our loved ones. It is still perceived as one of the worst insults against an individual. Furthermore, calling some men alcoholics deeply affects the integrity of their manhood. They feel there is no need to apologize for humorous behavior. And if an apology is needed, and if it is expected to show any level of intolerance for drinking, it is much harder to obtain.

Making amends has everything to do with the treatment of alcoholism. Alcoholics Anonymous places absolutely no blame on our "wrongs" or "shortcomings" as causes for alcoholism. These are the results of alcoholism. Nor does AA ignore the social influences in alcoholism. Alcoholics Anonymous does, however, present alcoholism as a disease, as has nearly every professional psychological and medical society or association.

Working with other suffering alcoholics can help us to remember whence we came. It can be used to view the changes in our own lives and help us to look into a mirror of our past. As recovering alcoholics mature into and through the various stages of recovery and put into action the Twelve Steps of Alcoholics Anonymous, they must also look toward the giving of themselves to others. The final Step in AA, the act of unselfish giving to others, is perhaps the single most important means by which to maintain an existing program of sobriety.

Giving It Back (to Keep It)

Stories abound in AA about the kind acts of the members once into recovery, from simply giving someone a ride home to an out-of-the-way location after a meeting to "Twelve Stepping" someone at three in the morning. The Big Book asks AA members to be of service to others. Often it is pointed out that giving begins as a selfish act for obtaining the good feelings associated with the giving. Giving the gift of love to another allows us to keep the love for ourselves. Helping with the gift of sobriety for another alcoholic allows us to keep the sobriety for ourselves.

The Big Book does not contain an actual requirement of helping only other alcoholics. It does, however, speak of helping others—anyone, anytime, anyplace. Only individually can we ascertain what level of helpfulness or what action we are capable of providing. At times, it may be the silent nod of a head during a conversation, compassion toward others in pain, or "just being there." This is a level of giving not offered while drinking and may include volunteer work, driving a hundred miles to help another alcoholic or friend in need, charity work, and sacrifice. Because the Big Book mainly discusses the lives and recovery of alcoholics, it is wrongly assumed that our giving must be aimed only at other alcoholics. Winston Churchill was quoted as saying, "We make a living by what we get, but we make a life by what we give."

When entering this stage of recovery, we must not try to force ourselves on others we think need our help. Once at an AA meeting, one of the participants was talking about his desire to help someone else. He said he had asked his sponsor why no one had come running up to him at one of his AA meetings asking him for his advice or help. His sponsor answered him by saying, "You don't have anything they need." This is not a stage in which we feel as though we are now recovered and the newcomers need our advice. First of all, alcoholics never recover and are always in recovery. Second, if the recovering alcoholic is not past the tendency to judge others, she or he is most certainly not ready to begin some type of self-righteous crusade. The best help an alcoholic can provide another alcoholic is to lend a compassionate ear and be a solid example of living life through God's will in service to God.

What it really involves is living a good, honest life, based on a spiritual understanding and connectedness to a Higher Power. It is the same goal I believe that most people would like to live, if only self-indulgence didn't take over. Living by example may be the only means for many to give back to others. *Not* doing some of the things we used to do when we were drinking may be another way. But in time, any "good person" will find a need and submit to efforts to be of service to fellow humans. This act of compassion and sobriety will provide a lifetime of rewards and a lifetime of happiness, to both the alcoholic and the codependent, as long as they work the program.

"SHAMEOBOROS"

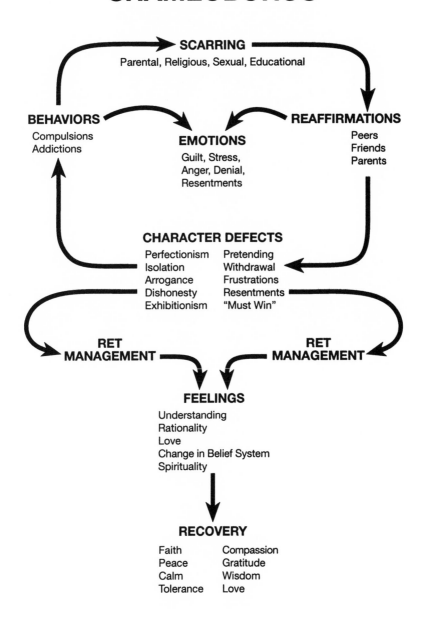

Chapter 8

Laughing, Listening, and Learning

One of the most important changes in recovery is finding the ability to enjoy life again. This includes not only the newfound talent to listen, but once again to laugh. This acts as a lifetime support to the recovery process. We can learn to listen to others, to listen to ourselves, to laugh at others, and to laugh at ourselves.

For example, in my own life, for the first time, I have begun to laugh even when I am alone. I now listen to the lyrics of songs. When others are telling me their side of a story, I no longer spend those moments formulating my response. One of the problems with AA meetings is that many of the meetings are frequented by newcomers. This can cause a depressing group at first glance. Upon further involvement in AA, one finds that without the newcomer to listen to and to help, we have little chance of continued recovery.

For newcomers, sad, scared, and lonely, to walk into one of these meetings, I can't help but wonder what they sometimes see that keeps them coming back. This alone is reason to frequent as many meetings as possible until one is found that also produces enjoyment and social benefits.

My home group, for example, is filled with laughter at virtually every meeting. Listening to the many stories of our members is often cause for great personal reflection, yet also great humor. The funniest thing is that I hear outrageous stories about past behavior and realize that I understand it perfectly.

In this vein, I present a few of the stories I have found humorous or intriguing, and a few of the jokes I have heard through AA meetings and friends. I hope they help bring a smile to the face of the reader.

An Alcoholic Goes to Church—Anonymous

One sad and lonely day an alcoholic decided to go to church. He sat in the front row and prayed hard for help. He said, "Dear Lord, please help me through this agonizing life. Just give me a sign, any sign at all that you are there and I will know I can make it. Help me, O Lord, I just need to know that you are real, that you are there for me, that my prayers don't fall on deaf ears."

He kept praying, over and over again, staring at the Christ figure on the crucifix hanging on the back of the church wall. "Please, Lord, just a small sign and I will never question you again. I will change my life forever. I only need one sign; just help me to believe, please, Lord."

After a while, the Christ figure slowly moved his head, looked directly at the alcoholic, and winked. The alcoholic, startled, looked up at the Christ figure and said, "Do it again!"

An Alcoholic Goes to Heaven—Anonymous

An alcoholic was giving his confession to a priest during a terrible storm when lightning struck the building and killed both men. They were met at the gates of heaven by St. Peter, who took them both on a tour and showed them their new homes. The first stop was the alcoholic's new home. It was a quaint little two-bedroom home, with a small garden out front, just down the street from the beach. The next stop was the priest's new home. It was a ten-thousand-square-foot mansion, complete with maid and butler service, a swimming pool, and tennis courts overlooking the ocean. The priest felt guilty and asked why he had such a wonderful new home and the alcoholic did not. St. Peter answered,

"Oh, we get lots of recovered alcoholics up here, but you are special. We hardly ever get any priests."

A Walk on the Beach—Anonymous

An alcoholic had died and gone to heaven after living the better part of his life in turmoil, full of problems and unhappiness before he had entered recovery. Once in heaven, he had the opportunity to spend some time with God to ask any questions he had regarding his life on earth. He asked, "Why was it that you were not always there for me? Even though once I had entered recovery, I prayed to you many times each day, you still were not always there for me." He went on, "I remember often that when walking on the beach alone, when things were going well for me you were always there. I could look behind me in the sand and there would be two sets of footprints in the sand. I knew the other set was yours." He then said, " But when things were going bad and my life was in turmoil, I would look back and there was only one set of footprints, and I knew you were not there." God interrupted, "Oh but my child, I was there. I was just carrying you."

Jump Off the Bridge—Modified from humor appearing in the *Tri-State Fax Times*

Paul (an alcoholic) and Jim, his friend, are in the bar watching the local news when suddenly a story is told of a man standing on the edge of the bridge threatening to jump. The television station cuts to the bridge and begins coverage of the full story. Paul says to Jim, "I'll bet you ten bucks the guy won't jump." Jim says to Paul, "It's a bet."

They continue watching the story unfold, when suddenly, the man jumps to his death. "You win," says Paul. "Here's your ten bucks." Jim tells Paul that he can't take his money because he saw the man jump on the early edition of the news. "I watched it too," says Paul. "But I just couldn't believe he would jump a second time."

The Nuclear Reactor—Craig McPherson

A nuclear engineer was retiring from his duties running the reactor for over thirty years. As this was an important job and took specific expertise, he invited his top two managers into the control room before he left, for one solid piece of advice. Both of these men were alcoholics. He told them, "Remember, no matter what else you do, you can never put too much water in the reactor, or there will be dire consequences, and you must put it in every hour on the hour." After some fond farewells, he departed and left the men to attend to their duties. As the first hour went by quickly, the bell sounded, and the two men hurried to get the water. As they met at the reactor, one was holding a cup of water, the other a hose. One said to the other, "What are you doing with only a small cup of water?" The other man answered, "He said you can't put in too much, so I got just a little bit of water to put in." "Oh, no," replied the other alcoholic. "He said you can never put in too much; that means you can put in all you want."

The Alcoholic on a Hike—Bob S., AA convention, 1989

An alcoholic decided to go on a nice long hike one day to meditate and think about his trust in God. Suddenly, as he got just a little too close to the edge of the cliff, the bottom fell out from underneath him, and he fell. The canyon was a half mile below him but luckily, as he was falling, he grabbed a small branch growing out of the side of the mountain.

As he was holding on for dear life, he began to yell, "Hello! Anyone up there? Help, help." With each second, his grip was loosening, and the alcoholic began to pray, "Lord, please help me, please save me, Lord, and I will forever do anything you ask of me. Oh, Lord, I beg of you to help me."

The man was now within a minute of falling to his death and his prayers became more promising: "Dear God, I ask you to forgive me for my sins and know that I am now your servant. If you can just save me, I will do whatever you ask of me for the rest of my life. I will become the living example of doing your will."

Just then a loud but humble voice came from above: "Let go of the branch." The alcoholic replied, "What? Who is it? Help me!" The voice answered again, "Let go of the branch, and I will catch you." "Who is this? Who's there?" the alcoholic yelled. "It is I, my child, your God, your Father. Let go of the branch and I will catch you."

The alcoholic began yelling again, "Is there anyone else up there?"

Jesus Knows Who He Is—Ed J., Recovery Is Forever series, *Hope*, 1981

Once when Jesus was speaking to the masses, an alcoholic had a front-row seat in the audience. After an hour-long talk, Jesus asked the man, "Who am I?"

The alcoholic, wanting to impress Jesus with his knowledge, answered, "You are the esoterical enigma of the successful battle of psychological manifestations of good over evil, the paranormal representation of the third realm of religious righteousness." Jesus looked at the man in complete puzzlement and said, "What?"

Jesus in a Bar—Attributed to Father Martin

An alcoholic goes to his favorite drinking establishment and has his usual seat at one end of the bar. Next to him sits a blind man and a handicapped man. As the evening progresses and they all begin to talk and buy each other drinks, the alcoholic notices a man sitting at the other end of the bar in a long white robe, with a beard and long hair. He says to the bartender, "That man down at the end of the bar looks like Jesus." The bartender answers, "It is Jesus. He comes in here all the time now, has a couple beers, and heals people."

The blind man, after hearing this, tells the bartender that he wants to buy a drink for the man who looks like Jesus. After the man finishes the drink, the handicapped man tells the bartender the same thing. "Send Jesus a drink, on me," he says. And after the man finishes that drink, the alcoholic tells the bartender to buy Jesus another drink from him.

After Jesus finishes the last drink, he gets up and walks over to thank the group for their kindness. He first puts his hands on the blind man's temple, and the blind man suddenly jumps up, runs around the room, and yells with joy, "I can see, I can see! Thank you, Jesus. I can see."

Then Jesus puts his hands on the handicapped man's legs, and he immediately starts walking for the first time in twenty years. "Thank you, Jesus, thank you so much," he says.

After that, Jesus holds out his hand to thank the alcoholic. But the alcoholic jumps up from his seat and yells, "Stay away from me," and runs out of the bar, preferring not to be healed.

Jury Duty—Modified from humor appearing in the *Tri-State Fax Times*

An alcoholic is called for jury duty but does not want to be involved. He tries to think of something he can tell the judge so he can be excused from his role as a juror.

On the first day, the judge goes around the room and asks if there is any reason anyone should be excused. The alcoholic says, "Yes sir, Your Honor, I really don't want to be away from my job for that long." The judge is silent for a few seconds, then asks the man, "Can't they do without you at work?" The alcoholic takes several deep breaths and, looking down at the floor, replies, "Yes, sir, they can. But I don't want them to find that out."

Who Took God?—Anonymous

Two friends who were known to be the town drunks were arrested again one night for disorderly conduct and drunkenness. All of the local police in this small town knew the men, and the judge was tired of seeing them so regularly. After they had slept off the drunk for the night, the men were brought in front of the judge one at a time the next morning.

When the first man was brought forward, the judge thought he might try something different this time. He had seen the man many times before and knew personally that nothing had helped the man stop drinking in the past. This time he spent a long time talking with the man, offering compassion and wisdom.

Eventually the judge said, "You have got to find God. God is the only thing that I believe can save you now, and you must find Him right away." The judge told the man, "I am simply going to let you go this time, but I beg you to spend some time looking for God." The judge continued, "If you find God, I promise you that all of your troubles will go away. If you don't find God, I can also promise you that your troubles will likely continue, and I will be the one who has to punish you."

After listening intently for some time, trying to understand in his drunkenness the importance of what the judge was saying, the drunk was returned to his jail cell. His friend, who had been waiting for his return in his own state of fear, immediately asked, "What happened? What did the judge say? What did the judge tell you?"

The drunk replied, "They think we took God, and we better find him right away."

Two Brothers—Anonymous

An alcoholic went to the same bar every night for years. Each time he would order the same thing for every round of drinks: two beers and two shots of bourbon. Every time a new bartender would start work at the bar, the alcoholic would have to explain that one set of drinks was for him and the other set of drinks was for his brother, back home in Ireland. Every time he took a sip, he would make a toast to his brother, drink part of one of the drinks, put it down, then drink part of the other drink, and on and on.

One day the man sat down and ordered only one drink and one shot. The bartender, seeing this, thought immediately that something terrible might have happened to the man's brother and offered his condolences. The man replied, "Oh no, everything is fine with my dear ol' brother back in Ireland. But I just found out that I am an alcoholic, so now I can only drink for him."

A Fly in Your Drink—Rob M.

An alcoholic and his nonalcoholic friend went into their favorite bar to have a few drinks. After the bartender set the drinks in front of them, two flies were flying around, and one of them landed in each of the drinks. The friend immediately grabbed the fly out of his drink and threw it to the floor. The alcoholic gently lifted the fly out of his drink and, bringing it to eye level, yelled, "Spit it out! Spit it out!"

The Plane Ride—Peter B.

An alcoholic took a trip for his yearly vacation and was put on a plane that ended up heading into a severe thunderstorm. As the bumpy and extremely scary flight went on, he began to order drink after drink. After about an hour, there was a loud bang and the pilot came on over the intercom. He said, "Folks, we just lost our number one engine, so the flight may get a little bumpier. We apologize for the inconvenience, and we may be a little late on our arrival."

The alcoholic proceeded to order a couple more drinks. After another half hour, another loud bang occurred, and the pilot made another announcement: "Hello, folks, we just lost our number two engine, so things may get a little rough the rest of the ride. We apologize for any inconvenience, as this may add another half hour to our flight time."

Again, the alcoholic ordered a couple of drinks. It wasn't more than fifteen minutes later when again a loud noise came from the rear of the plane, and the plane began to shake. The pilot came on again and said, "Hello again. We just lost our number three engine, so we'll have to ride out the storm for the rest of the way. We apologize for any inconvenience, but we will be about an hour late." The alcoholic ordered a double.

About five minutes later, the loudest sound yet came from the rear of the plane, followed by a whirling noise. The pilot blurted over the intercom, "Folks, we just lost our number four engine; please fasten your seat belts." The alcoholic looked at the person next to him and said, "At this rate, we'll be up here all night."

Ten Shots—Modified from humor appearing in the *Tri-State Fax Times*

A man runs into a bar and orders ten shots of whiskey at the same time. The bartender quickly pours the shots, and the man drinks them without delay, one at a time. The bartender asks the man why in the world he is in such a hurry and why he is drinking so fast. The man tells the bartender, "You would drink as fast as I am if you had what I had." "Oh my," said the bartender. "What do you have?" The man answered, "One dollar."

An Alcoholic Dreams—Jim B., from a lecture at Hazelden in 1997

I dreamed one night I passed away and left the world behind,
I started down that lonely trail, some of my friends to find.
I came to a signboard on the trail, the directions it did tell:
KEEP RIGHT to go to heaven, TURN LEFT to go to hell.

I hadn't been too good on earth, just a hopeless boozing rake,
And knew there at the crossroads the path I'd have to take.
So I started on that rocky path that leads to Satan's place,
And I shook without knowing just what I'd have to face.

Old Satan met me at the gate, "What's your name my friend?"
I said, "I'm just old sober Sam that's come to a very sad end."

He glanced through some yellow files, "You've made a mistake
  I fear.
You're listed as an alcoholic, we do not want you here."

I said, "I'm looking for my friends," and a smile stole o'er his face.
"If your friends are alcoholics, they're in the other place."
So I went back the way I came, till the crossroads I did see.
Then turned right to heaven, as happy as I could be.

St. Peter smiled and said, "Come in, for you I have a berth.
You are an alcoholic, you've been through hell on earth."
I saw Al, Dud, and ol' Pat too; Bill R., and a friend called Bell.
And brother was I tickled, 'cause I thought they'd gone to hell.

So brothers, all take warning, learn something from my trip.
You've got a place in heaven, if you try hard not to slip.
If someone tempts you with drug or drink when you're not
  feeling well,
Tell him you're going to heaven, and he can go to hell!

I Am Today—Ed J., Recovery Is Forever series, *Hope,* 1981

I am today, I greeted you with the crimson of dawn.
I met you with a challenge of hours yet to come.

I am a friend as old as the years you know.
I am today, in one small sprinkling of time I should become
  yesterday.

I shall have lived and looked and lingered yet a while with
  you, and then be gone forever.
Look at me well for I am your time of promise.

Do not use me lightly for I affect your tomorrows.
Remember me for what I am, opportunity for whatever you
  may choose.

I am today, I have lived as long as man.
A thousand times a thousand times, since God made night
  and day.

I have seen the earth green with the grace of peace, and
  also black with the curse of war.

I have held the fragile promises of men until tomorrow,
then watched them shattered with disrespect.

I am today, I am no babe in the woods, no wide-eyed child
of time.

I am your hope, for I give you your chance to remake your
yesterdays.

The Doctor—Modified from humor appearing in the *Tri-State Fax Times*

Charlie, the alcoholic, gets a call from his doctor. The doctor says to him that he has good news and he has bad news. Charlie says, "Oh, no. Well, give me the good news first." The doctor says, "You have an incurable disease, and you will be dead in twenty-four hours." "Oh, my God," cries Charlie. "What's the bad news?" "I was supposed to call you yesterday," replies the doctor.

CHAPTER 9

SLOGANS FOR RECOVERY

Alcoholics Anonymous is threaded with many slogans aimed at keeping the program in front of the alcoholic in an easily identifiable way. Originally given birth by Bill Wilson himself in the Big Book and at many of the AA conventions at which he spoke, slogans have become the mainstay of AA meetings, the AA program, and in most references to Alcoholics Anonymous. As they speak for themselves, only simple descriptions have been included. This chapter offers just a small sampling of some of the slogans used.

The most complete list I have found to date is located in a book by Bill Pittman, *Stepping Stones to Recovery*. He includes nearly thirty pages of the most comprehensive list of slogans available. (His fine work was part of the impetus for my first step into recovery.) Pittman provides to the recovery movement what Bill Wilson provided to Alcoholics Anonymous—a thorough and complete understanding of alcoholism as a disease and the need to give back what you have taken away.

On the need to live in the moment and not worry about yesterday or tomorrow:

1. "A person with one eye on yesterday and one eye on tomorrow is living cockeyed."
2. "One day at a time."

3. "Live in the now."
4. "Let go of old ideas."
5. "This too shall pass."
6. "First things first."
7. "Just for today."
8. "Living in the here and now."

On giving up control and turning things over to your Higher Power:

1. "But for the grace of God."
2. "Let go and let God."
3. "Turn it over."
4. "You will be amazed."
5. "Willingness is the key."
6. "God is never late."
7. "Quit playing God."
8. "Our need is God's opportunity."
9. "God will never give you more than you can handle."
10. "God will only do for you what you can't do for yourself."

On not allowing our mind to think and overreact:

1. "Think, think, think."
2. "K.I.S.S. = Keep it simple, stupid."
3. "Identify, don't compare."
4. "Take it easy."
5. "Wherever you go, there you are."
6. "Replace guilt with gratitude."
7. "Don't intellectualize. Utilize."

On working the program in any way we can, with faith:

1. "Act as if."
2. "Expect miracles."
3. "Who is the one who moved, if God seems too far away?"

4. "Faith is spelled A-C-T-I-O-N."
5. "Faith without works is dead."
6. "Don't quit five minutes before the miracle."
7. "I came, I came to, I came to believe."
8. "You are not alone."
9. "Count your blessings."
10. "I can't handle it, God. I give it to you."
11. "More will be revealed."
12. "When man listens, God speaks."

On sobriety:

1. "To keep it, you have to give it away."
2. "Try not to place conditions on your sobriety."
3. "What goes around, comes around."
4. "Let it begin with me."
5. "Practice an attitude of gratitude."
6. "Have a good day, unless you've made other plans."
7. "You can't give away what you don't have."
8. "Our worst day in sobriety is better than our best day drinking."

On the Alcoholics Anonymous program:

1. "Keep coming back. It works if you work it."
2. "Sobriety is a journey, not a destination."
3. "Stick with the winners."
4. "Take what you need and leave the rest behind."
5. "AA = Altered Minds."
6. "No one is too drunk for the program."
7. "If you don't want to slip, avoid slippery places."
8. "Bring the body and the mind will follow."
9. "Clean up your side of the street."
10. "No one is too dumb for the program, but many are too smart."
11. "Ninety meetings in ninety days."
12. "Don't drink, read the Big Book, and go to meetings."

13.   "When all else fails, listen to your sponsor."
14.   "It works. It really does!"
15.   "Be part of the solution, not part of the problem."
16.   "No pain, no gain."
17.   "Pass it on."
18.   "It's in the Book."
19.   "This is a selfish program."
20.   "What you see here, what you hear here, when you leave here, let it stay here."
21.   "Principles before personalities."
22.   "The surest way to AA is to first go all the way to hell."
23.   "You need a meeting."

On not drinking:

1.   "Nothing is so bad that a drink will not make worse."
2.   "You are exactly where God wants you to be."
3.   "Drink, drank, drunk."
4.   "Remember your last drunk."
5.   "To thine own self be true."
6.   "Bend your knees before you bend your elbow."
7.   "There is no chemical solution to a spiritual problem."
8.   "Your best sponsor is the Big Book."
9.   "You are not alone."
10.   "Let go of old ideas."
11.   "Change is a process, not an event."
12.   "Stay sober for yourself."
13.   "Call your sponsor before, not after, you take a drink."

On the alcoholic mind-set:

1.   "Poor me, poor me, pour me another drink."
2.   "We are only as sick as our secrets."
3.   "Utilize, don't analyze."
4.   "Pain is constant. Suffering is a choice."
5.   "You know you are sharing a feeling when you do not need a reply."

6. "H.O.W. = Honesty, Openness, Willingness."
7. "We are not responsible *for* our family. We are responsible *to* our family."
8. "E.G.O. = Edge God Out."
9. "Don't let them live rent free in your head."
10. "Let go of old ideas."
11. "You can act yourself into right thinking easier than you can think yourself into right acting."
12. "Stinking thinking."
13. "Pain is the fire that burns the heart pure."
14. "Sick and tired of being sick and tired."

On the disease:

1. "Cunning, baffling, and powerful."
2. "Alcoholism is an equal-opportunity destroyer."
3. "The only disease that tells us we are all right."
4. "Rule 62: Don't take yourself so seriously."
5. "Some people are so successful in recovery, they turn out to be almost as good as they thought they were while drinking."
6. "Alcoholism is incurable, progressive, and fatal."
7. "Like a wire stripped of its insulation."

Chapter 10

Prayer and Meditation

The most important ingredient in maintaining sobriety and finding an inner peace is a connection with your Higher Power. The only means available to us to achieve this connection is to pray and meditate. As a child, I could say in my mind the words I had been taught, while at the same time actually thinking about totally different, and at times inappropriate, things. In recovery, I have found a way to pray that allows a closeness with my Higher Power, whom I call God. It is simple: I just talk. I get on my knees, and I talk to Him about what is going on in my life.

This may sound corny and perhaps a little self-serving. However, any means that works for you is the right way to pray. I find myself praying in the shower, praying while driving, praying during work, or anytime at all. And I pray for all kinds of things. I ask God to give me patience, to help me forgive, to help me remove my defects of character, and even to help the little girl on the nightly news who was beaten by her father. It doesn't matter. It is what is on my mind at the time.

Each and every day starts with a period of inner focus, a period where I sit quietly. After taking several deep breaths, I try to clear my mind of any thoughts. I have a word I use that reminds me of God's presence, and if a thought comes to my mind, I say that word over and over again in my head until I refocus on my inner self. Some call this meditation. I call it a way in which to calm myself, focusing on the need to begin a connection with my Higher Power.

Once I have accomplished this calmness, I say the Serenity Prayer. I ask God to help me understand the things that I can control and to accept the things He needs to control for me. Then I use one or more of the many resource books I have collected that contain prayers and meditations for me to read out loud. Some days, I need to use the more religious and scriptural writings, including, at times, the Bible. Some days, I need to use the writings of other alcoholics in recovery. I use the Big Book prayers, and I use prayers from many different faiths—from American Indian to the Paramahansa Yogananda. It doesn't matter.

Many of these books have been written expressly to use one day at a time, with a different writing for every day. I may read the specific date from several books; I may read the entire week out of the same book. Sometimes I read my favorites over and over again. I can't remember a morning where I haven't started with the "Yesterday, Today, Tomorrow" reading out of the *Twenty-Four Hours a Day* book, as I have always had difficulty in frequently getting away from the moment. Again, it doesn't matter. This is what I do, not what you should do. The point is only that you do something. God talks to you only when you listen. Generally speaking, we find ourselves listening only when we make a conscious effort to let Him know we are there.

Once I have finished my readings, usually lasting about half an hour, I begin my personal prayers. These prayers are just that—personal. The subject matter runs the gamut. For the first time in my life, much time is taken praying for others instead of for my own needs. I also make a point each morning to pray in gratitude for something God has done for me and to pray for someone who I feel has wronged me or whom I simply do not like. By the time I ask something for myself, I often have realized that I am completely ready to accept God's will and only ask for that knowledge. In hopes of helping with the notion of prayer as I was once helped, I have included a few of my favorite prayers and meditations in this chapter.

At times, I find myself needing a formality in my moment with God. At those times, I use the strict and formal Christian prayers many of us have known for years. Other times, I feel a need for a subject matter from another author. Then I use contemporary writings. I have included both and offer them to you as a means to find your connection to your own Higher Power, as you understand Him.

It is impossible to acknowledge the sources of all of these readings, but perhaps those people I have left out will be made happy by the thought that I believe their readings truly came from God.

Desiderata—Max Ehrmann

Go placidly amid the noise and the haste, and remember what peace there may be in silence. As far as possible, without surrender, be on good terms with all persons. Speak your truth quietly and clearly; and listen to others, even dull and ignorant; they, too, have their story.

Avoid loud and aggressive persons. They are vexations to the spirit. If you compare yourself with others, you may become vain and bitter, for always there will be greater and lesser persons than yourself. Enjoy your achievements as well as your plans.

Keep interested in your own career, however humble; it is a real possession in the changing fortunes of time. Exercise caution in your business affairs, for the world is full of trickery. But let this not blind you to what virtue there is; many persons strive for high ideals; and everywhere life is full of heroism.

Be yourself. Especially, do not feign affection. Neither be cynical about love, for in the face of all aridity and disenchantment it is perennial as the grass.

Take kindly the counsel of the years, gracefully surrendering the things of youth. Nurture strength of spirit to shield you in sudden misfortune. But do not distress yourself with imaginings. Many fears are born of fatigue and loneliness. Beyond a wholesome discipline, be gentle with yourself.

You are a child of the universe, no less than the trees and the stars; you have a right to be here. Whether or not it is clear to you, no doubt the universe is unfolding as it should.

Therefore, be at peace with God, whatever you conceive Him to be, and whatever your labor and aspirations, in the noisy confusion of life, keep peace with your soul.

With all of the sham, drudgery, and broken dreams, it is still a beautiful world. Be careful, but strive to be happy.

The Serenity Prayer

> God grant me the serenity
> To accept the things I cannot change,
> The courage to change the things I can,
> And the wisdom to know the difference.

Sanskrit Proverb— *Twenty-Four Hours a Day*

> Look to this day,
> For it is life,
> The very life of life.
> In its brief course lie all
> The realities and verities of existence,
> The bliss of growth,
> The splendor of action,
> The glory of power—
>
> For yesterday is but a dream,
> And tomorrow is only a vision,
> But today, well lived,
> Makes every yesterday a dream of happiness
> And every tomorrow a vision of hope.
>
> Look well, therefore, to this day.

Yesterday, Today, and Tomorrow— *Twenty-Four Hours a Day,* July 29, 30, 31

There are two days in every week about which we should not worry, two days which should be kept from fear and apprehension. One of these days is yesterday, with its mistakes and cares, its faults and blunders, its aches and pains. Yesterday has passed forever beyond our control. All the money in the world cannot bring back yesterday. We cannot undo a single act we performed. We cannot erase a single word we said. Yesterday is gone beyond recall. *Do I still worry about what happened yesterday? . . .*

The other day we should not worry about is tomorrow, with its possible adversities, its burdens, its large promise, and perhaps its poor performance. Tomorrow is also beyond our immediate control. Tomorrow's sun will rise, either in splendor or behind a mask of clouds, but it will rise. Until it does, we have no stake in tomorrow, for it is as yet unborn. *Do I still worry too much about tomorrow? . . .*

This leaves only one day—today. Anyone can fight the battles of just one day. It is only when you and I add the burden of those two awful eternities, yesterday and tomorrow, that we break down. It is not the experience of today that drives us mad. It is the remorse or bitterness for something which happened yesterday or the dread of what tomorrow may bring. Let us therefore do our best to live but one day at a time. *Am I living one day at a time?*

Thank You, God, for AA—Bill Pittman, *Stepping Stones to Recovery*

Thank you, dear God, for another day;
The chance to live in a decent way;
To feel again the joy of living,
And happiness that comes from giving.
Thank you for friends who can understand
And the peace that flows from Your loving hand.
Help me to wake to the morning sun

With the prayer, "Today Thy will be done,"
For with Your help I will find the way.
Thank you again, dear God, for AA.

The Lord's Prayer

> Our Father, Who art in heaven, hallowed be Thy
>   name.
> Thy kingdom come, Thy will be done,
> on earth as it is in heaven.
> Give us this day our daily bread,
> and forgive us our trespasses,
> as we forgive those who trespass against us.
> And lead us not into temptation,
> but deliver us from evil,
> for Thine is the kingdom, and the power, and the
>   glory forever and ever.
> Amen

The Prayer of St. Francis of Assisi— *Twelve Steps and Twelve Traditions*, p. 99

Lord, make me a channel of thy peace—

that where there is hatred, I may bring love—

that where there is wrong, I may bring the spirit of forgiveness—

that where there is discord, I may bring harmony—

that where there is error, I may bring truth—

that where there is doubt, I may bring faith—

that where there is despair, I may bring hope—

that where there are shadows, I may bring light—

that where there is sadness, I may bring joy.

Lord, grant that I may seek

rather to comfort than to be comforted—

to understand, than to be understood—

to love, than to be loved.

For it is by self-forgetting that one finds.

It is by forgiving that one is forgiven.

It is by dying that one awakens to to Eternal Life. Amen.

Live for Today—Joe McPherson

> Live for today, not tomorrow.
>
> For if everyone lived for endless tomorrows,
>
> everyone would be left with empty yesterdays.

Third Step Prayer—*Alcoholics Anonymous,* p. 63

God, I offer myself to Thee—to build with me and to do with me as Thou wilt. Relieve me of the bondage of self, that I may better do Thy will. Take away my difficulties, that victory over them may bear witness to those I would help of Thy Power, Thy Love, and Thy Way of life. May I do Thy will always!

Seventh Step Prayer—*Alcoholics Anonymous,* p. 76

My Creator, I am now willing that you should have all of me, good and bad. I pray that you now remove from me every single defect of character which stands in the way of my usefulness to you and my fellows. Grant me strength, as I go out from here, to do your bidding. Amen.

For the Grace of Humility—*My Prayer Book,* p. 75

Most righteous and everliving God, whose standard is perfection and whose justice punishes sin . . . I bow before Your majesty, and humble myself in Your holy presence. Make me understand that the way of the sinner leads to eternal disaster. Impress Your will on my heart. Grant me true repentance. For Jesus' sake forgive my sins and shortcomings, my ignorance and hardness of heart.

Give me grace to pattern my conduct after Your Word. Destroy in me the spirit of pride. . . . Preserve me from the spirit of the Pharisee who would make himself more important than others. Help my heart to be merciful to all people. And by Your mercy grant that I may finally enjoy the light and joy of heaven.

Freedom to Be Unique — *Touchstones,* July 4

Each of us is a unique creature and has special gifts to contribute to the world. We were not free in the past because we were slaves to addictions and codependency. We know that freedom is precious. Compulsions and pressures for conformity stifle our creativity and erode our dignity. As we grow in our relationship to our Higher Power, we get stronger and more balanced in our unique qualities. Some of us have a talent for empathizing with others, some for writing and art, others for sports and physical activities.

There is no recipe that prescribes exactly what kind of [people] we should be. Because we're free, it is our creative task to discover what it means to be honest . . . contributing [people] within our circumstances. We don't get a list of directions for each day, only guidelines for progress. Through groups and friendships, we develop in our own ways and learn to respect each other's freedom.

Overcoming Perfectionism —
Jim Conway, *Men's Devotional Bible,* p. 1,307

It may sound strange, but frequently a person with a poor self-image tends to be a perfectionist. If you feel inadequate, unsure of other people's love, then you start saying to yourself, "If only I try harder, if I achieve more, if I'm a better person, then . . . other people will love me."

Perfectionism, however, is never satisfied! If you can't accept any good things that people say of you, then even if you do great things, your accomplishments will not satisfy that insatiable, gulping appetite of perfectionism.

The perfectionist never asks the question, "How much is enough? At what point can I stop? How much perfection will I have to accomplish to receive the love from people that I really want?" There never is an end; only God is perfect.

The perfectionism also fails to realize that God loves unconditionally. God doesn't withhold love until we arrive at perfection. He loves us while we are growing and even while we are his enemies. His love enables us to change and mature.

Tragically, perfectionists think other people will like them better for their perfection. But truthfully, it is just the opposite. People like to be around flexible, tolerant, imperfect people—like themselves. Perfect people frighten them and cause them to withdraw.

Perfectionists are always paying a debt. The irony is that no one is asking that any debt be paid. Perfectionists do all of this because their poor self-images manipulate them into doing it.

Sharing—Sally Coleman and Nancy Hull-Mast, *Our Best Days,*
April 30

Sharing our problems is one way to get rid of our internal garbage. It has been said that we are as sick as the secret we keep. . . . If we have turned our wills and lives over to the care of God, we have nothing to be afraid of.

By honestly sharing what we think and feel, we are admitting that we own these thoughts and feelings, and they are part of our lives. Anything that we own we can give away. What we get in return is freedom.

Today let me have the courage to share a secret fear.

God's Answer—Neale Donald Walsch, *Meditations from Conversations with God,* January 3

[God's words through Neale Donald Walsch:]
I have always been here to help you, I am here now. You don't have to find the answers on your own. You never had to.

Develop Your Compassion—Richard Carlson, *Don't Sweat the Small Stuff...*, p. 17

Nothing helps build our perspective more than developing compassion for others. Compassion is a sympathetic feeling. It involves the willingness to put yourself in someone else's shoes, to take the focus off yourself and to imagine what it's like to be in someone else's predicament, and simultaneously, to feel love for that person. It's the recognition that other people's problems, their pain and frustrations, are every bit as real as our own—often far worse. In recognizing this fact and trying to offer some assistance, we open our own hearts and greatly enhance our sense of gratitude.

Compassion is something you can develop with practice. It involves two things: intention and action. Intention simply means you remember to open your heart to others; you expand what and who matters, from yourself to other people. Action is simply the "what you do about it." You might donate a little money or time (or both) on a regular basis to a cause near to your heart. Or perhaps you'll offer a beautiful smile and genuine "hello" to the people you meet on the street. It's not so important what you do, just that you do something. As Mother Teresa reminds us, "We cannot do great things on this earth. We can only do small things with great love."

Compassion develops your sense of gratitude by taking your attention off the little things that most of us have learned to take too seriously. When you take time, often, to reflect on the miracle of life—the miracle that you are even able to read this book— the gift of sight, of love, and all the rest, it can help to remind you that many of the things that you think of as "big stuff" are really just "small stuff" that you are *turning into* big stuff.

Foundation for Life—Bill Wilson, *As Bill Sees It*, p. 33

We discover that we receive guidance for our lives to just about the extent that we stop making demands upon God to give it to us on order and on our terms.

In praying, we ask simply that throughout the day God place in us the best understanding of His will that we can have for that day, and that we be given the grace by which we may carry it out.

There is a direct linkage among self-examination, meditation, and prayer. Taken separately, these practices can bring much relief and benefit. But when they are logically related and interwoven, the result is an unshakable foundation for life.

"Help Me" Prayer—Dale Mitchel

Dear Lord, I have had enough. I cannot run my life myself. I beg you to take it over for me, to help me put things in the order that would please you. Give me only the will to find the will, to accept your will. Amen.

Rejecting Shame—Melody Beattie, *The Language of Letting Go,* February 3

Shame can be a powerful force in our life. It is the trademark of dysfunctional families.

Authentic, legitimate *guilt* is the feeling or thought that what we did is not okay. It indicates that our behavior needs to be corrected or altered, or an amend needs to be made.

Shame is an overwhelming negative sense that who we are isn't okay. Shame is a no-win situation. We can change our behaviors, but we can't change who we are. Shame can propel us deeper into self-defeating and sometimes self-destructive behaviors.

What are the things that can cause us to feel shame? We may feel ashamed when we have a problem or someone we love has a problem. We may feel ashamed for making mistakes or for succeeding. We may feel ashamed about certain feelings or thoughts. We may feel ashamed when we have fun, feel good, or are vulnerable enough to show ourselves to others. Some of us feel ashamed just for being.

Shame is a spell others put on us to control us, to keep us playing our part in dysfunctional systems. It is a spell many of us have learned to put on ourselves.

Learning to reject shame can change the quality of our life. It's okay to be who we are. We are good enough. Our feelings are okay. Our past is okay. It's okay to have problems, make mistakes, and struggle to find our path. It's okay to be human and cherish our humanness.

Accepting ourselves is the first step toward recovery. Letting go of shame about who we are is the next important step.

Today, I will watch for signs that I have fallen into shame's trap. If I get hooked into shame, I will get myself out by accepting myself and affirming that it's okay to be who I am.

Having Love —*Day by Day*, August 7

The program is not a religious affair, but a beloved spiritual fellowship. Spirituality is a manifestation of the living God. If we take explicit directions from the emotion-divorced voice within ourselves, we find freedom.

Many of us discovered that our former . . . experiences left us with a residue of wreckage. Having exposed ourselves to their effects for several years, we found ourselves having to scrape the mire off our souls to let in the sunshine of the spirit.

When we line ourselves up with the spirit of love, we find that it leaves no residue. Do I have the spirit of love?

Father, let me make each of my decisions today in accordance with the direction that is coming to me through love's eyes.

Saying No —Karen Casey and Martha Vanceburg, *The Promise of a New Day*, July 10

In the early years it often seems to the growing human child that most of civilization consists of saying "No!" Parents and teachers sometimes act as if that were so. Everyone who has ever raised, taught, or cared for small children knows what a totally involving commitment it is, and knows, too, that it is impossible to do everything right. Parents struggle with their children over trivia; teachers may punish small infractions and ignore large ones. Humans raise humans; if it were possible to do it perfectly, surely we would all be angels by now.

Often we are fully grown before we're able to let go of some of the rigid rules we learned. Often it may seem that our task as adults is to *un*learn what we learned as infants. The "housebreaking" that has made us considerate to one another and peaceable in adjusting our differences may also have squelched some of our capacity for feeling.

We can recover our feeling selves, without violating the rules of society, if we can remember not to be afraid. Feelings are only frightening when we repress them; when we let them out and let them sweep through, then they are gone.

Finding Peace—Norman Vincent Peale, *Positive Thinking Every Day,* March 16

Saturate your thoughts with peaceful experiences, peaceful words and ideas, and ultimately you will have a storehouse of peace-producing experiences to which you may turn for refreshment and renewal of your spirit.

Seeking Balance— *Touchstones,* August 6

We seek balance in our lives. The greatest sign of unmanageability in our past was the unbalanced lives we led. This is no easy lesson to learn. We are inclined to grasp for a single answer, thinking we now have the key insight to a happier way of life. . . . Many of us have pursued our happiness in work with little time for anything else. Perhaps, for some, the singing and playing we have done were part of our addiction or participating with someone else in their addiction. This makes it feel dangerous or frightening now to be playful in recovery.

We can find ways to have more balance in our lives. Spiritual vitality grows when we make room in our day for lighthearted play as well as the serious tasks.

Answers to Prayer—Ruth Stafford Peale, in Norman Vincent Peale, *Words I Have Lived By*

There are three answers to prayer: Yes, no, and wait a while. It must be recognized that no is an answer.

About Lying—Debbie Butcher Wiersma, *Prayers for Boys and Girls,* p. 24

I told a lie today, God.

It didn't seem like a big lie. It didn't seem like it would hurt to tell one little lie. But it did hurt, God. It hurt me to know that I lied. Even if no one ever finds out, I will always know.

Please help me to tell the truth from now on. If I want to tell a lie, please remind me how awful it will make me feel. I want always to tell the truth so people will always believe what I say.

Please forgive me for lying, God.

Amen.

A Prayer for Forgiveness—Dale Mitchel

Dear God, please forgive me for forgetting that You are there, for the things that I have done that have disappointed You and others. I forgot that You love me and that You want me only to be happy. I forgot that in order to achieve happiness, I need You guiding my life. I cannot control life as I thought and ask for Your forgiveness for believing that I might. I ask for Your forgiveness for the fact that I simply forgot how to keep score. I began to judge myself more by what I had than by who I was.

Walk beside me, Lord, holding my hand gently to pull me in the direction that I need to go. Help me to remember the pain I feel now, in order that I may someday forgive another. Help me to find the compassion for others that I am asking for myself.

Make me strong, Lord, give me the power I need to overcome my temptations and to move forward with self-confidence. Help me to fight the need to control, and give me the knowledge that I am no better or worse than anybody else. Teach me humility, and give me the grace of humbleness.

Help me to eliminate the shame of my actions without shutting the door on my past. Help me to use these actions as a means to learn, to grow, and to grow closer to You. I want to find a peace that I know only You can grant. It is a peace that I am ready to work hard to find, but I know I need Your help in finding.

I ask, therefore, Lord, my only prayer: that You give me the knowledge of Your will, that I may step away from my expectations and do as You please. Let me be an example to others of Your love.

Give me the strength to overcome gossip and ridicule, and for what actions I have taken in the past. Give me the strength to follow Your will as You would desire and to find the strength to forgive myself.

Amen.

God, I Give You Me—Anonymous

Dear God, I am powerless and my life is unmanageable without Your help and guidance. I come to You today because I believe that You can restore and renew me to meet my needs today. Since I cannot manage my life or affairs, I have decided to give them to You. I put my life, my will, my thoughts, my desires and ambitions in Your hands.

I give You all of me: the good and the bad, the character defects and the shortcomings, my selfishness, resentments and problems. I know that You will work them out in accordance with Your plan. Such as I am, take all of me and use me in Your service. Guide and direct my ways and show me what to do for You.

I cannot control or change my friends or loved ones, so I release them into Your care for Your loving hands to do with as You will. Just keep me loving and free from judging them. If they need changing, God, You'll have to do it; I can't. Just make me willing and ready to be of service to You, to have my shortcomings removed, and to do my best.

Help me to see how I have harmed others and make me willing to make amends to them all. Keep me ever mindful of thoughts and feelings that harm myself and others, and which separate me from Your light, love and spirit. And when I commit these errors, make me aware of them and help me to admit each one promptly.

I am seeking to know You better, to love You more. I am seeking the knowledge of Your will for me and the power to carry it out.

A Prayer of Gratitude—Anonymous

Lord, thank you for all that you are. Thank you for providing me the things that I cannot do for myself. Thank you, Lord, for the ability to work, to provide for myself and my family. Thank you for the grass, for the sky, for the rain, the wind, the sun, and the snow. Thank you, Lord, for allowing me to experience it.

Thank you, Lord, for allowing me the knowledge of right and wrong, and the ability to decide between them for myself. Thank you for the friends and for the enemies, both of whom teach me your ways.

Thank you, Lord, for all the things that come from you and for all the things that don't. Thank you for the knowledge that you have control of my life and that if I stay out of your way, all will be taken care of that you feel I need.

Lastly, Lord, thank you for showing me the infinite love you have for your children as an example of the love I need to have for others, for the compassion, tolerance, and understanding of those I come in contact with, and for the assurance that you are always there, that I am never alone. Thank you, Lord. Amen.

Wholeness—*In God's Care,* January 1

Observing the stately calm of an elderly couple on a park bench or watching children boisterously chasing their playmates; noting the comfort of a worn path through a park or hearing the wildness of wind in a tree filled with chirping birds can bring home to us the miracle of God's world—a world teeming with life, full of contrasts. It's a world that has a special place for each of us.

Letting the rapture of this miracle wash over us changes us wholly, in the wholeness of the moment. We cannot doubt God's love for the universe when we enter undemandingly, unquestioningly the wondrous current of life.

And how remarkable, how miraculous our recovery is: yet another gift from God, one we show gratitude for each time we offer a loving glance or thoughtful, caring remark to another of God's miracles.

We will grow in understanding and appreciation and self-assurance with each loving action we take.

Jesus Speaks—The Holy Bible, Matthew 5:3–12

> Blessed are the poor in spirit; for theirs is the kingdom of heaven.
>
> Blessed are they that mourn; for they shall be comforted.
>
> Blessed are the meek; for they shall inherit the earth.
>
> Blessed are they who do hunger and thirst after righteousness; for they shall be filled.
>
> Blessed are the merciful; for they shall obtain mercy.
>
> Blessed are the pure in heart; for they shall see God.
>
> Blessed are the peacemakers; for they shall be called the sons of God.
>
> Blessed are they who are persecuted for righteousness' sake; for theirs is the kingdom of heaven.

> Blessed are you, when man shall revile you, and persecute you, and shall say all manner of evil against you falsely, for my sake.

> Rejoice, and be exceedingly glad, for great is your reward in heaven; for so persecuted were they the prophets who came before you.

To Conclude

I therefore do not wish you joy without sorrow,
nor endless days without the healing dark.
Nor brilliant sun without the restful shadow,
nor tides that never turn against your bark.

I wish you faith, strength, love and wisdom,
goods, gold enough to help some needy one.
I wish you songs, but also blessed silence,
And God's sweet peace when the day is done.

—Father Martin

" . . . faith without works is dead . . . "

—James 2:26

Research, References, and Suggested Readings

Ackerman, R. 1983. *Children of Alcoholics*. New York: Simon and Schuster.

Alcoholics Anonymous. 1976. 3d ed. New York: Alcoholics Anonymous World Services. Also referred to as the Big Book.

Ball, S. 1996. Type A and Type B Alcoholism: Applicability Across Sub-populations and Treatment Settings. *Alcohol Health & Research World* 20, no. 1.

Bandler, R. 1978. *They Lived Happily Ever After*. Capitola, Calif.: META Publications.

Beattie, M. 1990. *The Language of Letting Go*. Center City, Minn.: Hazelden.

Berger, G. 1992. *Addiction*. New York: Franklin Watts.

Blane, H. 1968. *The Personality of the Alcoholic— Guises of Dependency*. New York: Harper and Row.

Bloom, I. 1970. The Evaluation of Primary Prevention Programs. In *Comprehensive Mental Health*. Edited by L. Roberts, N. Greenfield, and M. Miller. Madison, Wis.: University of Wisconsin Press.

Blum, E. M. 1966. Psychoanalytic Views of Alcoholism: A Review. *Quarterly Journal of Studies on Alcohol* 27, no. 2.

Blum, K., et al. 1991. An Allelic Association of Human D2 Receptor Genes in Alcoholism. *Journal of the American Medical Association* 263.

Blume, S. 1983. *The Disease Concept of Alcoholism*. Minneapolis: The Johnson Institute.

Bradshaw, J. 1988. *Healing the Shame That Binds You*. Deerfield Beach, Fla.: Health Communications.

Brickman, P., et al. 1982. Models of Helping and Coping. *American Psychologist* 37.

Briscoe, J. 1997. *The One Year Book of Quiet Times with God*. Wheaton, Ill.: Tyndale House Publishers.

Brown, H. J. 1991. *The Complete Life's Little Instruction Book*. Nashville, Tenn.: Rutledge Hill Press.

Brown, S. 1995. *Treating Alcoholism*. Edited by Irvin Yacom. San Francisco: Jossey Bass.

Bruun, K. 1963. Outcome of Different Types of Treatment of Alcoholics. *Quarterly Journal of Studies on Alcohol* 24, no. 2.

Bufe, C. 1998. *Alcoholics Anonymous—Cult or Cure?* Tucson, Ariz.: Sharp Press.

Cahalan, D. 1970. *Problem Drinkers: A National Survey*. San Francisco: Jossey Bass.

Carlson, R. 1997. *Don't Sweat the Small Stuff... and It's All Small Stuff*. New York: Hyperion.

Carlson, R., and J. Bailey. 1997. *Slowing Down to the Speed of Life*. San Francisco: HarperCollins Publishers.

Casey, K., and M. Vanceburg. 1991. *The Promise of a New Day*. Center City, Minn.: Hazelden.

Chafetz, M. 1970. *Frontiers of Alcoholism*. New York: Science House.

———. 1974. Various articles in *The Alcoholism Report*.

———. 1982. Safe and Healthy Drinking. *The Encyclopedia of Alcoholism*. Edited by E. M. Pattison and E. Kaufman. New York: Gardner Press.

Chafetz, M., H. Blane, and M. Hill. 1971. Children of Alcoholics: Observations in a Child Guidance Clinic. *Quarterly Journal of Studies on Alcohol* 32, no. 3.

Chafetz, M., and H. Demone. 1962. *Alcoholism and Society*. New York: Oxford University Press.

Chapman, P., and I. Huygens. 1988. An Evaluation of Three Treatment Programmes for Alcoholism: An Experimental Study with 6- and 18-month Follow-Ups. *British Journal of Addiction* 83 no. 1.

Chopra, D. 1994. *The Seven Spiritual Laws of Success*. San Rafael, Calif.: Amber-Allen Publishing.

Cloninger, C. R. 1987. Neurogenetic Adaptive Mechanisms in Alcoholism. *Science* 236.

Cloninger, C. R., M. Bohman, and S. Sigvardsson. 1981. Inheritance of Alcohol Abuse—Cross Fostering Analysis of Adopted Men. *Archives of General Psychiatry* 38.

Cloninger, C. R., S. Sigvardsson, A.-L. von Knorring, and M. Bohman. 1988. The Swedish Studies of the Adopted Children of Alcoholics: A Reply to Littrell. *Journal of Studies on Alcohol* 49, no. 6.

Cloninger, C. R., S. Sigvardsson, and M. Bohman. 1988. Childhood Personality Predicts Alcohol Abuse in Young Adults. *Alcoholism: Clinical and Experimental Research* 12, no. 4.

———. 1996. Type I and Type II Alcoholism: An Update. *Alcohol Health & Research World* 20, no. 1.

Coleman, S., and N. Hull-Mast. 1990. *Our Best Days*. Center City, Minn.: Hazelden.

Cook, P., and M. Moore. 1993. Economic Perspectives on Reducing Alcohol-Related Violence. In *Alcohol and Interpersonal Violence: Fostering Multidisciplinary Perspectives*, National Institute on Alcohol Abuse and Alcholism Research Monograph, no. 24 (NIH Pub. No. 93-3496).

Cotton, N. S. 1979. The Familial Incidence of Alcoholism: A Review. *Journal of Studies on Alcohol* 40, no. 1.

Crewe, C. A. 1974. *Look at Relapse*. Center City, Minn.: Hazelden.

Day by Day. 1974. Center City, Minn.: Hazelden.

Department of Health and Human Services (DHHS). 1974. Second Report to Congress on Alcohol and Health (Pub. No. ADM 75-212). Washington, D.C.: National Institute on Alcohol Abuse and Alcoholism, U.S. Government Printing Office.

———.1984. Report to Congress. Washington, D.C.: National Institute on Drug Abuse, U. S. Government Printing Office.

———. 1987. Sixth Report to Congress on Alcohol and Health (Pub. No. ADM 87-1519). Washington, D.C.: National Institute on Alcohol Abuse and Alcoholism, U.S. Government Printing Office.

———. 1990. Seventh Report to Congress on Alcohol and Health (Pub. No. ADM 90-165). Washington, D.C.: National Institute on Alcohol Abuse and Alcoholism, U.S. Government Printing Office.

———. 1991. *Drug Abuse and Drug Research*. Third Triennial Report to Congress. Washington, D.C.: National Institute on Drug Abuse, U.S. Government Printing Office.

Di Chiara, G. 1997. Alcohol and Dopamine. *Alcohol Health & Research World* 21, no. 2.

Drew, L. R. H. 1968. Alcoholism as a Self-Limiting Disease. *Quarterly Journal of Studies on Alcohol* 29, no. 4.

Foreman, J. 1996. Exercise Appears to Boost Immune System to a Point. *Boston Globe,* 1 January.

Froehlich, J. 1997. Opioid Peptides. *Alcohol Health & Research World* 21, no. 2.

Giesbrecht, N., and K. Pernanen. 1987. Sociological Perspectives on the Alcoholism Treatment Literature Since 1940. In *Recent Developments in Alcoholism.* New York: Plenum Press.

Glasser, W. 1976. *Positive Addictions.* New York: Harper and Row.

Glueck, S., and E. Glueck. 1950. *Unravelling Juvenile Delinquency.* New York: Commonwealth Fund.

Gonzalez, R., and J. Jaworski. 1997. Alcohol and Glutamate. *Alcohol Health & Research World* 21, no. 2.

Goodwin, D. 1971. The Alcoholism of Eugene O'Neill. *Journal of American Medicine* 216.

———. 1971. Is Alcoholism Heriditary? *Archives of General Psychiatry* 25.

———. 1974. Drinking Problems in Adopted and Non Adopted Sons of Alcoholics. *Archives of General Psychiatry* 31.

———. 1976. *Is Alcoholism Hereditary?* New York: Oxford University Press.

Goodwin, D., L. Schulsinger, S. Guze, and G. Winkour. 1973. Alcohol Problems in Adoptees Raised Apart from Biological Parents. *Archives of General Psychiatry* 28.

Goodwin, D., and S. Guze. 1974. Heredity and Alcoholism. In *The Biology of Alcoholism: Clinical Pathology.* Vol. 3. Edited by B. Kissin and H. Begleiter. New York: Plenum Press.

Gordis, T. 1976. What Is Alcoholism Research? *Annals of Internal Medicine* 85.

Gorski, T. 1976. Denial Patterns: A System for Understanding the Alcoholic's Behavior. Ingalls Memorial Hospital publication (June). HazelCrest, Ill: CENAPS Corporation.

————. 1979 *The Neurologically-Based Alcoholism Diagnostic System.* HazelCrest, Ill: Alcoholism System Associates.

————. 1989. *Passages through Recovery.* Center City, Minn.: Hazelden.

Gorski, T., and M. Miller. 1986. *Staying Sober: A Guide for Relapse Prevention.* Independence, Mo.: Herald House Independence Press.

Grant, I. 1987. Alcohol and the Brain: Neuropsychological Correlates. *Journal of Consulting and Clinical Psychology* 3.

Grant, I., et al. 1979. Normal Neuropsychological Abilities of Alcoholic Men in Their Thirties. *American Journal of Psychiatry* 13, no. 6.

Gross, L. 1985. *How Much Is Too Much?* New York: Random House.

Gustafson, R. 1994. Alcohol and Aggression. *Journal of Offender Rehabilitation* 21 (March 4).

Hauck, P. 1974. *Overcoming Frustration and Anger.* Philadelphia: Westminster Press.

Heath, D. B. 1975. A Critical Review of Ethnographical Studies of Alcohol Use. In *Research Advances in Alcohol and Drug Problems.* Vol. 2. New York: Wiley.

Higley, J. D. 1991. *Nonhuman Primate Model of Alcohol Abuse.* Proceedings of the National Survey of Sciences 88: 7261–65.

————. 1997. Various articles as referenced in *Alcohol Alert,* a quarterly bulletin produced by the National Institute on Alcohol Abuse and Alcoholism.

Higley, J. D., and M. Linnoila. 1997. A Nonhuman Primate Model of Excessive Alcohol Intake: Personality and Neurobiological Parallels of Type I and Type II Like Alcoholism. In *Recent Developments in Alcoholism.* Vol. 13. New York: Plenum Press.

Higley, J. D., S. J. Suomi, and M. Linnoila. 1996. A Nonhuman Primate Model of Type II Excessive Alcohol Consumption? *Alcoholism: Clinical and Experimental Research* 20, no. 4.

Hoffer, E. 1951. *The True Believer.* New York: Harper.

Hoffman, H., R. G. Loper, and M. L. Kammeier. 1974. Identifying Future Alcoholics with MMPI Alcoholism Scales. *Quarterly Journal of Studies on Alcohol* 35, no. 2.

Holy Bible, The. 1967. Authorized King James Version. Edited by C. I. Scofield. Scofield Reference Bible. New York: Oxford University Press.

Hyman, S. 1976. Alcoholics 15 Years Later. *Annals of the New York Academy of Science* 273.

In God's Care. 1991. Center City, Minn.: Hazelden.

Institute of Medicine. 1979. *Prevention and Treatment of Alcohol Problems: Research Opportunities.* Washington D.C.: National Academy Press.

J., Ed. 1981. *Hope.* Recovery Is Forever audiocassette series. Center City, Minn.: Hazelden.

Jellinek, E. M. 1952. Phases of Alcohol Addiction. *Quarterly Journal of Studies on Alcohol* 13, no. 4.

————. 1957. The World and Its Bottle. *World Health* 10: 4–6.

————. 1960. *The Disease Concept of Alcoholism.* New Haven, Conn.: Hillhouse Press.

Jennison, K. 1992. The Impact of Stressful Life Events and Social Support on Drinking Among Older Adults: A General Population Survey. *International Journal of Aging and Human Development* 35, no. 2.

Jones, J., and S. Pilat. 1993. Children of Alcoholics Screening Test. Children of Alcoholics Research Series. Chicago: Camelot Unlimited.

Jones, L. 1997. *Jesus in Blue Jeans.* New York: Hyperion.

Jung, C. 1963. *Memories, Dreams and Reflections.* Edited by R. Winston and C. Winston. New York: Pantheon.

Kalant, H. 1990. Stress-Related Effects of Ethanol in Mammals. *Critical Reviews in Biotechnology* 9, no. 4.

Kellerman, J. 1991. *Alcoholism: A Merry-Go-Round Named Denial.* Center City, Minn.: Hazelden.

Kissin, B., and H. Begleiter. 1972. *The Biology of Alcoholism.* New York: Plenum Press.

Knupfer, G. 1972. Ex-Problem Drinkers. In *Life History Research in Psychopathology.* Edited by Roff, Robbins, and Pollock. Minneapolis: University of Minnesota Press.

Kolb, L. 1973. Article found in *Modern Clinical Psychiatry.* Noted in G. Vaillant, *The Natural History of Alcoholism* (Cambridge, Mass.: Harvard University Press, 1983).

Kurtz, E. 1979. *Not-God: A History of Alcoholics Anonymous*. Center City, Minn.: Hazelden.

L., Mark. 1994. *An Evening of Twelve Step Humor*. San Jose, Calif.: Insanity Inc. Audiocassette.

LeBlanc, A. E., R. J. Gibbins, and H. Kalant. 1973. Behavioral Augmentation of Tolerance to Ethanol in the Rat. *Psychopharmacologia* 30.

Lieber, C. S. 1976. The Metabolism of Alcoholism. *Scientific American* (March).

Lieber, C. S., T. Hasumara, R. Teschke, S. Matsuzaki, and M. Korsten. 1975. The Effect of Chronic Ethanol Consumption on Acetaldehyde Metabolism. In *The Role of Acetaldehyde in the Actions of Ethanol*. Vol. 23. Edited by K. Lindros and C. Eriksson. Helsinki: Finnish Foundation for Alcohol Studies.

Lindstrom, L. 1992. *Managing Alcoholism*. Oxford: Oxford University Press.

Litman, G. 1982. Personal Meanings and Alcoholism Survival: Translating Subjective Experience into Empirical Data. In *Personal Meanings*. Edited by Sheppard and Watson. New York: Wiley.

Littrell, J. 1988. The Swedish Studies of the Adopted Children of Alcoholics. *Journal of Studies on Alcohol* 49, no. 6.

Lovinger, D. 1997. Seritonin's Role in Alcohol's Effects on the Brain. *Alcohol Health & Research World* 21, no. 2.

Ludwig, A. 1988. *Understanding the Alcoholic's Mind*. New York: Oxford University Press.

Ludwig, A., A. Winkler, and L. Stark. 1974. The First Drink: Psychobiological Aspects of Craving. *Archives of General Psychiatry* 30.

Ludwig, A., L. Levine, L. Stark, and R. Lazar. 1969. A Clinical Study of LSD Treatment in Alcoholism. *American Journal of Psychiatry* 126.

Mack, J. 1981. Alcoholism, AA and the Governance of the Self. In *Dynamic Approaches to the Understanding and Treatment of Alcoholism*. Edited by M. Bean and N. Zinberg. New York: Free Press.

Madill, M.-F., D. Campbell, S. G. Laverty, R. E. Sanderson, and S. L. Vandewater. 1966. Aversion Treatment of Alcoholics by Succinylcholine-Induced Apneic Paralysis: An Analysis of Early Changes in Drinking Behavior. *Quarterly Journal of Studies on Alcohol* 27, no. 3.

Madsen, W. 1974. *The American Alcoholic*. Springfield, Ill.: C. C. Thomas.

Marlatt, G. A., B. Demming, and J. B. Reid. 1973. Loss of Control Drinking in Alcoholics: An Experimental Analogue. *Journal of Abnormal Psychology* 83.

Marlatt, G. A., and J. R. Gordon. 1985. *Relapse Prevention*. New York: Guilford Press.

Maslin, B. 1994. *The Angry Marriage*. New York: Skylight Press.

Matheny, K. B., and R. J. Riordan. 1992. *Stress and Strategies for Lifestyle Management*. Athens, Ga.: Georgia State University Press.

McCord, W., and J. McCord. 1960. *Origins of Alcoholism*. Stanford, Calif.: Stanford University Press.

McCormick, R. 1982. *Facing Alcoholism*. San Diego: Oak Tree.

McCusker, C. G., and K. Brown. 1990. Alcohol-Predictive Cues Enhance Tolerance to and Precipitate "Craving" for Alcohol in Social Drinkers. *Journal of Studies on Alcohol* 51, no. 6.

Menninger, K. 1938. *Man Against Himself*. New York: Harcourt Brace.

———. 1973. *Whatever Became of Sin?* New York: Hawthorn Books.

Men's Devotional Bible. 1993. The New International Version. Grand Rapids, Mich.: Zondervan Publishing.

Meyer, R., T. Babor, and P. Mirkin. 1983. Typologies in Alcoholism: An Overview. *International Journal of the Addictions* 18.

Meyers, R. D., and W. L. Veale. 1968. Alcohol Preference in the Rat: Reduction Following Depletion of Serotonin. *Science* 160.

Miczek, K., et al. 1997. Alcohol GABA-Benzodiazephine Receptor Complex and Aggression. In *Recent Developments in Alcoholism*. Vol. 13. New York: Plenum Press.

Milam, J. R., and K. Ketcham. 1981. *Under the Influence: A Guide to the Myths and Realities of Alcoholism*. Seattle: Madrona Publishers and Bantam Books.

Miller, N., and D. Toft. 1990. *The Disease Concept of Alcoholism and Other Drug Addiction*. Center City, Minn.: Hazelden.

Murphy, H. B. M. 1980. Hidden Barriers to the Diagnosis and Treatment of Alcoholism and Other Alcohol Misuse. *Journal of Studies on Alcohol* 41, no. 5.

My Prayer Book. 1980. St. Louis, Mo.: Concordia Publishing House.

Nash, J., and R. Maickel. 1988. The Role of the Hypothalmatic-Pituitary-Adreocortical Axis in Post Stress Induced Ethanol Consumption by Rats. *Progress in Neuro-Psychopharmacology and Biological Psychiatry* 12.

National Council on Alcoholism. 1972. Criteria for the Diagnosis of Alcoholism. *Annals of Internal Medicine* 77.

National Highway Traffic Safety Administration. 1988. *Drunk Driving Facts.* Washington, D.C.

National Insitute on Alcohol Abuse and Alcoholism (NIAAA). 1972. *The Alcoholism Report.* Washington, D.C.: U.S. Government Printing Office.

———. 1996. *Alcohol Alert.* No. 33.

———. 1996. *Alcohol Alert.* No. 34.

———. 1998. *Alcohol Alert.* No. 39.

National Institute on Drug Abuse. 1988. *National Survey on Drug Abuse.* DDHS Publication No. ADM 88-1586.

Niehaus, J. T. 1997. Personal correspondence. Cincinnati, Ohio.

O'Brien, R., and M. Chafetz. 1982. In *The Encyclopedia of Alcoholism.* Edited by E. M. Pattison and E. Kaufman. New York: Gardner Press.

Ogborne, A. 1989. Some Limitations to Alcoholics Anonymous. In *Recent Developments in Alcoholism: Treatment Issues.* Vol. 7. Edited by M. Galanter. New York: Plenum Press.

Oswald, R. 1976. *The Development and Function of Personality.* Morristown, N. J.: General Learning Press.

Parham, A. P. 1987. *Letting God.* San Francisco: Harper.

Pattison, E. M. 1968. A Critique of Abstinence Criteria in the Treatment of Alcoholism. *International Journal of Social Psychiatry* 14.

Pattison, E. M., and E. Koffman, eds. 1982. Various articles in *Encyclopedia Handbook of Alcoholism.* New York: Gardner Press.

Peale, N. 1990. *Words I Have Lived By.* Norwalk, Conn.: C. R. Gibson Company.

———. 1993. *Positive Thinking Every Day.* New York: Simon and Schuster.

Pernanen, K. 1991. *Alcohol in Human Violence.* New York: Guilford Press.

Pickens, R., D. Svikis, M. McGue, D. Lykken, L. Heston, and P. Clayton. 1991. Heterogeneity in the Inheritance of Alcoholism: A Study of Male and Female Twins. *Archives of General Psychiatry* 48, no. 1.

Pittman, B. 1988. *Stepping Stones to Recovery*. Seattle: Glen Abbey Books.

Pittman, B., and T. Weber. 1993. *Drop the Rock*. Seattle: Glen Abbey Books.

Plaut, T. F. 1967. *Alcohol Problems: A Report to the Nation by the Cooperative Commission on the Study of Alcoholism*. New York: Oxford University Press.

Pohorecky, L. 1991. Stress and Alcohol Interaction: An Update of Human Research. *Alcoholism: Clinical and Experimental Research* 15, no. 3.

Polich, J., D. Armor, and H. Braiker. 1981. *The Course of Alcoholism*. New York: Wiley.

Potter-Efron, R., and P. Potter-Efron. 1989. *Letting Go of Shame: Understanding How Shame Affects Your Life*. Center City, Minn.: Hazelden.

Rado, S. 1933. The Psychoanalysis of Phanachothymia (Drug Addiction): The Clinical Picture. *Psychoannal.*

Reiss, A., Jr., and J. Roth, eds. 1994. *Understanding and Preventing Violence*. Vol. 3. Washington, D.C.: National Academy Press.

Rivers, P. C., ed. 1987. Various articles in *Alcohol and Addictive Behavior*. Nebraska Symposium on Motivation. Lincoln, Nebr.: University of Nebraska Press.

———. 1994. *Alcohol and Human Behavior*. New Jersey: Prentice Hall.

Roberts, A., and G. Koob. 1997. The Neurobiology of Addiction: An Overview. *Alcohol Health & Research World* 21, no. 2.

Robertson, N. 1988. *Getting Better: Inside Alcoholics Anonymous*. New York: William Morrow.

Roizen, J. 1997. Epidemiological Issues in Alcohol Related Violence. In *Recent Developments in Alcoholism*. Edited by M. Galanter. Vol. 13. New York: Plenum Press.

Rush, B. 1784. *An Enquiry into the Effects of Spirituous Liquors Upon the Human Body, and Their Influence Upon the Happiness of Society*. Brookfield, Mass.: E. Merriam and Company.

Russell, D. E. H. 1982. *Rape in Marriage*. New York: Macmillan.

S., Richard. 1988. *Communication Skills*. Center City, Minn.: Hazelden.

Sadava, S., and A. Pak. 1993. Stress-Related Problem Drinking and Alcohol Problems: A Longitudinal Study and Extension of Marlatt's Model. *Canadian Journal of Behavioral Science* 25, no. 3.

Sargent, W. 1957. *Battle for the Mind.* Garden City, N.Y.: Doubleday.

Schmidt, W., and R. S. Popham. 1975. Heavy Alcohol Consumption and Physical Health Problems: A Review of Epidemiological Evidence. *Drug and Alcohol* 1.

———. 1979. Data as printed in Y. Israel, Researching the Biology of Alcoholism: One Way of Seeing It, in Mark Keller, ed., *Journal of Studies on Alcohol,* supplement no. 8.

Schuckit, M. 1980. Alcoholism and Genetics: Possible Biological Mediators. *Biology Psychiatry* 15

———. 1992. Advances to the Understanding of the Vulnerability to Alcoholism. In *Addictive States.* New York: Raven Press.

Seixis, J., and G. Youcha. 1985. *Children of Alcoholism: A Survivor's Manual.* New York: Harper and Row.

Selzer, M. L., A. Vinokur, and L. van Rooijen. 1975. A Self-Administered Short Michigan Alcoholism Screening Test (SMAST). *Journal of Studies on Alcohol* 36, no. 1: 124.

Shapiro, F. 1988. *Rapid Eye Movement and Desensitization.* New York: Guilford Press.

Shepherd, G. 1994. *Neurobiology.* 3d ed. New York: Oxford University Press.

Sherfey, M. 1955. Psychopathology and Character Structures in Chronic Alcoholism. In *Etiology of Chronic Alcoholism.* Edited by O. Diethelm. Springfield, Ill.: C. C. Thomas.

Shoemaker, S. 1954. *Psychological Rehabilitation of Alcoholics.* Pleasantville, N.Y.: Reader's Digest, Inc.

Snyder, C. 1962. Culture and Jewish Sobriety: The Ingroup–Outgroup Factor. In *Society, Culture, and Drinking Patterns.* Edited by D. Pittman and C. Snyder. New York: John Wiley and Sons.

Solly, R. 1995. *Call to Purpose.* Center City, Minn.: Hazelden.

Springborn, W. 1992. *Step 1: The Foundation of Recovery.* Center City, Minn.: Hazelden, 8–9.

Syme, L. 1957. Personality Characteristics and the Alcoholic: A Critique of Current Studies. *Quarterly Journal of Studies on Alcohol* 18, no. 2.

Tahka, V. 1966. *The Alcoholic Personality.* Helsinki: Finnish Foundation for Alcohol Studies.

Thompson, P. 1994. *Finding Your Own Spiritual Path.* Center City, Minn.: Hazelden.

Tiebout, H. M. 1953. Surrender Versus Compliance in Therapy: With Special Reference to Alcoholism. *Quarterly Journal of Studies on Alcohol* 14, no. 1.

———. 1957. Therapeutic Mechanisms of Alcoholics Anonymous. In *Alcoholics Anonymous Comes of Age: A Brief History of A.A.* New York: Alcoholics Anonymous World Services.

———. 1969. *The Act of Surrender in the Therapeutic Process.* New York: The National Council on Alcoholism.

Touchstones: A Book of Daily Meditations for Men. 1986. Center City, Minn.: Hazelden.

Trice, H., and P. Roman. 1970. Sociopsychological Predictors of Affiliation with Alcoholics Anonymous: A Longitudinal Study of "Treatment Success." *Social Psychiatry* 5.

Trotter, T. 1804. An Essay, Medical, Philosophical and Chemical, on Drunkenness and Its Effects on the Human Body. London.

Twelve Steps and Twelve Traditions. 1981. New York: Alcoholics Anonymous World Services.

Twenty-Four Hours a Day. 1994. 40th Anniversary Edition. Center City, Minn.: Hazelden.

Vaillant, G. 1983. *The Natural History of Alcoholism.* Cambridge, Mass.: Harvard University Press.

———. 1985. *The History of Alcoholism Revisited.* Cambridge, Mass.: Harvard University Press.

———. 1993. *The Wisdom of the Ego.* Cambridge, Mass.: Harvard University Press.

Virkkunen, M., and M. Linnoila. 1996. Serotonin and Glucose Metabolism in Impulsively Violent Offenders. In *Aggression and Violence.* Edited by D. Stoff and R. Cairns. Mahwah, N.J.: Erlbaum.

Vogel-Sprott, M. 1979. Acute Recovery and Tolerance to Low Doses of Alcohol: Differences in Cognitive and Motor Skill Performance. *Psychopharmacology* 61, no. 3.

Vogel-Sprott, M., et al. 1991. Mental Rehearsal of Attack Under Ethanol. *Alcohol* 8, no. 6.

Volger, R. E., T. Weissbach, and J. Compton. 1977. Learning Techniques for Alcohol Abuse. *Behavior Research Therapy* 15.

Volpicelli, J. 1987. Uncontrollable Events and Alcohol Drinking. *British Journal of Addiction* 82, no. 4.

Wallerstein, R. 1956. Comparative Study of Treatment Methods for Chronic Alcoholism: The Alcoholism Research Project at Winter Veterans Administration Hospital. *American Journal of Psychiatry* 113.

Wallgren, H., and H. Berry. 1970. *Actions of Alcohol.* New York: Elsevier.

Walsch, N. D. 1997. *Meditations from Conversations with God.* New York: Berkeley Books.

Wanberg, K., and J. Knapp. 1970. A Multidimesional Model for the Research and Treatment of Alcoholism. *International Journal of the Addictions* 5.

Warner, J. 1993. "Resolv'd to Drink No More": Addiction as a Pre-Industrial Construct. *Journal of Studies on Alcohol* (November): 685–91.

Wegscheider-Cruse, S. 1985. *Choice Making: For Co-Dependents, Adult Children and Spiritual Seekers.* Deerfield Beach, Fla.: Health Communications.

West, J. 1997. *The Betty Ford Center Book of Answers.* New York: Pocket Books.

White, W. 1998. *Slaying the Dragon: The History of Addiction Treatment and Recovery in America.* Bloomington, Ill.: Chestnut Health Systems, Lighthouse Institute.

Whitfield, C. L. 1987. *Healing the Child Within.* Deerfield Beach, Fla.: Health Communications.

Wiersma, D. 1989. *Prayers for Boys and Girls.* Nashville, Tenn.: Precious Moments, Tommy Nelson.

Wilson, B. 1959. Basic Concepts of Alcoholics Anonymous. Presented to the Medical Society of the State of New York, Neurology and Psychiatry, annual meeting.

————. 1967. *As Bill Sees It.* New York: Alcoholics Anonymous World Services.

World Health Organization. Report of Expert Committee on Alcohol. 1954. First Report, World Health Organization Report Series, no. 84.

————. Report of Expert Committee on Alcohol. 1955. Technical Report, no. 94.

Yankelovich, Skelly and White, Inc. 1979. The General Mills American Family Report: Family Health in an Era of Stress. Minneapolis, Minn: General Mills.

Zucker, R. 1987. The Four Alcoholisms: A Developmental Account of the Etiological Process. In *Alcohol and Addictive Behavior.* Edited by P. C. Rivers. Nebraska Symposium on Motivation. Lincoln, Nebr.: University of Nebraska Press.